A Frontier Doctor

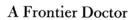

Henry F. Hoyt.

The Lakeside Classics

A FRONTIER
DOCTOR

By Henry F. Hoyt

EDITED BY
Doyce B. Nunis, Jr.

The Lakeside Press

R. R. DONNELLEY & SONS COMPANY

CHICAGO

Christmas, 1979

PUBLISHERS' PREFACE

THIS is the seventy-seventh volume of *The Lake-side Classics*—a series that we have continued without interruption since 1903.

Producing this book is dependent upon the combined skills of many people. A number of production steps are repeated from one volume to the next with only an occasional change or updating, but not so when it comes to searching for and selecting a suitable manuscript or reprint.

Through the years, we have discovered or have been introduced to prospective titles through a variety of circumstances. The paths we have taken have led us in all directions and at times there have been unexpected twists and turns. The events leading to finding this year's manuscript are rather unusual and we believe are worth relating.

On March 23, 1968, Mrs. Dortha Patrick, a quality inspector in our Crawfordsville Manufacturing Division, was at home watching television. The program was an episode from the then-popular series *Death Valley Days*. The storyline featured General Lew Wallace, the author of *Ben Hur* and a noted soldier, politician, and former resident of Crawfordsville. Mrs. Patrick suggested that we investigate for possible *Classic* material. What followed could probably qualify as a first-rate detective story.

We contacted the Indianapolis television station

manager who identified the episode that Mrs. Patrick had seen. We asked the program sponsor for
the name of the producer. We wrote the producing
company to determine what resource materials the
writer had used for that particular episode. Our request drew a lengthy delay while the producers
sought the writer who in turn worked to remember
his source material. Finally, we learned that several
books were used but the only title remembered was
A Frontier Doctor by Henry F. Hoyt and published
by Houghton-Mifflin in 1929.

Finding a copy of the out-of-print book was far
from routine. After an extensive search, a copy was
located in the Evanston (Illinois) Public Library.
The book was read by the members of our screen-
ing committee and reviewed by a historian for its
authenticity. Everyone who read Dr. Hoyt's book
enjoyed it and were agreed that it would meet the
requirements for the series.

In 1976 we offered the editorship of this volume
to Professor Doyce B. Nunis, Jr., a distinguished
member of the History Department of the University of Southern California. Dr. Nunis is the author of
several books about the American West and has had
extensive experience as an editor. We were delighted when he accepted our offer.

Our editor has done a scholarly job in contacting
members of Dr. Hoyt's family, researching names,
places and events for historical accuracy. He supplied all but one of the photographs that appeared

in the original book and added other pictorial material to enhance this fast-moving autobiography.

Early in 1979, the editor's work was complete. The three maps were researched and prepared by the Donnelley Cartographic Service. Composition was performed by our Electronic Graphics Central Division. Printing, binding, cartoning and distribution were accomplished through our Crawfordsville Manufacturing Division.

THE PUBLISHERS' PREFACE has become an appropriate place for us to comment on our past year of business operation; the problems and challenges we face; and our plans for the future.

This past year, 1979, continued our growth in sales and profits to new records, thanks to an overall healthy demand for our services. We continue to be the leading manufacturer of catalogs, tabloids, magazines, books and directories in the United States. Profit margins suffered slightly under the pressure of inflation and continued heavy start-up costs. The latter is the price of continued growth, without which the future would be bleak indeed. We have maintained our long-standing policy of reinvesting in the business two-thirds or more of our after-tax profits. This policy permitted in January a dividend increase to one dollar per share on an annual basis. Results for the year fully justified this action by our Board of Directors, even though anticipated capital expenditures exceeded all sources of funds, retained earnings, depreciation charges, and deferred taxes, by a significant amount. However, our financial position remains strong.

Construction has now begun for new divisions at Harrisonburg, Virginia, to expand our highly successful short run book capacity, and at Spartanburg, South Carolina for gravure printing, for which demand remains remarkably high. We have been made to feel most welcome in both these communities, and look forward to a healthy atmosphere of cooperation. An existing building of 445,000 square feet in Lancaster, Pennsylvania was purchased. This building is being remodeled and equipped as a gravure printing operation and will initially produce a major part of *TV Guide*, portions of which we were already producing in an existing Division. These plants will commence production in late 1980.

Substantial expenditures were made during the year to expand many of our existing facilities. Major expansions were made in our Gallatin, Glasgow, Warsaw, Mattoon and Dwight divisions. The printing industry continues to experience rapid technological development, and we are determined to maintain our competitive lead in this regard. In the 1977 Publishers' Preface we speculated on the use of satellite communications. Now it is an actuality. To help us evaluate and apply available and developing technology, we have established a Technical Advisory Council of scientists outstanding in their respective fields. We have also added considerable strength to our own several staffs in this area.

During the past year there have been some real problems in the availability of lightweight coated paper, extensively used in magazines and catalogs. Shortages may continue for paper purchased both by our customers and ourselves. We are also concerned about the energy situation and lack of effective action in Washington. Fortunately, we have had ample gas, partly thanks to our own wells.

The main problem is inflation, which we share with everyone. The costs of materials, services, equipment and buildings have escalated, in some cases far beyond the increase in the Consumer Price Index, which as of this writing is rising at an annual rate in excess of 13%. Inflation also overstates our profits and retained earnings. Our planned growth becomes increasingly expensive and difficult to finance with internally generated funds.

A most serious impact of inflation is on our employees. We began the year resolved to take the maximum action possible under the President's guidelines on wages. In keeping with this objective, we granted a special adjustment in October, in addition to the annual increase in wages earlier in the year. Even so, our employees see the value of their dollar decrease under the impact of inflation. They have every right to see their standard of living increase because of their efforts and skills and the Company's increasing investment in equipment and technology to improve their productivity and opportunities. However, inflation is causing a decline in the standard of living for almost everyone. Investment by the Company is essential for our employees' job security in the highly competitive marketplace for printing. Yet, due in large part to inflation's impact on costs, the return on the increased stockholders investment did not improve appreciably and the portion of the sales dollar remaining as profit had actually declined as of this writing.

As a means of arresting the inflation for which the Federal government must stand primarily responsible, we fervently wish the Administration and Congress would recognize these essential needs:

1. Immediate and effective limits on government spending;

2. Elimination from the Federal budget of deficits that cannot be supported by real growth in the nation's economy;

3. Reduction and rationalization of present chaotic regulation;

4. The importance of encouragement of capital formation through savings and tax policy;

5. Facing the energy question squarely and honestly, recognizing that controls don't work, but put a burden on the economy.

To make business, and especially the oil industry, scapegoats for our present predicament is only evading the issue. It behooves everyone to make their views known where it will do the most good.

At the time of writing this preface, the future is

not at all clear, but the economic indicators point
to some sort of recession as being already underway.
While we have weathered previous downturns rather successfully, any such development will have
some effect on our business, how much no one can
predict. In spite of this, our Company is embarked
on the largest and most aggressive expansion program in our history. Capital appropriations for 1979
will approximate $145 million with capital expend-
itures at $140 million. Most of the appropriations
this year will call for expenditures in 1980 and beyond. Cash and investments now earning record
high interest rates will be converted temporarily
into nonearning assets as we make progress pay-
ments on buildings and equipment. Following will
come the inevitable heavy training and start-up expenses. Fortunately, the major additions to our capacity are presold. It has long been our custom to
plan and execute expansion on a continuing basis,
recognizing there will be cyclical swings in the
economy. To maintain a strong company, it would
be difficult to do otherwise. Projects once begun
can be halted, usually at considerable expense. Also
the lead time from the decision to proceed to full
production is long, as much as four or five years.
Hopefully, at the end of this period the economy
will be booming, and the demands for our services
will be even greater. Apart from the timing of the
business cycle, we are confident of the basic sound-
ness of the markets this expansion will serve.

For the first time in over twenty years we will undoubtedly need to borrow capital, but it will be modest in relation to stockholders' equity, and in all probability within one year's flow of funds. We approach the future with confidence, then, but with the full recognition of many challenges and problems, known and unknown.

In our endeavor we will continue to rely on the skills, talents, efforts, and dedication of many others, inside and outside our Company, our customers, suppliers, and employees. The investment of our stockholders' will be at some risk, but we believe it a prudent and reasonable one. We appreciate the support we enjoy from them all, and at Christmastime extend our very best wishes for this season and next year.

THE PUBLISHERS

Christmas, 1979

CONTENTS

Contents — xvii

ILLUSTRATIONS

HISTORICAL INTRODUCTION

HENRY FRANKLIN HOYT'S lifetime spanned three-quarters of a century, decades in which the United States underwent profound and vital changes. Born in the middle of the nineteenth century, he lived to see America transformed from a rural to an urban nation; an agrarian way of life replaced by the world's largest industrial economy; bickering states, who fought each other in a bitter civil war, emerge as a dominant world power. Born in the political crisis surrounding slavery and states rights, Hoyt died in the midst of the nation's greatest economic crisis, the Depression. Born on the pioneer fringe of settlement on the Mississippi River, he witnessed the closing of the Far Western frontier. In his own quiet way, he played a role in the last surge of the nation's westward movement and a small part in the emergence of the United States as a world power.

A man of modest accomplishments, Hoyt's name does not appear in the nation's annals, although he made positive contributions to his native state during his tenure as Commissioner of Health for the city of St. Paul, Minnesota, and served his country ably during the Spanish-American War. Yet he has earned a unique place in the history of the American West, a place achieved by his autobiography, *A Frontier Doctor*, penned in the twilight of his life.

Published by the Houghton Mifflin Company in 1929, Hoyt's book was well received. One review noted that Hoyt wrote "easily with good powers of description" and that his story was "interesting and enjoyable as a straightforward narrative of personal adventures. A clean, honest man has told a reminiscent story well." Another reviewer declared: "This narrative of days in the Northwest and the Southwest, away back in the '70s and the '80s, when the frontier was a definite, dramatic, picturesque, dynamic and deadly region, makes a contribution of real interest and value to the story of that unique section of our American history. Moreover, it is highly entertaining." A third critic described the book as "a picaresque novel, like a Wild West thriller" which brimmed with "travels, prospecting, Indians, bad men, shootings, hangings, coincidences and hairbreadth escapes." There was little question, Hoyt was "an old hand at telling stories, and often tells them well."[1] Frankly, the book deserved the warm critical praise it received as any reader of it quickly learns.

The book's intrinsic worth, indeed its true secret, is that Hoyt, by sheer happenstance, found himself in the right place at the right time. His was not a life of contrivance; rather it was one of coincidence. Thus his recollections begin with the tragic Santee Sioux uprising in Minnesota and culminate in the

[1] *The Book Review Digest for 1930* (New York, 1931), 26: 513–514.

equally tragic suppression of the Filipino insurrection which followed the termination of the Spanish-American War.

Perhaps as a presage of what was to come, Hoyt was born on the frontier of American settlement in Minnesota Territory. In 1848 his parents emigrated from Illinois and settled in the near vicinity of the fledgling community of St. Paul. At the time, the settler population of the territory was no more than 4,000 and St. Paul was just a hamlet of 910 residents. Within a decade that small population rose to over 10,000.

When Congress enacted a territorial bill for Minnesota in 1849, the year of the California gold rush, St. Paul became the territorial capital. It was here that Hoyt was born on January 30, 1854, the same year in which the city was incorporated. Four years later when statehood was approved, St. Paul was designated the state capital.

Hoyt was a descendant of pioneers drawn to the West. Grandfather Benjamin J. Hoyt, Connecticut born, married Elizabeth Haney, whose birthplace was Pennsylvania. Hoyt's father, Lorenzo, was born in Richland County, Ohio, February 21, 1828. He took as his wife Sarah Philadelphia Terrell, a southern lady born in Virginia, August 30, 1832. Hoyt's maternal grandparents, Henry K. Terrell and Jane Camerose, were also Virginians.[2] Hoyt's parents

---

[2] Biographical data supplied by Hoyt's grandson, John Terrell Hoyt, Jr.

were typical—young people attracted to western
lands on the ever beckoning horizon of nineteenth-
century America. They established a farm in Ramsey County near the townlet of Rose. There they
reared their children, including two sons, Henry
and George, and two daughters.

When the Civil War ripped the nation asunder
in 1861, Minnesota was spared the scars of direct
conflict. Although the state supplied a large contingent of volunteers in support of the Union cause, it
was geographically removed from the fields of battle. Thus its populace was spared the sound of shot
and cannon, the piercing yells of charging infantry,
the rumble of sweating cavalry, and the clang of
slashing sabres. Unfortunately Minnesota did not
completely escape the ravages and vicissitudes of
warfare; it suffered terribly in a brief but bloody
Indian conflict.

In the summer of 1862, near starvation, poorly
supplied by Indian agencies, antagonized by ever-
growing white encroachment on their land, the
Santee Sioux commenced hostilities against Minnesota settlers on August 18. Quickly the southern part
of the state was engulfed in bloodshed. The Minnesota Uprising, although short-lived, reaped a heavy toll
of life. Within thirty-eight days 500 to 800 settlers
and soldiers were killed, along with an unknown
number of Indians, and some 300 whites were taken
captive. An expedition led by General Henry H.
Sibley finally subdued the Santee at the battle of

Lone Tree Lake, September 23. An enraged citizenry demanded retribution. As a result, thirty-eight Santee, convicted of murder and rape, were executed on December 26. Within two years the Sioux were completely driven out of Minnesota into the neighboring Dakota Territory and placed on reservations in present-day South Dakota. But peace proved illusive. Intermittent conflict with the Sioux continued in the ensuing decade, culminating in their 1877 subjugation in the wake of the annihilation of General George A. Custer's command at the battle of the Little Big Horn.

Far too young to participate in the Civil War or the Sioux uprising, young Henry never forgot those two events which seared his childhood memory. Later in life he was an associate and intimate of many Civil War veterans, and in 1877 found himself in Deadwood, Dakota Territory, the year after the Sioux, led by Sitting Bull, had triumphed over Custer, but who quickly tasted bitter defeat in the death of American Horse, the flight of Sitting Bull to Canada, and the abject surrender of Crazy Horse.

Contemporary with the Sioux problem, first in Minnesota and later in the Dakota and Montana territories, Hoyt grew to manhood during the railroad building era. Congressional enactment of the railroad acts of 1862–1864 made possible the eventual completion of four major transcontinental routes in the trans-Mississippi West. The northern route, which ran from Lake Superior to Portland,

Oregon, was undertaken by the Northern Pacific
Railroad Company, chartered in 1864. Initially fi-
nanced by the New York banker, Jay Cooke, the
railway company was reorganized in 1881 by Henry
Villard, who managed to complete the road successfully in 1883. Hoyt, as a St. Paul resident, participated as a spectator in the lavish ceremonies that
marked the grand opening of the new rail link to
the Pacific Coast that year.[3]

While construction on the Northern Pacific route
languished from financial difficulties, a second effort to push a railroad connection between Minnesota and the Pacific Northwest had been launched
in 1878 by the St. Paul and Manitoba Railroad. As a
prelude to a larger effort, the St. Paul and Pacific
Railroad Company commenced local construction
shortly after the end of Civil War hostilities in
1865. As a young eighteen-year-old, Hoyt's first
gainful employment was with one of the company's
surveying parties. Subsequently, in 1878, when several local railroad companies were organized by
James J. Hill into the Great Northern Railroad,
Hoyt was appointed the railroad's physician and
surgeon, in 1883. Thus as a youth, later a medical
practitioner, Hoyt's life was directly influenced by
the railroad, as was most of his fellow countrymen.
In addition, Hoyt witnessed the arrival of the Atchi-

---

[3] These festivities are amply recorded in Nicolaus Mohr,
Excursion Through America, edited by Ray A. Billington
(Chicago, 1973), a *Lakeside Classic*, pp. xliii-lii.

son, Topeka and Santa Fe in the Territory of New Mexico while residing there. He early came to appreciate the extraordinary impact wrought in communities linked by the railroads. He saw at first hand the dramatic and startling changes which were produced by the ever-expanding web of steel rails. Indeed, he witnessed during his lifetime the transition from stagecoach to railcoach, from horse to automobile.

Fortunately for Hoyt, he made his career decision early: he decided to become a doctor. Most likely that decision was influenced by his uncle, John Henry Murphy, M.D., hailed as "the Nestor of the medical profession of Minnesota."[4]

Dr. Murphy, born in New Brunswick, New Jersey, January 22, 1826, was the son of an Irish immigrant. In 1834 his family moved to Quincy, Illinois, where young Murphy attended high school. Upon graduation, he undertook the study of medicine with Dr. Abram Hill in Lewiston, an accepted medical educational practice, commonly called the preceptorial method. Marriage followed on June 28, 1848, when he took as his bride Mary A. Terrell, sister to Hoyt's mother, in Fulton County, Illinois. The next year the young newlyweds settled in St. Anthony (later to be called Minneapolis), Minnesota, where Murphy opened his medical practice. Aware that his training was deficient, Murphy enrolled in

---

[4] General C. C. Andrews, ed., *History of St. Paul, Minn.* (Syracuse, N.Y., 1890), p. 176.

Rush Medical College, Chicago, in the winter of
1849–1850, and completed the requirements for his
M.D. degree. Returning home, in 1851, he became a
partner with Albert A. Ames, M.D. Both men became prominent citizens in the state. Murphy was
elected to a term in the territorial legislature and a
delegate to the 1857 state constitutional conven-
tion, and served with distinction in the medical
service during the Civil War. After 1864 he made
St. Paul his home.

In many ways Hoyt's uncle was a career model.
Like him, Hoyt took his first year of medical training through the preceptorial method, studying with
his uncle. In the spring of the following year he
received solid clinical training as an intern (then
called steward) in Church Hospital, founded in
1857, and later renamed St. Luke's, in St. Paul.
This experience was followed by a year of medical
courses at Rush Medical College, 1876–1877.

The fledgling young doctor returned to St. Paul
in March 1877. Six feet tall, lean, blue-eyed, with a
thick mat of wavy red hair, Hoyt was a dashing 23-
year-old, the same age as Dr. Murphy when he first
brought his bride to Minnesota in 1849. Hoyt also
found himself in the same predicament as had his
uncle: his medical education was incomplete. He
still had a year's course work before him to earn his
M.D. degree. But apparent "itchy" feet, perhaps his
pioneering heritage, coupled with an empty pocket,
beckoned. Instead of completing a second year of

medical courses as required in the 1870s, the restless young man headed West like so many of his
generation—West to a once-in-a-lifetime opportunity of exciting adventures.

The West that lured Hoyt was still largely un-
tamed and wild. In the aftermath of the Civil War,
the coming of the railroad brought with it a steady
influx of settlers. Dakota Territory, created by Congress in 1861, did not boom until railroad engineers
began inching westward into the northern portion,
the present town of Bismarck being established in
1872. The far-flung territory had a population of
20,000 in 1872, a figure that increased dramatically
within two years. In August 1874, the nation was
electrified with the news of the Black Hills gold
discovery. By 1876 some 20,000 people crowded
into the mining district sprawling around the new
towns of Custer and Deadwood. That influx provided the fatal catalyst in extinguishing the uneasy
peace existing between the Sioux and the encroach-
ing whites. The Sioux War of 1876–1877 was the
ultimate price for the Black Hills gold rush; at the
end, the Sioux were broken and vanquished. This
pattern of Indian confrontation would be repeated
along every perimeter of settlement contact and in-
cursion. Indian conflict was a dominant motif in the
history of the Far West in the two post-Civil War
decades.

The railroads, too, played a major role in shaping
the post-bellum Far West. Their coming stimulated

settlement; settlement exacerbated Indian conflict; such outbreaks insured military oppression of the hostile tribes. In the end, the settler triumphed.

Building railroads in the West also greatly stimulated economic development and growth. A notable example was the emergence of the "cattle kingdom," replete with that rich panoramic imagery so familiar to the American West—droving herds of longhorn cattle loping across dusty, distant vistas; mulling herds fording turbulent streams; wide skies streaked with threads of lightning or ablaze with sun or stars; the thunder of wild stampedes; the ominous threat from stalking Indians and marauders; twangy-speaking cowhands twirling lariats; the solitary chuck wagon; and slouched figures of cowboys bobbing in the saddle.

By the end of the Civil War railroads already had slashed through much of the Kansas and Nebraska landscape. In the bargain the Union Pacific was hard at work racing west to meet the Central Pacific building east from California to complete the central route, an accomplishment realized in Utah at Promontory Point, May 10, 1869. Meanwhile, to the south in Texas, a surfeit of cattle, accumulated during war years, significantly depressed prices on the local market, while demand in the Midwest soared in the face of short supply. An enterprising handful of adventurous cattlemen seized the opportunity and initiated the "Long Drive," trailing herds of cattle north from the Brazos to Kansas and Nebraska railheads. Between 1865 and 1879 some four million head of cattle reached midwestern and eastern markets by this arduous means.

In efforts to shorten the trail distance to the railroads, veteran cattlemen, joined by determined novices, searched for new ranges to feed and stock their herds. This search led to the opening of the Texas Panhandle in 1876, ranching expansion into western and southwestern portions of the Territory of New Mexico, with like development in southern Colorado and the adjacent Indian Territory, which eventually became present-day Oklahoma. This raw frontier attracted young men by the scores, a hardy breed who welcomed the prospect of life in the open in lands unencumbered by the trappings of civilization; indeed, the excitement of being involved in the opening up of America's last virgin frontier. It was a region whose lifestyle quickly separated the men from the boys and made boys men overnight. Henry Hoyt at age twenty-four was drawn to this cowman's new domain. He became a part of that milieu, first as a cowboy, then as a pioneer physician, on this new frontier of the cattlemen's range.

Gradually the heyday of the "Long Drive" faded as the railroads came ever closer. And as the railroads came ever closer, increasing numbers of settlers appeared along the right-of-ways. Railroad hamlets became towns; towns became cities; cities meant a new lifestyle. The days of rambunctious herds, unruly cowhands, flamboyant gunfighters, overnight vigilantes, and violent conduct gradually withered in the wake of increased demands of the populace for law and order, public decency, and respectability. The requirements of an urban environment muted the way of life mirrored in the cattlemen's frontier. Change was mandated; accommodation was required. Perhaps sensing this, Hoyt decided to leave the West he had first encountered; the West he loved, a West that was open and unfettered, was a West that was slowly vanishing. If he had to live in an orderly and stable society, he may well have pondered, Minnesota would do just as well as New Mexico.

There is little question that Hoyt could have remained in the West had he elected to do so. His last place of residence before returning east was Bernalillo, New Mexico, where he had a good medical practice. From his first appearance in the Dakota Territory at Deadwood, he always relied on his medical training as the source of his income and considered himself a "doctor" in every sense. However, doctoring was not always profitable or possible in his peripatetic wanderings. He found this out in Tascosa in the Panhandle. Undaunted, he hired out as a cowboy and was schooled in those basic skills by a young cowpoke, Charlie Siringo, who became his lifelong friend. Again, in Las Vegas, New Mexico, bartending provided his livelihood, along with several other odd employments. In the end, however, the practice of medicine called him to Bernalillo. There he prospered, not lavishly, but modestly. His future was secure.

Why he decided to return east from the West, where he had established himself in comfortable circumstances, is unknown. One could speculate that like so many others before him, Hoyt went West in hopes of striking it rich, with the steady intent of one day returning home. It is obvious why he went to Deadwood—a gold rush was underway. A mining venture there proved a bust. Again, in New Mexico, a second mining interest failed to pan out as well. Yet, when Hoyt headed east, he had amassed $3,000, money earned from a prudent investment in a drugstore and a lucrative practice, which included tending railroad workers. Perhaps it was that accumulated bankroll that provided the final basis for his decision to leave New Mexico. One thing is clear: he had a definite motive; he wanted to complete his medical education.

In March 1882, Hoyt completed the required course of study at Columbus Medical College in Ohio and received his M.D. in a class of fifty-nine. Now a full-fledged doctor of medicine, Hoyt returned to St. Paul. It proved to be a wise choice. His uncle, Dr. Murphy, was a man of considerable influence. He held the office of state surgeon as well as physician-surgeon to several of the large railroad companies headquartered in the city. His reputation was such that he was elected vice president of the National Association of Railroad Surgeons and served as president, 1892–1893. Unquestionably, Dr. Murphy came to the aid of his nephew, for in a very short time Hoyt became physician-surgeon to several railroads, including the Great Northern, as well as becoming a member of the same railroad surgeons' association.

Secure in his job as a railroad physician-surgeon, Hoyt soon found romance. Nothing is known of the circumstances that brought Ella Herrick Owens Gray and Hoyt together. All that is known is that she was the widow of Charles Gray of Des Moines, Iowa, had a son, Owen Herrick Gray, born in February 1876, and had been a widow for some years prior to her marriage to Hoyt on May 23, 1888. The year following, on August 11, the Hoyt's only child, John Terrell Hoyt, was born in St. Paul.

In the same year of his marriage, Hoyt was appointed Commissioner of Health for the city of St. Paul; it was a demanding and important job. He served in that capacity until March 10, 1895. During his tenure, he proved himself a model public health official.

St. Paul was typical of what was being experienced across the nation by one-time rural towns that were being transformed rapidly into cities through industrial and transportation technology. In 1850 St. Paul was a rural hamlet of less than 1,000, but by 1883 it boasted 90,000, an increase due, in part, to railroads which had made the city a major rail center. By 1890 the population had doubled to 185,000! Such spectacular growth in seven years created many serious health hazards and medical problems, especially from epidemical and infectious diseases. Sanitary controls, a good water supply, proper inspection and quarantine provisions, coupled with diligent enforcement became essential for survival of the urban community. Such requirements gave rise to the development of public health. In this respect, Hoyt was among the early pioneers in the field. As he candidly remarked: "The sanitary condition of a city can always be judged by its death rate." His strong advocacy of public-sponsored sanitation programs and his close attention to the handling of infectious diseases, particularly diphtheria and typhoid fever, were praiseworthy. Statistics reflected the effectiveness of the health measures taken: the death rate in 1882 was 16.52 per thousand, but was reduced to 10.48 by 1889. The marked decrease in the death rate was due in no small part to Hoyt's campaign for vaccination and inoculation for epidemical diseases, as well as strong public sanitary policies.

By 1898 Hoyt was an established physician with a family. He was a vigorous forty-four, a citizen of repute. As a reflection of the esteem he had garnered by his career in medicine, from 1895–1898 he was a member of the governing board of St. Joseph's Hospital. Perhaps a bit of complacency and routine tinged his daily living. However, his ordered and staid existence was quickly altered in 1898 with the advent of the Spanish-American War.

When the United States declared war on Spain, April 20, 1898, public sentiment had been whipped to a fury by the sensational journalism practiced by William Randolph Hearst and Joseph Pulitzer in their New York based newspapers, the *Journal* and the *World*. The exile residence in the United States of José Martí, the leading Cuban revolutionary leader, and his tragic death on his native isle in the cause of freedom, had stirred many. The cruel and harsh repressive measures imposed by Spain on Cuba in the island's struggle for independence had long dominated headlines. But the ultimate factor in determining American public opinion was the destruction of the *U.S.S. Maine* in Havana harbor, February 15, 1898. The sinking of the battleship proved the point of no return.

Two days after declaring war, Congress authorized the creation of a volunteer force of 200,000 men and subsequently approved an increase in the regular army from 28,000 to 60,000. Responding to the call for volunteers, Hoyt enlisted on May 26 in the Medical Department of the United States Volunteers as chief surgeon with the rank of major. Reared in the post-Civil War generation in which pride of service in the cause of the Union was widespread, Hoyt leaped at the opportunity afforded. Mayhap a surge of his youthful wanderlust and craving for adventure helped spark his patriotic sensibilities. He was followed by thousands, including the hundreds of westerners who flocked to join Teddy Roosevelt's Rough Riders.

Within a few months, the United States Navy was victorious both in Cuba and the Philippines. By July, Cuba and Puerto Rico were under American control; Manila fell on August 13. Peace was restored by the Treaty of Paris, signed on December 10, 1898. Under its terms Spain relinquished sovereignty over Cuba, ceded Guam and Puerto Rico outright to the United States, and ceded the Philippines for a payment of $20 million. The latter provision in the treaty triggered the tragic Filipino insurrection.

Shortly after the Spanish-American War commenced, the United States arranged for the return to the Philippines, from exile in Hong Kong, of Filipino patriot Emilio Aguinaldo, leader of the independence movement from Spain. He was to lead a native resistance movement while the United States launched its military and naval expeditions. Upon reaching Luzon Island, Aguinaldo recruited a Filipino army and established a provisional government, on June 12, 1898, which declared the Philippines independent of Spain.

In early January 1899, when Aguinaldo learned of the peace treaty's Philippine provision, he felt betrayed by the United States. On January 5 he raised the cry of independence. Mediating efforts on behalf of the federal government failed to blunt

Filipino outrage. By February 4 an armed revolt against American rule erupted. A bitter and cruel guerrilla war ensued in which both sides utilized brutal and ruthless tactics. Although Aguinaldo was captured on March 23, 1901, Filipino resistance continued for another year until an uneasy peace was effected in mid-1902 with the promise of eventual independence for the Philippines.

Hoyt, as well as a large contingent of other war volunteers, continued to serve during the Filipino insurrection. Like many other officers, as the conflict with the insurgents waned, he brought his wife and son to live with him while on duty at Nueva Caceres, Camarines Sur. One night an accidental fire swept their rooms, almost claiming their lives, and seriously burning John, the Hoyts' son. There is every reason to believe that Hoyt would have remained in army service as a medical officer had it not been for the tragic fire in his private quarters. But the injury his son suffered, which greatly jeopardized the boy's health, forced Hoyt to resign his commission.

Literally, Hoyt's recollections end with his military discharge, October 10, 1902, when he was only forty-eight years old. He modestly concludes his narrative with the comment that "after visiting our Eastern cities and making a tour through Old Mexico, I again took up the practice of my profession at El Paso, Texas, later settling in Long Beach, California, the queen of the beach cities in this State, which has now been my home for nearly twenty years . . ." This statement was penned in 1928. Thus we learn that he lived in Long Beach at least from 1908 or 1909. What of the intervening years between discharge and Long Beach?

A slender outline of those years can be gleaned from Hoyt's pension file in the National Archives in which he recorded his places of residence after his discharge from service, in October 1902: "Salt Lake City, Utah: Muskogee, Okla: Des Moines, Iowa: Minneapolis, Minn: Durango, Colo: Mexico City, Mexico: San Luis Potosi, Mexico: Washington, D.C.: New York City: El Paso, Texas: Los Angeles, Calif: Long Beach, Calif. Don't remember dates."

It is clear that Hoyt was restless after his military service. Equally important, his recollection is silent in respect to his son and wife, with no mention at all of his stepson. An educated guess is that Hoyt encountered some marital difficulties, as his pension petition candidly admitted, "On account of health and climate my wife has been for some years residing with her two sons at Salt Lake City, Utah."

While residing in Long Beach, Hoyt was joined by his widowed mother. She died there on April 13, 1915. Also joining him, as he had during a portion of his New Mexico sojourn, was his brother George. And it was sometime during those same years that Hoyt's wife rejoined him, their marital difficulties apparently resolved. But both George and Mrs. Hoyt would precede Hoyt in death.

When Hoyt turned sixty-five in 1919, he may well have looked forward to retirement from active medical practice. Certainly as he entered the last decade of his life, he began to recall his youthful past. No doubt his recollection was stirred by a renewal of his friendship with Jack Ryan, a friendship dating back to his early days in old Tascosa in the Texas Panhandle. Friendships were also renewed with James H. East, residing in Douglas, Arizona, and with Charles A. Siringo. Another nudge to Hoyt's memory may well have been stimulated by his acquaintance with John Chisum's nephew, William J. Chisum, a resident of Los Angeles, as well as new acquaintances with western writers Emerson Hough and Randall Parish.

In an endeavor to share his recollections, Hoyt began to write letters to former friends and to various publications. Among his earliest letters was one to Siringo, June 9, 1921. The occasion was provoked by Hoyt's reading of Siringo's *The Lone Star Cowboy*, published in 1919, "recently handed to me by our mutual friend, Jack Ryan." Pointedly, Hoyt declared, "it is quite evident that you have forgotten me." He continued:

> I have the distinction of being the first physician that ever located for the practice of medicine in the Panhandle of Texas. I mean, of course, in civil life, as there were doubtless army doctors at Ft. Elliott prior to the time I arrived at Tascosa in November, 1877 with hdqrs. for a time at

Howard and McMasters store on north side of the plaza, Rinehart's being on the west side, Henry Martin (I think that was his name) blacksmith shop on the south and a mexican adobe residence on the west.

Then, in an autobiographical vein, Hoyt highlighted some of his experiences, ending with a capsule of his return east and Spanish-American War service. "If you ever come to Calif. don't fail to look me up," Hoyt wrote. "I would sure enjoy a 'harked back' with you." There is little question: this sevenpage letter was a prelude to a larger memoir which would eventually be written.[5]

The following year Siringo moved to Los Angeles, settling in Hollywood. There he resided until his death, in 1928. The two former cowboys probably shared many an evening together "harking back" to their Panhandle days. For Siringo's last book, *Riata and Spurs*, published in 1927, Hoyt provided as an illustration a copy of the receipt given him by Billy the Kid for a horse, an illustration also used by Hoyt in his book. Siringo reciprocated in kind by providing Hoyt with a photograph of their former boss, Bill Moore, foreman of the LX Ranch, under whom they had worked as cowboys. It probably was Siringo who had suggested Houghton

---

[5] Typescript, Panhandle-Plains Historical Museum, Canyon, Texas. Siringo added this postscript to Hoyt's letter: "I knew the writer of this letter well, when he was an LX cowboy."

Mifflin Company, the publisher of his *Riata and Spurs*, as a possible outlet for Hoyt's recollections.

A lengthy correspondence between Hoyt and Mrs. Annie Dyer Nunn, related to Colonel Charles Goodnight, famed Texas cowman, developed after Hoyt read an article by Mrs. Nunn on her illustrious kinfolk, which had appeared in *The Dearborn (Michigan) Independent*. Hoyt's letters fleshed out numerous details, many of them being incorporated directly into his final effort, *A Frontier Doctor*. No doubt there are other letters of a similar nature scattered among Hoyt's "old timers."

Perhaps additional correspondence was stimulated by Hoyt's detailed letters to various publications. Two examples have been located. The first appeared in a letter to the editor of the *International Book Review*, in January 1925. Written on December 1, 1924, the text focused on Hoyt's New Mexico experiences, with some reference to the Panhandle, and was headlined "Bad Men of the Pioneer West." This was subsequently reprinted in the *Childress (Texas) Index*, March 23, 1925, under the heading "Bad Men Who Lived in the Panhandle."

From these seedlings sprang Hoyt's *A Frontier Doctor*. However, such was not his objective when he first communicated with Houghton Mifflin editor Ira Rich Kent. Writing on February 15, 1928, Hoyt was blunt:

> I mailed you a letter a short time ago but have been thinking and a new idea has occurred to me.

In the matter of putting out a book its success naturally depends largely upon the ability and reputation of the writer, or writers.

As my name is but a -o- in the book game, the greater the name and reputation of the person I can rope in as 'co-respondent' the bigger the results. I am also well aware that the greater one becomes in the literary world the desire to *share* this greatness with a *tyro* becomes correspondingly *less*. That being true I will have to depend more upon old lady luck in hand-cuffing myself with a real celebrity than anything else.

Obviously, Hoyt was unsure of his skill and talent in writing a memoir that would be publishable. He sorely lacked confidence in his literary ability. The solution he proposed was simple: recruit Frederick Palmer for the job. Palmer had served as a correspondent in the Philippines during the Spanish-American War, thus was acquainted with one dimension of Hoyt's experiences. During that time they had become "very good friends." Besides, Palmer had a name. He had served as chief of the Intelligence Bureau during World War I and had been made a colonel. In the bargain Palmer had published a number of books, including a novel, *The Last Shot*, which Hoyt hailed as "one of the most remarkable prophecies (unintentional, too) that I ever read."

With the assistance of Palmer, Hoyt envisioned an authentic account of the Aguinaldo campaign, one which had yet to be written. To strengthen that side of the proposal, he informed Kent, "I have a diary that I kept of the entire campaign that would come in OK. It has blood stains still perceptible on notes I made with bloody hands after giving first aid on battle fields." Gleefully Hoyt exclaimed, "Now, if I *could* have the wonderful luck of interesting Frederick Palmer to take up my early career and wind up with the story of our joint experiences in the Philippines, say, wouldent [sic] it be a winner?" In closing, Hoyt asked the publisher to initiate the contact with Palmer, and he concluded, "Here's to good luck."[6]

Nothing ever came of this suggestion. Unfortunately the replies to Hoyt's letters have not survived, or if they have, they have yet to be located. Thus one is left to surmise as to Kent's response.

In the weeks intervening between the February letter and the next one which survives, June 9, 1928, Hoyt had written his recollections. Addressing Kent again, he remarked:

> Not hearing from you after sending the sample of my corrected manuscript . . . I decided you were satisfied with the sample and have acted accordingly.
>
> My manuscript has been corrected, revised,

[6]Houghton Mifflin Papers, Houghton Library, Harvard University. It is interesting to note that Hoyt's letters were typed by himself, training which probably reflects a year he spent in a St. Paul business school in his youth.

and rewritten and, as you see, is now in your hands to do with as you think best.

In surrendering editorial control over the copy to the editor, as well as the matter of illustrations, Hoyt placed one stipulation, one made at the outset of publication negotiations—"if a book is published of my story I want my army career as a wind up, to be just as prominent as my ups and downs, mostly 'ne'er do well,' during my five or six years experience in the early west."

With the acceptance of the manuscript for publication, the question of title became a prime consideration. Several friends and well-wishers who had learned about Hoyt's "'alleged' book . . . asked 'what is the title' and upon being informed it was still 'up in the air' . . . made several suggestions and each one contains either 'Red Head' or 'Red Headed,' for example—'The Thrilling Adventures of a Red Headed Medico'—'The Experiences and Adventures of a Red Headed Doctor,' etc., etc." Later two additional suggestions surfaced: "Pills and Thrills by a Red-headed Medico" and "True Tales of a Red-headed Doctor, Pioneer in Texas Panhandle and the Philippines." The good sense of the Boston-based publisher prevailed and the dignified title, *A Frontier Doctor*, was selected.

A Frontier Doctor was released by Hoyt's publisher on November 10, 1929. A short time after, on November 18, Hoyt, joined by his sister Sue, Mrs. George S. Wilson of Minneapolis, and her husband, took passage on the *S.S. President Cleveland* from Los Angeles via San Francisco for Manila. At Honolulu, Mr. Wilson disembarked while Hoyt and his sister proceeded to Manila. They planned to spend three weeks visiting their other sister, Mrs. George R. Harvey. While en route to Honolulu, Hoyt had the pleasant surprise of hearing a San Francisco broadcast of a review of his book.

Two days east of Yokohama, Hoyt penned a letter to his son and daughter-in-law. He commented wryly, "I have always been rather long on *coincidents* and yesterday ran across another." On board ship he ran into Miss Ann Livingstone of New York City, the same lady he had met at a party given by General Frederick Grant when he was stationed in the Philippines. "We sure had a great hark back all right," he wrote. "She and a brother veteran of the Spanish and World Wars are en route to Manila, her first visit since 1900."

Hoyt also met on the ship George W. Hunt, "a man who worked as a laborer at a dollar a day for a contractor building the S.P.R.R. [Southern Pacific Railroad] in New Mexico when I was there 50 years ago—later moved to Arizona, served in the legislature of that ter[ritory] & state for 14 years—governor for 13 years and Minister to Siam for 6 years. . . ." Hoyt concluded:

> . . . I was perfectly astonished to learn who he was—I won't tell you just what I said to him, but I found him to be a great old scout and as we had

many mutual friends among old timers we
pass[ed] many pleasant hours harking back. . . .

When the passenger ship docked at Manila on
the morning of December 19, the Harveys were at
the pier "with their big limousine & liveried Filipino chauffeur" to greet Hoyt and his sister Sue.
Three crowded weeks ensued. Since his brother-in-
law George Harvey was Judge of the Court of the
First Instance, the highest trial court in the Philippine judiciary, Hoyt quickly found himself being
introduced to all the leading figures in Manila.
Among those he met were the new governor general, Dwight F. Davis, who as secretary of war under
President Coolidge had signed Hoyt's Silver Star
citation for gallantry during his war service, and
Major General Douglas MacArthur, son of Lieutenant General Arthur MacArthur under whose command Hoyt had served in the Spanish-American
War. On a subsequent visit with Major General
MacArthur, the general autographed a photograph
portrait, "With affectionate regards from the son of
your old comrade-in-arms. Jan. 4, 1930." Hoyt was
equally impressed with Emilio Aguinaldo whom he
heard speak at a banquet with General MacArthur.

Other than sharing Christmas with his two sisters
in the Harvey bungalow, the greatest thrill for Hoyt
was to retrace his tour of duty. Mrs. Harvey placed
her car at his disposal and for a week the one-time
Spanish-American War volunteer revisited many of
the scenes of his wartime service.

The three-week visit ended on January 10, 1930, when Hoyt and his sister Sue boarded the *S.S. President Jackson* for their return voyage. Two days later, while at anchor in Hong Kong, Hoyt scribbled a note to his son and daughter-in-law on the back of the ship's dinner menu in which he boasted:

> . . . Had about the biggest 3 weeks of my life while in the Philippines. Toured over the trail of our big campaign of 30 years ago in Ray's Studebaker President Eight Limousine, driven by her liveried Filipino chauffeur, the best driver I ever rode with except Barney Oldfield—then a fine visit with Maj. Gen. Douglas MacArthur, now commanding all troops in the Islands & last but not least I spent P.M. New Years day with Gen. Emilio Aguinaldo at his palatial home near Cavite, and was treated like a brother. . . .

There would be no more letters. On January 21, while the ship was docked in Yokohama, Hoyt died. He would have celebrated his seventy-sixth birthday on January 30. His body was brought back to Long Beach for the funeral. Harrison Leussler, head of Houghton Mifflin's San Francisco office, attended to all details since Hoyt's son, accompanied by his wife, was in Europe.[7]

[7] Hoyt's son, John Terrell, carved a fine career for himself as a mining engineer. Highly successful and prosperous, he died in Darien, Connecticut, February 7, 1962, survived by his widow and two sons, John Terrell Hoyt, Jr., and Owen Franklin Hoyt, both of whom were born after the death of their grandfather. *The Darien Review*, February 8, 1962.

Leussler expressed his condolences to Hoyt's son and described the final rites for his "good friend":

. . . The services were beautiful, and I felt that the tribute by the Spanish American Veteran's Camp with its military dignity was a real 'last farewell.' I cannot recall a time in my life, when the passing of a relative has effected me as it did today. The notes of 'Taps' in the ending closes the day of a good friend, and Father. There were many beautiful flowers and the services were well attended. Your uncle Mr. Wilson and I accompanied the body to the crematory.

Hoyt's one-page holigraphic will was specific; he wished to be cremated and his ashes scattered on the Pacific Ocean in front of Long Beach. That wish was fulfilled.

Although Hoyt Street in St. Paul, Minnesota, was named to honor the memory of his father, the enduring testimonial of Henry Franklin Hoyt's life is his autobiography, *A Frontier Doctor*. It is a fitting epitaph to his life of coincidences as it harkens back to yesteryear when the West was ripe for adventure for those who dared.

EDITOR'S ACKNOWLEDGMENTS

Because of the broad geographical sweep of Henry F. Hoyt's *A Frontier Doctor*, coupled with the expanse of subjects included in the book, I have had to call upon the assistance and expertise of a number of individuals. Some have rendered major assistance, others have supplied answers to limited queries. It is fitting and proper that this invaluable aid, large and small, be duly acknowledged.

Those who have responded to limited queries include: James de T. Abajian, San Francisco; Doris A. Beaven, assistant clerk, Court of Probate, Darien, Connecticut; Jack K. Boyer, director, Kit Carson Foundation, Taos; Donald M. Duke, San Marino, California; Jeff C. Dykes, College Park, Maryland; Louis A. Hieb, head, Special Collections, University of Arizona, Tucson; Ruth E. Kelly, Rosenberg Library, Galveston, Texas; Robert J. Moes, M.D., Los Angeles; Lynn I. Perrigo, professor emeritus of New Mexico Highland University, Las Vegas; Larry Remele, editor, *North Dakota History*, State Historical Society of North Dakota, Bismarck; Philip J. Roberts, Wyoming State Archives and Historical Department, Laramie; Orlando Romero, New Mexico State Library; Albert Shumate, M.D., San Francisco; Lawrence T. Suess, administrator, Saint Joseph's Hospital, St. Paul, Minnesota; Robert A. Weinstein, Los Angeles; John R. Wills, associate professor of history, University of Southern California.

Special searches were undertaken for me on a number of matters by Anthony J. Amodeo, Department of Special Collections, Newberry Library, Chicago; Ruth Ellen Bauer, reference services aide, Minnesota Historical Society, St. Paul; Stephany Eger, Museum of New Mexico, Santa Fe; Elaine C. Everly, assistant chief, Navy and Old Army Branch, Military Archives Division, National Archives, Washington, D.C.; Peter D. Olch, M.D., deputy chief, History of Medicine Division, National Library of Medicine, Bethesda, Maryland; James H. Purdy, New Mexico State Records Center, Santa Fe; Pauline Rankin, curator, Adams Memorial Hall Museum, Deadwood, South Dakota; Dorothy Ross, archives assistant, Ohio State University, Columbus; Mrs. Helen M. Rowland, assistant librarian, Association of American Railroads, Washington, D.C.; W. R. "Bill" Schroeder, Citizens Savings Athletic Foundation, Los Angeles; Mary Kay Snell, Public Library, Amarillo, Texas; Jean-Jacques L. Strayer, Darien Library, Darien, Connecticut; Vivian Lee Welch, Phoenix, Arizona.

Two individuals rendered invaluable assistance of a more extended sort: Edward R. Eberhardt, Public Health Services Manager, Department of Community Services, Division of Public Health, St. Paul, and Mrs. Claire R. Kuehn, archivist-librarian, The Panhandle-Plains Historical Museum, Canyon,

Texas. Mr. Robert N. Mullin, South Laguna, California, made a notable contribution based on his extensive files relating to Billy the Kid.

I owe a particular debt of thanks to the Reference Department, Doheny Library, University of Southern California, for handling my many requests for interlibrary loan materials, and to the History Collection, University Library, New Mexico Highlands University, Las Vegas, for courtesy in responding to a number of queries and supplying a microfilm of the *Las Vegas Optic*.

Invaluable aid was given me by the grandson of Henry F. Hoyt, John Terrell Hoyt, Jr., Stockbridge, Massachusetts. He placed at my disposal the surviving materials relating to his grandfather's book, all of which has been incorporated into this new edition. His brother, Owen F. Hoyt, San Francisco, was the catalyst in arranging for this fortunate circumstance which so greatly enhances this book.

Lastly, I am most grateful to Mrs. Eleanor Kelman, my typist, for her careful eye and efficient skill in rendering final copy.

DOYCE B. NUNIS, JR.

December 15, 1978

A Frontier Doctor

I

A Pioneer Boyhood

URING State Fair Week in September, 1927, I visited a flying-field at the southeast corner of Snelling and Larpenteur Avenues, St. Paul, Minnesota. Planes were humming through the air in every direction, when suddenly a young woman dropped from one as it passed over, a parachute unfolded, and she made a graceful landing but a few paces from where I first appeared on the screen of life.

In 1854, this flying-field was a typical Minnesota farm, owned by my father, Lorenzo Hoyt, who had arrived in Minnesota as a pioneer in 1848. Our farm then was practically a self-sufficing unit. Not only did we raise all our own food, including a coffee substitute composed of several varieties of parched cereals, but we even provided our own clothing by raising and shearing our own sheep, carding the wool and spinning it, and on our own loom making our own cloth.

There were no railroads in St. Paul in those early days. All our transportation was by stage or steamboat. Two of my uncles were rivermen and one of my pleasures was driving down to the levee at the foot of Jackson Street to meet the boats coming upriver from New Orleans. Sometimes as my father and I sat in the buggy watching the unloading of the boat, very often a fine-looking, strongly featured young man would come over and chat with us. This was James J. Hill, then working as a freight clerk at forty-five dollars a month.[1] Many years later, when, by his remarkable foresight and acumen, he had risen to be one of the great railway magnates of the country, the head of the Great Northern Railway lines, I became chief surgeon of all his properties.

Very well do I remember also the many bands of Indians who visited the old farm, coming from the West with furs, buckskins, pemmican, and maple sugar to sell or trade. They camped all about our home during their annual visits, and as my father spoke their language they became very friendly. I attracted their special attention because I had a profusion of curly red hair. This they seemed to admire greatly, and I received many presents of moccasins, leggings, etc. My complacency with this state of affairs, however, was shattered by one of our hired men who told me that the reason they paid so much attention to my red curls was because they were preparing to go on the warpath, and as red scalps were very scarce, they would be after mine the first thing. At once there was a noticeable cooling in my friendship for the visitors.

[1] All prominent individuals mentioned in Hoyt's text have been identified for the convenience of the reader. They can be found at the end of the last chapter in *Biographical Notes*, arranged in alphabetical order.

Father had always bought from the Indians quantities of their maple sugar, which, with buckwheat cakes, was an ever-popular item on our winter morning breakfast menus. One day it was found out that they always strained the maple sap through their blankets, and from that time Indian maple sugar was taboo in the family, and syrup from home-grown sorghum became the favorite sweetener.

It was the usual thing for these Indians to file silently into our kitchen in the early morning, squat around the kitchen stove, and gratefully eat the abundant leavings from our table that mother scraped into a dish and passed to them. Later on many of these very Indians were active in the terrible massacres that took place in Minnesota in 1862.

Father was a Major of the militia that organized for protection against this outbreak. Excitement was tense when one evening word came that the savages were within a few miles of Long Lake, or about twenty miles north of St. Paul, and the militia were instructed to meet at our farm at daybreak and march against them. How distinctly I remember sitting up the most of that night helping my father mould bullets for the anticipated encounter on the morrow. The militia assembled according to schedule and galloped away, leaving a weeping family at our home. The wily enemy, however, had disappeared, and no blood was shed.

Shortly after this, while going through the woods one day, my father ran across an old muzzle-loading army musket, which he brought home, and, as I had just been taught to operate a shotgun, he gave it to me. It was very rusty, but I spent several days cleaning it up, and, as we had a fine twenty-acre grove just north of our house where game was always abundant, I loaded it and sallied forth. Soon I ran across an animal which appeared to be a rabbit and immediately blazed away, bringing down both myself and the quarry, for the old musket worked forcefully at both ends. Almost stunned, I finally got up, retrieved my game, and staggered home, only to be informed that I had been mistaken in my diagnosis of the species, and a burial of my clothes was ordered.

My memories of childhood also include episodes of the Civil War, in which five uncles and several cousins participated, receiving their training at Fort Snelling, just a few miles from home.[2] I remember particularly the intense pleasure experienced on occasional visits there when watching General Gorman putting the raw recruits through their paces. Two of my uncles were members of the famous First Minnesota Volunteer Infantry which so distinguished itself at Gettysburg.

I grew into a strong, healthy lad, tall and athletic, and at thirteen was doing a man's work on the farm.

[2]All important and unusual places referred to by Hoyt are identified in *Place Notes* at the end of the last chapter, following *Biographical Notes*. They are arranged in alphabetical order.

This meant that I could shoulder a two-bushel bag of wheat without help and perform similar feats of strength and dexterity. My schooling was the usual sort that a country boy got at country schools, with the addition of a term at Lake City, Minnesota, a course at the Faddis Business College, St. Paul, and the sessions of 1870 and 1871 at the Minnesota State University.

My school term at Lake City was my last one in public school. While there I lived with my maternal grandfather, Henry K. Terrell, a former Virginian who had gone out to California in '49, and come from there to Minnesota in 1850. He was an ardent hunter, and while I was there he took me on my first deer hunt in the area near Mazeppa and the Zumbro River, the very district where my friend, William S. Hart, passed many of his childhood days.

The Faddis Business College was located on Third Street, St. Paul. One evening when I was about to start home, an argument arose as to who was the best runner in the class. To settle the dispute, a course was measured down Third Street, judges were selected, and another student, James Aherne, known to his friends as 'Slim Jim,' was paired off with me for the contest. Away we dashed in the moonlight. Soon Jim found I was gaining on him and being a great practical joker, he stopped suddenly, yelling at the top of his voice, 'Stop thief!' A big policeman appeared from somewhere, and before I could get him to listen to me, he had me well on the way to the station house. His name was Andy Call, now a special guard at the First National Bank of St. Paul.

My father decided that he could not afford to send me through college. I then asked and received permission to leave home and see if I could not earn enough to educate myself. I was convinced that he gave his consent with the idea that sooner or later I would be glad to return to the farm, but if this were so, he was mistaken.

My first inclination was to become a civil engineer, and learning that the St. Paul and Pacific Railroad was sending out a surveying party, I applied to the chief engineer for a job. He looked me over, asked a few questions, and took me on. The proposed survey was to be from Glyndon to St. Vincent, paralleling the course of the Red River of the North. The party was in charge of C. A. J. Morris, a son of the chief engineer, and he had two assistant engineers, Henry Hollingshead and a Mr. Wheaton. I was given the position of rodman and worked with Mr. Wheaton, who operated the level.

Our outfit left St. Cloud for Glyndon in three covered wagons, the members of the party perching on top of the loaded vehicles as best we could. Our route ran along the east bank of the Mississippi by way of Little Falls—later the home of 'Lindy'—to Brainerd, thence to Glyndon.[3] The country dirt road was very rough, ruts and deep mud holes being

[3]Though born in Detroit, Charles A. Lindbergh, Jr.'s childhood home was near Little Falls, Minnesota.

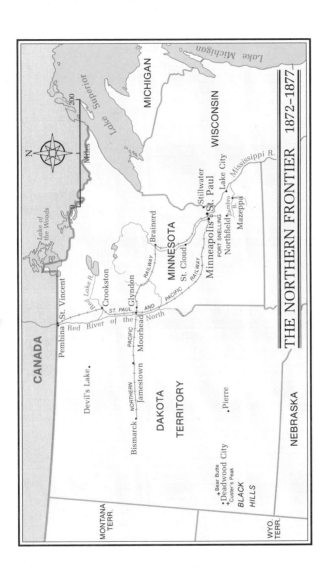

THE NORTHERN FRONTIER 1872–1877

much in evidence. One of these holes would have written 'finis' to my earthly career had I been in less perfect physical trim. In passing through Little Falls, the right front wheel of the wagon dropped into a hole with a lurch that pitched me headfirst between the front and hind wheels. As my head was sinking in the mud, I somehow threw myself clear of it all just as the rear wheel crushed my fur cap deep in the mire with the weight of over a ton.

Reaching Glyndon, the party was organized. I knew nothing of the different positions, but it appeared that the rodman's job paid fifteen dollars a month more than the rest. Most of the party had been out before and knew this, so each was doing his best to pick the plum.

It was early in the spring of 1872, snow and ice were melting fast, and all the streams were swollen with rapid currents. It became necessary to cross the one at our camp. The stream was too deep and rapid to ford, so a raft was constructed and Engineer Morris called for a volunteer to swim across with a rope with which to pull the raft to and fro. There was plenty of floating ice and the stream was about twenty-five yards wide. I was the first to respond and, being a strong swimmer, I soon had the rope over and tied to a tree.

Next morning the men were assigned their duties by Mr. Morris, and I was selected as rodman, which I learned later was due to my alacrity in coming to the front at the ford.

Our course ran through a level country, mostly prairie, with an occasional strip of timber and underbrush. In some places the entire prairie would be literally covered with grasshoppers, a scourge that virtually devastated western Minnesota for some years. To one fresh from our beautiful farm home, this seemed the most worthless country imaginable.

Reaching Red Lake River, the largest in that section, we found it high, with a swift current and plenty of ice still floating. Again it became necessary to use a raft. A clumsy one was built of green timber and started on an experimental trip, with Billy Gooding, son of the St. Paul Chief of Police, who was a chainman in our party, and myself, as the crew. Each of us had a long, strong pole to keep off the cakes of ice. At first all went well, but, when we struck the swift current and floating ice, our 'Injun yacht' began to whirl around and around. Then suddenly, like a stricken submarine, she sank to the bottom, leaving us swimming for dear life. Billy, who was a strong swimmer like myself, bumped into a chunk of ice that nearly sent him after the raft, but he shook it off and soon joined me in a downward career which, as usual, was not slow. We found to our dismay that the banks on either side were so precipitous that we could not climb out. We were forced to keep on swimming. The other members of the party were pacing along the bank, but powerless to help us. We must have been carried down at least a half-mile, chilled and almost exhausted, when we saw wild grapevines hanging over the bank. These proved our salvation. We grasped and hung to them while the boys quickly improvised a kind of sling with some willow withes and pulled us up. A rousing log fire soon dried and put new life in us. Crookston, Minnesota, with a population of seven thousand, now occupies the site of this near tragedy.

II

Marking the Boundary

Early in the spring of 1873, I became interested in the Government Expedition sent out to survey the boundary line between the United States and Canada, from the Lake of the Woods on the northern line of Minnesota, west on the forty-ninth parallel of latitude to the foothills of the Rocky Mountains.

The English Government sent out a similar expedition to coöperate with the Americans. Since the route was through a perfectly wild country, a strong escort was supplied by both governments, ours sending Troops D and I of the famous Seventh Cavalry, U.S.A., officered by Captains Weir and Keogh, Lieutenants Edgerly and Porter, and Captain A. A. Harback's company of the Twentieth Infantry.

Troop I, with Captain Keogh and Lieutenant Porter, was one of the five troops later wiped out with General George A. Custer at the battle of the Little Big Horn River in Montana, June 25, 1876. Troop D, with Captain Weir and Lieutenant Edgerly, I am told, was in Captain Benteen's command in this same memorable battle.

In St. Paul I had formed a close friendship with a young man about my age, Charles W. Paist by name, and we decided to make this venture together. We made application to join the expedition as civilian employees, were accepted, and shortly entrained on the Northern Pacific Railway for Moorhead, Minnesota, where we took a steamer down the Red River of the North for Pembina, Dakota Territory, where there was a small army post and where the expedition was to organize.

We arrived there about the first of May, 1873, with the mercury over 100° in the shade.[1] There was great activity in every direction, and, after unloading the steamer and drawing all kinds of supplies from the Post, our camp sprang up as if by magic. Until our military escort arrived, we civilians were obliged to stand guard at night.

Nothing very exciting happened the first night until about 3 A.M., when a bunch of hungry hogs from a nearby half-breed's ranch made a raid on the commissary tents. The sentry there took them for thieves and opened up strong with a Sharp's carbine, and in a moment the entire camp was in an uproar. Everybody turned out and contributed his share. The result was that we were rationed with fresh pork for several days thereafter.

The military escorts soon began to roll in, accompanied with extensive mule trains, six mules to

[1]Hoyt's memory is faulty here. The steamboat *Selkirk* reached Pembina on June 1. The surveying party departed from the post on June 9. John E. Parsons, *West on the 49th Parallel: Red River to the Rockies, 1872–1876* (New York, 1963), p. 61.

a wagon, driven by a 'mule skinner,' who rode the nigh wheeler, and steered his team with a single rein fastened to the bit of the nigh leader. A steady pull was the signal for a left turn, and several quick jerks meant that a turn to the right was desired. The rein was carried in the left hand, and its efficiency was reënforced by a whip, the handle of which was about two feet long and the lash about thirty, carried in the right hand of the 'skinner.'

When the expedition had assembled, the wagons were loaded to the limit with all kinds of supplies, and off we started. The column was divided into three divisions, Astronomical, Line, and Topographical. I was assigned to the first mentioned, and my friend Paist to the Line. The Astronomical Division was in charge of Captain Gregory, U.S.A., and the Line Division in charge of Lieutenant Greene, U.S.A. I have forgotten who commanded the Topographical Division.[2]

The Astronomical party would take reckonings both day and night, establish the latitude and longitude, and sink a large post on the forty-ninth parallel of latitude. This accomplished, we would break camp and wend our way westward for sixty miles and proceed as before.

The British expedition was doing likewise, but

[2]Lieutenant Francis V. Greene was in charge of the Line and Topographical Divisions. Archibald Campbell and W[illiam] J. Twining, *Reports upon the Survey of the Boundary* . . . (Washington, D.C., 1878), 44th Cong., 2nd Sess., *Senate Executive Document No. 41*, p. 69.

they would plant their posts just halfway between ours, so there would be an astronomical post on the forty-ninth parallel of latitude every thirty miles. The Line party would follow, survey a straight line between the thirty-mile posts, and plant a post or put up a stone monument every mile. I am told that these original posts have since been supplanted by iron monuments. The Line party was then followed by the Topographical party making topographical maps of the country.

As I was very fond of hunting, I had taken with me a good shotgun, the only one with the expedition. Game was plentiful, and as I was a good shot I kept our party well supplied with all kinds. The cavalry officers had a fine pack of hounds and as everybody had good horses to ride there was no limit to the sport we enjoyed. Captain Keogh's Comanche, later the only survivor of Custer's battle of the Little Big Horn, was one of the best among the Americans, and there were some splendid mounts among the English contingent also.[3]

[3]When found, Comanche had been wounded five times. He was taken downstream on the *Far West* and recuperated at Fort Lincoln. Honorably retired, when the 7th Cavalry was posted to Fort Leavenworth, Comanche went along. There he died on November 6, 1891. Unable to raise sufficient money for a taxidermist, the soldiers of the 7th turned over the remains to the University of Kansas. The horse stands today in the Lawrence institution's museum. Daniel O. Magnussen, ed., *Peter Thompson's Narrative of the Little Bighorn Campaign, 1876* (Glendale, Calif., 1974), p. 274, and *note* 26, pp. 275-276.

There was often but a short distance between our camps, and when this happened, there was always more or less rivalry, athletic and otherwise, between us. I had received a course of training from Ned Moulton, at that period a very famous professional sprinter, during my last year at the University of Minnesota, and could cover one hundred yards in ten and three-quarters seconds, which is rather fast for a non-professional six-footer weighing close to two hundred pounds. Ned had presented me with a very fine pair of calfskin, spiked running shoes, and I can truthfully say I was beaten but once on this expedition, although I raced many times.

One day a bunch of our British neighbors came over and announced that they had heard we had a runner in our camp. If that was so they had a race to propose. They declared they had a man who would carry any one in our camp on his back and run with him fifty yards to our sprinter's one hundred. As we had a man weighing over two hundred pounds, our boys were all keen for the contest.

I consented readily enough to run, but advised my friends not to wager anything on me, as I had never heard of any such race and had no idea what might be the outcome. The course was measured off, the preliminaries arranged, and we took our places. Anatomically my opponent was a freak. He was about five feet tall, with shoulders and chest very broad, body and arms very long, legs very short, body and limbs very hairy. In fact, as I looked at him fifty yards away, he seemed more like an animal than a human. Later I learned he was a Welshman, born and reared in the coal district of Wales.

Our heavyweight mounted his back, the pistol cracked, and away we went. This was many, many years ago, but I can still visualize him as if it were but yesterday. His short legs worked with the rapidity of one of these modern movie stunts where the policeman is chasing a victim, only this was real, not reel.

I was in splendid form, never ran better in my life, but I was beaten by a few inches.

An opportunity soon presented itself, however, to get even with our British brethren. McCarthy, our champion mule skinner, had a joke he used to spring on any 'sucker' who would bite. He would place a coin on top of a tent pin sticking loosely in the sand or soft earth and at a distance of from ten to twenty feet would deftly remove the coin with a crack of his whip, without disturbing or touching the tent pin.

Then he would declare he could crack the coin from the seat of any one's trousers without touching the wearer. One of his mates would offer to bet quite a sum that he could *not*. This would lead to an exciting argument, the money would be put up, and the next move was to get the victim to hold the coin. In this instance, by considerable Western diplomacy, the one secured was from our neighbor's camp, he to have half the winner's stake.

The poor victim, full of visions of what a good time he would have with his share, would get down on all fours, the whip would crack—as would also about six inches of trousers and integument beneath. I can still see vividly the skyward jump our visitor made. If there had been an amplifier and loud speaker then, his yell would have been broadcast all over Canada. When he came down, he was ready to whip the entire Yankee camp and it took another half hour of diplomacy to avert war.

Before I left home I had been taught by a young German a novel race which I introduced whenever I had an opportunity on this survey. I would run a hundred yards, turn a stake, and sprint back to the starting line against a man on horseback. At this stunt I never was beaten. Out West where good horsemen were the rule it was little trouble to arrange this race if it had never been seen before. However, it soon became well known through the expedition and it became difficult to find anyone to compete with me. Occasionally, however, we would meet a roving band of half-breeds on a hunt, or a small party of traders from the Blackfeet Indian country, and, as they were always mounted and eager for sport, my race was soon in evidence.

We passed through all kinds of country. For days it would be level plain in every direction, then we would find the famous Bad Lands in spots along the Dakota and Montana line. Once we came to a valley near a stream and discovered a vast field of wild strawberries, the largest and most deliciously flavored of any I have ever tasted, with the possible exception of the famous Mexican strawberry that can be obtained every day in the year at Irapuato, a station on the Mexican Central Railway some distance north of the city of Mexico.

On another occasion farther west, I started out from camp one day on a hunting expedition in the hope of bringing back a deer for the camp larder. I followed a trail up the side of a mountain for some distance until it led me into a little valley that formed a perfect natural amphitheater. Beside the sloping rocky sides nothing was to be seen except a pyramid of boulders in the very middle. On approaching it I could see the projecting ends of poles upon which the stones had been piled, as though something were secreted beneath. Visions of buried treasure prompted further investigation. I worked strenuously for about an hour heaving the rocks to one side, till finally I was able to pull out a few of the poles. Below them was revealed a large cavity dug right out of the rock. The first object visible was a buffalo hide almost decomposed, and on tearing it away I saw a skeleton, sitting upright, surrounded by many skins of buffalo and bear. As strict orders had been issued to us that all Indian graves were to be unmolested, and as dark was coming on, I hastily replaced a few of the stones and returned to camp at a good sprinter's pace.

Although we traversed the very heart of an Indian country, some tribes of which were known to be hostile, we never had a glimpse of any Indians, until quite late in the season. Our scouts, of which we had several who were quite famous, often reported the proximity of Indians, and whenever we were near high lands or mountains, we would see their smoke signals.

Somewhere along the Montana line we were awakened in the middle of one night by the most unearthly yells, the thunder of many hoofs dashing over the ground, and the *crack-crack-crack* of rifles. It did not take long to realize that we were attacked by Indians. I was hardly awake when I heard the quick commands of the officers, and in less time than it takes to write about it, our troopers were returning the fire. My shotgun in its case was the foundation of my pillow at night. I rolled over on my face, lying flat, unlimbered my gun, slipped in a couple of buckshot shells, and lay there awaiting developments. This was my first experience under fire and I was neither frightened nor excited. I had heard and read a lot about Indian fighting and decided to keep as near the ground as possible and so crawled out of the tent with my gun cocked, to reconnoiter and see if there was anything to do.

In a very short time, however, our enemies vanished and the horrible din ceased. The attack was for the purpose of stampeding our animals, but thanks to our system of corralling them, the drive was an utter failure. Morning disclosed three bullet holes through our tent, as well as many through others, but there was not a casualty on our side. Scouts found traces of blood in two places on the prairie and one dead Indian pony.

Later, when we were near the foothills of the Rocky Mountains, although still on the plains, the Indians set fire to the grass, during a very strong west wind, and this nearly developed into a tragedy. Our men at once started counter-fires, but before the ground cooled enough to allow us to take advantage of the cleared space, immense volumes of smoke overtook us, and for a time we were all in danger of suffocation. We covered our heads with our garments and kept as near the ground as possible. Troopers and drivers did their best to keep covers over the animals' heads, but some became unruly, rushed into the flames, and perished.

Late in the fall we neared the end of the season's work. Camp was made near a small stream fed by a spring. A terrific snowstorm, in the West termed 'blizzard,' came up and raged in all its fury for about a week.[4] When it subsided, snow was twenty inches deep on the level, and wherever there was any obstruction, there were gigantic drifts. It was so fierce at its height that antelope came in bunches and huddled up on the leeward side of our tents.

The snowfall was so heavy that it absorbed all

[4]The blizzard struck on September 23 in the Coteau, the plains region of northwestern North Dakota and lasted until the 29th. Campbell and Twining, *Reports,* p. 277.

the water from both spring and stream. Many of our horses and mules perished and the situation rapidly became very serious. Fortunately, however, when everyone had just about lost hope, a grand old Chinook wind came pouring down from the mountains, the snow melted as rapidly as it had come, and the danger was over.[5]

A conference of the officers was held and it was decided unanimously to take the home trail without delay. On account of the loss of mules, a number of wagons were abandoned and all baggage was reduced to a minimum. This was bad news to me, as I had collected during the summer a two bushel canvas bag of all kinds of curios, souvenirs, and mineral specimens, all of which I was now obliged to leave behind.

The homeward trail was a little south of the line and was uneventful with one exception. Somewhere in northwest Dakota, as the Line party halted late one afternoon to pitch camp for the night, a flock of wild geese lit on the prairie a short distance away. My friend Paist borrowed a gun from one of the soldiers and started after a goose with the one cartridge that was in the piece.

Before he was close enough for a good shot, the geese became frightened and flew some distance to

[5] A Chinook wind is a warm, dry wind from the west or north which descends on the eastern slope of the Rockies. It was first named because it came from the direction of the Chinook Indian territory in the Pacific Northwest.

another resting-place. Paist, keen for a shot, kept after them until this had happened a number of times. Finally the chance came. He took good aim, fired, and missed.

It was cloudy when he left camp and when he now looked about for the way back, no camp was in sight. It grew dark very rapidly and at the same time a fierce blizzard came on. Paist quickly realized that he was lost, without an overcoat or mittens. He could see but a few feet in any direction.

He was soon missed at camp, but no one knew just what direction he had taken and the intensity of the storm precluded any systematic search. Guns were fired every few minutes all night, but the gale carried the sound the wrong way.

Paist had been familiar with life on the plains for some years and, when he realized he was lost, instead of trying to make camp, he began to tramp in a circle. This kept him from freezing, and he was certain that if he could weather the night his comrades would find him in the morning. Following this plan saved his life, although it was a very close call. His hands and feet were badly frozen and it was a long time before he recovered.

During the preceding summer, Paist and I had interviewed a number of the fur traders. We learned of the enormous profits of the business, so decided to pool our resources upon our return and blossom out the next spring as *bona-fide* Indian traders with a string of Red River carts loaded with cheap calico, beads, etc. After his terrifying experience in the storm, Paist most emphatically vetoed the proposed venture and vowed that nothing could tempt him from civilization again.

III

I Begin to Study Medicine

FROM the post at Devil's Lake, Dakota, we hiked south to Jamestown, then the terminus of the Northern Pacific Railway. There we entrained and reached St. Paul about the first of December, 1873.

By this time, having thought much about plans for my future, I decided to become a doctor. I began the study of medicine and surgery with the late Dr. J. H. Murphy, of St. Paul, a well-known physician and surgeon of that period, and an uncle of mine by marriage. At the same time, my erstwhile partner, Paist, began the study of law in the office of John B. Brisbin, also of St. Paul.

Making good progress, I accepted, in the spring of 1875, the place of steward of the Church Hospital, an institution maintained by the ladies of the Episcopal Churches of St. Paul and now known as St. Luke's Hospital. I remained there one year, gathered a great deal of practical experience in my chosen profession, and then resigned to prepare to enter Rush Medical College for the session of 1876–77. Work was scheduled to begin the first week in September, and so about August first I went to visit the Centennial Exhibition of Philadelphia, going by way of Chicago, Baltimore, Washington, and New

York, making my first acquaintance with a large city.

I saw everything worth seeing at the great exhibition, including the first telephone. Dom Pedro, Emperor of Brazil, who, when he first listened to this new device, sprang back exclaiming, 'My God, it talks!' Best of all I had the pleasure of meeting Sir Joseph Lister, the famous English surgeon, father of antiseptic surgery.

On September 7, 1876, while I was enjoying the Centennial, a band of eight, splendidly mounted, each armed with a brace of Colt's forty-fives, galloped into the quiet, peaceful little village of Northfield, Minnesota, and halted in front of the First National Bank. Two dismounted and ran into the bank. The others sat on their horses, firing off their revolvers and cursing furiously with the idea of terrorizing any passers-by.[1]

J. L. Heywood, the cashier, was alone in the bank when the two outlaws entered, threw their guns down on him, and ordered him to open the safe. He refused to open the safe or to give the combination, and after cursing and threatening him without avail, one of them put a bullet through his brain.

[1] Hoyt, who was not present in Northfield during the raid, has garbled numerous details in respect to this fateful attempt. The curious reader can find accurate accounts in Robertus Love, *The Rise and Fall of Jesse James* (New York, 1926), pp. 189–242; William A. Settle, Jr., *Jesse James Was His Name or, Fact and Fiction Concerning the Careers of the Notorious James Brothers of Missouri* (Columbia, 1966), pp. 93–101, and in Dallas Cantrell, *Youngers' Fatal Blunder: Northfield, Minnesota* (San Antonio, 1973).

Henry F. Hoyt,
1876

In the meantime there was something doing outside. A young medical student, Wheeler by name, was in a doctor's office upstairs just across the street. Hearing the racket, he rushed to the window, took in the situation at a glance, tore down an old Spencer carbine that had been hanging on the wall since the Civil War, and, without hesitating a moment, opened up on the mounted bandits across the street, killing one of them, Clell Miller by name, in short order, and shattering the right elbow of another, Bob Younger; while a Mr. Manning with a rifle killed another, Bill Chadwell.

The two men in the bank, having failed to get the safe open, dashed out, sprang on their mounts, and made a quick getaway. As they fled, they met an inoffensive Swede along the roadway and, with a curse, fired a volley at him, killing him outright.

The six that galloped from the bank scene were the three Younger brothers, Bob, Cole, and Jim, Jesse and Frank James, and Charley Pitts. The entire country was quickly aroused and posses were hot-foot after them in every direction. They began to realize their danger and, as they disagreed about the best route to follow, they separated, the James brothers going one way, the Youngers and Pitts another. The second day the latter were rounded up in a swamp, and, as they refused to surrender, they were all shot down and Pitts was killed.[2]

The Youngers finally recovered and were sent to

[2] Pitts' real name was Samuel Wells.

the penitentiary at Stillwater, Minnesota, for life.
The body of Charley Pitts was taken to St. Paul,
where my preceptor, Dr. Murphy, who was Surgeon
General of the State, secured it and had it em-
balmed and preserved for dissecting purposes. Minnesota laws allowed all unknown or unclaimed
bodies to be used in that way.

When I arrived home from Rush Medical College
in March, 1877, the remains were turned over to
me. Pitts was a fine specimen of physical manhood
and I decided to retain and mount his skeleton for
use in my office after my graduation. A good method of preparing a skeleton after dissecting is to
bleach the bones under water for a year or so. En-
listing the help of one of my brothers, I packed the
bones in an ordinary shoe box, putting in a few
large rocks as sinkers. We drove out to the south
branch of Lake Como, just inside the city limits of
St. Paul, Minnesota, took the box out in a boat, and
sank it about at the middle of the lake. We shall
hear of that box later on.

While I was attending lectures at Rush Medical
College in Chicago, I boarded at the home of one
Addison Snell, located at 771 West Van Buren Street.
Two other students, Van Dusen from Michigan,
and Joseph G. Henderson from Iowa, resided in the
same house.

We were coming from downtown one afternoon
and saw two women, richly dressed, approaching.
Just before we met, one gave a cry and fainted away.

The other screamed for help. Henderson was first on the scene, picked up the woman who had fainted, and carried her to a passing street car that was going in their direction.

The other woman was very profuse in her thanks. We went on our way, both Van Dusen and I sorry that Henderson had 'beaten us to it.' Nearing home Henderson reached for his watch, a valuable one, a present from his mother. It was gone. Our sorrow vanished.

At that time Allan Pinkerton lived not too far from our place. We just about ran to his house and Henderson reported the incident. After asking a few questions, Pinkerton laughed heartily and told Henderson not to worry, he would get the watch back. Sure enough, the next day it was returned and Pinkerton would take no fee for his services.

The first Tuesday in November, 1876, a President was to be elected. I never had voted for one. The Sunday morning before election day, while we were at breakfast, I heard some one say that the Republican and Democratic State Committees were giving passes on railroads to students in Chicago who would like to go home and vote.

Idea! I made a quick trip to the Grand Pacific Hotel on Clark Street, headquarters of one of the Committees—I never knew which one—found a group of men around a large table and told them what I had heard. They asked me a few questions and said that I had come to the wrong place, that I should go to a **Mr. Keep** at an address on **Michigan** Avenue. I noticed a sly wink or two and realized they were putting something over on me, or trying to. Thanking them for their kindness, I retired and smiled to myself as I heard them laughing.

I called at the office, asked the clerk who 'Mr. Keep' was, giving the number and street, and was informed that he was president of the Chicago and Northwestern Railroad Company and that the address was that of his residence.

I decided that it would do no harm to call and walked down the avenue. It was Sunday morning, but I rang the bell. A maid came, and I asked if Mr. Keep was at home. She replied that he was and asked me what my business was. I replied 'Personal,' when I heard a voice exclaim, 'Bring him in.'

I was ushered into a large parlor to the left of the hall and was cordially greeted by a middle-aged man with a kindly face. I told him my story exactly as it all occurred, word for word, winks, laughs, and all. When I finished, he laughed as heartily as the committee and then began to ask me all kinds of questions about myself. I felt perfectly at home with him and gave him a lot of my experiences out West, in which he seemed very much interested. Finally, he pulled out a bunch of letters from a pocket, selected a yellow envelope and wrote something on its back and handed it to me.

'Take that to the address I have written, as early as you can in the morning, and if not too late you will have a chance to cast your first vote for a President of the United States.'

I was there not less than an hour, and with all his questioning he never said one word about politics, nor hinted as to which man I should vote for.

On my way home that Sunday, I called at the Grand Pacific Hotel and thanked the men for their kindness. Their surprise at the outcome of their jest was a sweet morsel to me.

Next morning I was at the depot early, my order for a round trip to St. Paul was honored, and I surprised my parents by walking in Tuesday forenoon in time to vote for Rutherford B. Hayes.

Many years afterward, when I was chief surgeon of the Great Northern Railway Lines, I attended at Chicago an annual meeting of the National Association of Railway Surgeons, to which I belonged, and while there I called on Mr. Keep, who was still in the saddle as Chairman of the Executive Board of the Chicago and Northwestern Railroad Company. When I reminded him of my adventure in 1876, he remembered it and we had a good laugh over it.

December 20, 1876, my old friend, Charles W. Paist, now a law student at St. Paul, surprised me with a visit. We had a fine time together, and on Christmas Eve dined at the Palmer House. After dinner I walked with him to the train, at the Northwestern depot, and bade him good-bye. From that moment no one who knew him has ever seen him. He simply vanished from the face of the earth. He traveled on two trip passes, one from Chicago to Elroy and another from Elroy to St. Paul. The first was taken up by the conductor, so he must have disappeared between Chicago and Elroy. A detective agency hunted for him for months, but never found the slightest trace. To this date, 1928, his fate has remained an unfathomable mystery.

IV

Off for the Black Hills

FIFTY years ago, to obtain the degree of Doctor of Medicine, it was necessary to study a year or two under a preceptor and attend two courses of lectures at some reputable medical college. I had completed one course and was now ready to earn the necessary funds to enable me to graduate.

At this period, there were no laws regulating the practice of medicine and surgery, so I decided to locate in some live town and practice. Newspapers were full of the discovery of gold in the Black Hills. Deadwood was classed as the liveliest mining town in the country, so I selected that for my adventure.[1]

Learning that Blakely, Carpenter, and Siams, of St. Paul, were preparing to put on a stage line running from Bismarck to Deadwood, I decided to take that

---

[1] The discovery of gold in the Black Hills was a direct result of the U.S. Cavalry expedition, commanded by George A. Custer, which explored and surveyed the terrain during July and August 1874. Beginning in 1875, thousands flocked to the hills, hoping and searching for placer deposits. One of the most populous mining areas was concentrated within a ten-mile radius of Deadwood City, which was organized on April 26, 1876. Donald Jackson, *Custer's Gold: The United States Cavalry Expedition of 1874* (New Haven, 1966), pp. 83–85; Herbert S. Schell, *History of South Dakota* (Lincoln, Nebr., 1961), pp. 140–141.

route. Bismarck was then the terminus of the Northern Pacific Railroad, and when I arrived there about the first of May, 1877, I found that the first stage over the new route would leave in a few days. I was lucky enough to secure the last seat in the coach that was to make this historic journey.

I made the acquaintance of the clerk at the hotel, who told me that there was a passenger booked for Deadwood whom I should meet, as he was well known all through the West and could do me a lot of good should he take a fancy to me. He also added that he was a famous gambler.

Among the boarders at the Snells,' where I had lived in Chicago, was a beautiful young woman, Mrs. John Bull, and her five-year-old son. Mr. Bull was supposed to be a traveling man. Mrs. Bull had told of his being a close friend of Mark Twain, and to support her claim, exhibited with pride a beautiful, autographed *de luxe* edition of all Mark Twain's works up to that time.

I had seen Mr. Bull only once during that winter. The Snells had given a Christmas dinner to the boarders and he had been one of the guests. He had the appearance of a gentleman, was well mannered and well dressed, and in response to an inquiry during the dinner, he told of his acquaintance with the famous author.

Years before, he had known Clemens as a newspaper man at Virginia City, Nevada. The story of the 'hold-up' by a party of his comrades one night when

Clemens was coming home alone from some town across the divide, the tragic description he gave of it all when he arrived, and his chagrin when the 'joke' was exposed and his valuables returned is all a matter of history. John Bull was one of the party and laughingly told us how the young newspaper man could never see any joke in the affair. It was carried out much too realistically for any laughs.

'Dr. Hoyt, meet my friend Mr. Bull,' said the Bismarck hotel clerk. I turned around and much to my surprise, Mr. Bull, the 'famous gambler,' and the handsome, suave traveling man of Chicago, were one and the same person. The surprise was mutual and he seemed pleased to meet me again. 'I am well acquainted with the Black Hills,' he informed me later, 'and will be glad to help you get a start.'

That evening he confided to me that he had a partner, but did not want it known. They had arrived late and so were obliged to sit on the front seat in the coach, and when he learned I was on the same seat, he asked me to sit between his partner and himself. He had in the meantime pointed out his partner to me on the street and informed me that his name was Fish.

The Concord coaches used at this period had three seats, each seating three passengers, the rear and middle seats facing the boot, the front facing the rear. The boot also carried three persons, up in front. The company superintendent, W. J. Gidney, was present and very much to the fore at this time.

Everything was in readiness and we all piled in. As was usual at that time, most of the passengers were well armed. Bull and Fish, however, had no arms in sight. Fish, myself, and Bull occupied the front seat facing the other six. In front of Fish sat a man whom I will call Prentice, a capitalist from Minneapolis. In the middle of the back seat was a young man from Minnesota who had sold out his business and was to try his luck at gold-digging. Superintendent Gidney, a big, good-natured, typical Westerner, sat on the boot with the driver.

The first day out, everybody got acquainted and all the men, except Fish, told more or less about themselves. He was a small man with features of Jewish type, having dark eyes, hair, and skin. He sat wrapped up in a heavy overcoat with collar turned up, and was silent as the Sphinx.

The next day he began to thaw out. The recounting of various personal experiences was on the wane when suddenly Fish opened up with a line of Rube talk that would fool almost any one.

'Fellers,' he began, 'I was bawn on a meule fa'm in Missoury and last fall pa sent me to Chicago with a cyarload o' meules t' see if I had any business in me. I sold them ar meules for a lot of money and lit out for home.

'In the smoking cyar I met a couple of fellers playing cyards. One of 'em laid three little cyards face daoun with a pictur on one, and sez he to me and his pard, "I'll bet neither of yous kin pick out the pictur cyard." I seed the pictur cyard all right, an' was sure I knowed jest which one it was. The feller that laid daoun the cyards took out a big roll of money. I was so dang sure I cud pick up that pictur that I did not want to let the other feller get ahead. I saw a big chance to make a lot, so I jerked my money out as quick as I could, put it by his roll, and reached over to pick up the pictur cyard, but the cyard I grabbed didn't have a thing on it.

'Gosh, but I was mad. I reached to grab my money, but they was too quick. The train stopped at a station and away they went. But they left them three cyards on the seat, so I tuk 'em home and have been working with 'em ever sinse. I got so I cud skin all the boys around the old fa'm, so I'm going to the Black Hills to skin some of them gold miners.'

Whereupon the young Missourian took off his overcoat, folded it across his lap, pulled a red bandanna from an inside pocket, and shook out of it three worn and dirty playing cards, two with spots and the other the queen of hearts. After producing a large roll of bills, he began to shuffle the cards back and forth on his lap in a very awkward manner. He finally turned the cards face downward, threw them back and forth carelessly in such a way that any one could easily pick the queen, counted out one hundred dollars from his roll and invited any of the passengers to cover it and pick out the queen.

Bull quickly pulled a roll of bills from his pocket, counted out one hundred dollars, and of course turned over the queen. Fish frowned, seemed quite vexed, shuffled again. Bull bet and won.

Fish now became quite enraged, threw the cards about, and refused to let Bull bet any more, but extended an invitation to the rest. By this time the six men facing us were quite certain that Fish was the raw product he seemed to be.

When he invited the rest, I saw Prentice's right hand slip toward his pocket, but, before he could get to his cash, the young Minnesotan in the middle of the back seat sprang up and, reaching over the passengers in the middle seat, threw down a roll of bills. Then he reached for the card—but it was a two-spot!

His face registered chagrin, disappointment, and horror all at the same time, and he collapsed into his seat. The cat was now out of the bag and everybody, except the victim, roared. Bull shook his finger at the Minnesotan, exclaiming, 'You foolish man. Prentice here was the man we were after, and if you had kept out, we had him. I saw him reaching for his money.

'Never mind, we'll get him yet'—this to Prentice, who quickly replied, 'Yes, you will, like Hell.'

'Mid jest and banter, the coach jolted along over the wild prairie. Shortly we ran into a prairie-dog town, the driver pulled up for a few minutes, and everybody jumped out. Prairie dogs were in every direction, barking an invitation to us to try our marksmanship. Out came revolvers and several volleys were fired without result, as Mr. Prairie Dog is wary and very hard to hit.

Bull watched the scene for a time. Suddenly his hand flew to his hip; a big six-shooter of the dragoon type with a short barrel was drawn. The gun barked, and a dead dog was the result. He apparently took no aim at all.

Toward evening we met the coach that had left Deadwood at the same time that we left Bismarck. It had been sent to Deadwood by way of Pierre. As we stopped a few moments to visit and get the latest news from Deadwood, Bull's victim decided he had enough of frontier life, and he was permitted by Superintendent Gidney to use the rest of his transportation in returning to Bismarck on the northbound coach. That left a vacancy in our coach.

Some hours after, we overtook a covered wagon, driven by three young men. Two were brothers from Minnesota, druggists who had sold out and expected to go into business in Deadwood. Their team was well fagged out and very slow. They were in a hurry to get to the hills and inquired if they could get passage on our stage.

Gidney told them there was only one vacancy. They drew lots for it and the winner took the middle seat in the back. We had jogged along for a short time when Fish began to spin his yarn again, but this time he told an entirely new story, and instead of three cards, he worked with only two. Bull won as before several times, and was barred.

While talking and idly shuffling the two cards, Fish, apparently without knowing that he did so, tore a tiny bit from the corner of the picture card. This bait proved too much for the new victim. His roll came out as rapidly as that of number one.

Later the victim explained that he and his brother had divided their funds and he was so sure he would win that he wanted to give him a very pleasant surprise when he joined him at Deadwood. It was the old story. He was sure Fish had blundered and he was quick enough to bet on what he thought was a *sure thing*. He appeared afterward 'a sadder and a wiser man.'

During the forenoon of our last day on the plains, we crossed what Superintendent Gidney and the driver, both old-time Western men, declared was an extensive Indian trail, not over three hours old. Later it was learned that it was the trail of Red Cloud, the Sioux chieftain, on the war path with several thousand warriors. It was a wonderfully narrow escape for us. Although we were all armed, our little party would have lasted but a few minutes had we encountered that army of savages.

Some time before sundown we came in sight of Bear Butte, a lone rock that rises majestically from the plains, a landmark which can be seen for many miles and which is not very far from the entrance to the Black Hills on the way to Deadwood. Here we overtook another covered wagon drawn by a team of horses. The occupants were a man, his wife, and

Main Street, Deadwood, Dakota Territory, 1877
Courtesy Adams Memorial Hall Museum, Deadwood, South Dakota

a hired hand, all from Minnesota and en route for
the Black Hills. We halted, told them of the near-
ness of the Indians, doubtless on the war path, and
urged them to get into the hills as rapidly as they
possibly could.

The men laughed at us, saying that they were
Westerners, knew all about Indians, and were well
armed and able to take care of themselves.

We drove on, entering the hills about dusk, and
arrived at the metropolis of the Black Hills before
midnight.[2] There was only one street, built along
the gulch, Main Street, in fact as well as in name,
and although the hour was late it was swarming
with humanity. Saloons, gambling and dance halls
on both sides of the street were in full blast. All in
all, it was a wonderful sight for a tenderfoot.

While in Deadwood I met many who had been in
every mining camp in the country since '49, and
the universal opinion was that Deadwood was, at
that time, by far the wildest of them all.

The coach pulled up in front of the I. X. L. Hotel, fronting on Main Street on the opposite side
from the stables and office of the North-Western
Express, Stage & Transportation Company, the line
by which we had come.

We all put up at the hotel, a two-story frame

[2]Hoyt's arrival was announced in the local paper: "H. F.
Hoyt came in last evening by way of Bismark [sic]. He in-
tends having a medicine talk soon. Is now at the IXL." *Black
Hills Daily Times* (Deadwood), May 12, 1877.

building, with rooms divided only by canvas partitions. The owner and landlord, Johnny Van Danager, turned out to be an old friend of John Bull, as they had been together in the South African mining camps some years previously.[3] He was a most genial 'mine host' and did what he could to make us as comfortable as possible.

Next morning the news was brought that our party in the covered wagon from Minnesota had disregarded our warning, gone into camp at Bear Butte, and had been attacked in the night by Indians. They were all massacred and frightfully mutilated.[4]

If my memory is correct, a mounted party was soon made up and was fortunate enough to overtake a small bunch of the savages. Two scalps were brought in as trophies.

[3]The *Black Hills Daily Times,* of February 3 and November 26, 1877, indicates that James Vandaniker (not Johnny Van Danager) and Patrick McHugh were the proprietors of the I. X. L. Hotel and Restaurant.

[4]Hoyt's memory has failed him in respect to the date of the murder and mutilation of the Wagner family. The tragedy occurred on July 17, 1877. John S. McClintock, *Pioneer Days in the Black Hills* (Deadwood, 1939), pp. 178–179.

V

I Hang Out My Shingle in Deadwood

I SPENT my first forenoon in Deadwood searching for something to rent for an office but could not find even an available drygoods box from one end of the gulch to the other. Returning to the I. X. L. Hotel for dinner, I made a strong effort to rent a room or two from my landlord, but was promptly turned down. 'Impossible,' he decided.

At this juncture John Bull entered and I was greeted with, 'What's the good word, Doc?' Hearing my predicament, he called the landlord, Van Danager. 'Van, meet my friend Dr. Hoyt. I want you to let him have a room where he can hang out his shingle and go to work.'

'Johnny,' replied Van, 'I would be glad to, but I'm chuck *full* all the time and it's impossible.'

'I know you are,' said John, 'but he doesn't want *you*, he wants a room in the hotel.'

'Nothing doing, John. As I told you before, that settles it.'

Bull's genial smile, usually present, faded away. His eyes flashed, and stepping close up to Van, he remarked in a low tense tone, 'Did you hear what I said? Dr. Hoyt is my *friend*.'

Not another word was said, but Van showed a

sickly grin on his face and I was given the best room in the house.

Although I was mighty glad to get this room, I was certainly practicing medicine under difficulties. The room was about twelve feet square, a bed on each side with about a three-foot strip between as one entered, leaving a space of about six feet from the foot of the beds to the outside wall, where there was one small window with a cheap washstand, bowl and pitcher beneath. The hotel was not exactly what would be termed soundproof, as all partitions were canvas. Two small chairs completed the equipment.

Once between midnight and morning, while I was there, a man occupying a bed in the rear room on my side of the hall came in slightly drunk, found someone in his bed, started a row, and gun play was made, resulting in both being badly wounded. In the morning it was found that two bullets had passed through every partition on that side of the building, about five feet from the floor. I was about the only one who profited by that affair.

I purchased a small gold-scales outfit, had an old miner in the house teach me how to weigh dust, and after putting a card in the paper announcing the arrival of a new doctor, I spread out my few drugs and instruments, and was ready for business.

I held my office hours from 9 A.M. to 4 P.M. I had a roommate of course every night, in the other bed, and this often made it more or less awkward, as not infrequently the man-on-the-other-side would come in after midnight well soused and want to sleep all the next day. Being big and strong, I would pick him up, like a movie villain abducting the hero, and dump him into an empty bed in another room.

A few days after I began my practice I got a call to go ten miles over the mountains. I responded on horseback and found a man with an arm badly shot up. He had lost a good deal of blood and was weak. I fixed him up, was paid a fat fee in dust—very little money was in circulation at that time in the Black Hills—and returned home.

The day after my mountain trip, I went to the bank, and to my dismay was told that a good part of my dust was 'phony.' I mounted my mustang, made another fast ride over the mountains, determined to bring back some good dust or a scalp, but when I arrived I found that the bird had flown. I never ran across him again. As the result of this experience I provided myself with a bottle of testing acid, so this trick was never duplicated.

Mr. Prentice also put up at the I. X. L. Hotel, and both he and Mr. Bull usually dropped by my office sometime during the day for a friendly chat.

One day Bull burst in, wildly exultant over something. This was unusual, as he was ordinarily rather quiet and dignified.

'I got him! I got him!' he cried, slapping his leg.

'Got who?' I asked.

'Prentice, I told you I'd get him. I finally landed

him in my game and cleaned him for five hundred dollars. I have laid for him for days and have got him at last.'

Bull had not been gone ten minutes before in came Prentice, scarcely less mirthful and excited than Bull. 'By gosh, Doc,' he said, 'I got him.' 'John Bull,' he added, seeing a quizzical expression in my eyes. 'Cleaned him up to the tune of five hundred dollars.'

I indulged in a hearty laugh and with the remark, 'Now I'll tell one,' and gave Bull's side of the story. To this Prentice replied:

'He did think so, but it was thought only. This is the way it was. I sat in his game and got hung up for five hundred dollars. I said I'd have to cash in. 'I need all the money I've got with me for business to-morrow, so I'll have to ask you to take this draft!' He bit, accepted the draft, and counted out five hundred dollars in change. The draft was for one thousand dollars and it was *no good*!'

Such was life in the Far West fifty years ago. John Bull was a character in his way, one of the best in his line, and withal a kind-hearted man and a mighty good friend. This sketch would hardly be complete without a description of our last meeting.

After leaving the Black Hills in September, 1877, I lost all track of Bull. Some time in the nineties I entered a car at St. Paul, Minnesota, my home at that time, on my way to the City Hall at Minneapolis. As I sat down in the only vacant place, I recognized John Bull as my seat mate. He gave me a cold stare when I spoke, evidently taking me for some former victim, but was most cordial when I identified myself.

At the end of the ride, I invited him to dine with me that evening and hark back to the old frontier days. Hesitating a moment, he replied, 'Doc, I would be delighted, but I have a deal on and if it goes, I shall fade away; if not, I will sure be there.' He did not appear and the newspapers next morning explained the 'deal,' amounting to several thousand dollars, all of which accounted sufficiently for his 'fade-away.'

We have never met since. At the time of this writing (1928) I learned from good authority that with all his experiences and ups and downs, he has never been behind the bars, which fact demonstrates both brains and an unusual efficiency of its kind.

He had, however, one very close shave.

Before we parted at the Minneapolis depot that day, we chatted for a few moments, then he went in one direction while I went in another. I was quite elated over the meeting, as Bull had been kind to me in every way when I needed help, and I anticipated a pleasant visit that evening.

To see if I was on time for my appointment, I reached for my watch, which was a very fine one and had been a present, and which I carried in my right-hand vest pocket without chain or fob. *It was gone.*

It would take a number of pages to describe my thoughts for the next minute. I do not remember ever being more furiously angry. The idea that I, a man of the world, mixing with all kinds of people all over this country, Mexico, and Canada, had finally run across a supposedly old-time friend and he had picked my pocket!!! Whew!

My appointment was at the City Hall. I was well acquainted with both the chief of police and the detectives. I hadn't forgotten how to sprint, so I resolved to fly to the Hall and in a few minutes set the entire force on poor John Bull's trail. I started up Washington Avenue at a gait that astonished the people on the sidewalk. Some one had opened a hydrant and a stream of water about six feet wide was pouring from an alley across the sidewalk into the gutter. Reaching the stream, I cleared it with a leap, and as I landed on the other side, I felt something bump me in the right groin. Slowing up, I reached down and there was *my watch* down in the corner of my long vest. The lining of the pocket had become worn through and the last time the watch went in, it had kept on going.

It will take a strong imagination for my readers to realize my revulsion of feeling at my discovery. But for that stream of water, John Bull would have been behind the bars in a very short time and I should never have forgiven myself.

VI

I Go after Gold

AMONG my patients in Deadwood was a young mining engineer, Bailey by name, who had a contract with a Chicago syndicate to prospect for gold in the Black Hills. If he discovered a quartz proposition that would average twenty-five dollars to the ton, they would finance and develop it, giving him fifty per cent.

Fifty years ago, no one would look at a lode mine that averaged less than twenty-five dollars a ton. There has certainly been some progress in mining methods since then, when one of the best gold mines in this country is the Homestake, right in that district, that averages a trifle less than two dollars to the ton.

One day we went to visit the grave of the most famous 'two-gun man' the West has ever known, Wild Bill Hickok. It was located on an eminence to the left of the gulch not far from the center of the town, going west, and was marked only by a pine slab driven into the ground at the head. The name and inscription were both written on the slab with a carpenter's pencil. I have been informed that a monument now has been placed at Hickok's grave.[1]

Wild Bill was murdered in Deadwood in 1876 by one Jack McCall. They were in a poker game and Bill reprimanded Jack for some breach of poker ethics. A day or two later, McCall walked up behind Bill when he was sitting in a game and shot him dead. Jack escaped, but was captured about a week later near Fort Pierre and hanged.[2] In the fall of 1877 I met Wild Bill's partner, Colorado Charley (Charley Utter), at Santa Fé, New Mexico, and he showed me Bill's sombrero with the small bullet

[1]Mount Moriah Cemetery is the final resting place of Hickok and is well marked. The grave was transplanted to it in 1879. His grave has been marked by a succession of monuments, both plain and fancy. The first was raised by his friend Colorado Charley on the occasion of his burial, August 3, 1876, and is the one Hoyt alludes to.

[2]There is some dispute over the assertion that Hickok and McCall were gambling on the night before Hickok was slain. The most authoritative biographer supports the contention, but merely notes that McCall lost. There is no reference to any Hickok reprimand. When McCall shot Hickok the next day in Saloon No. 10, August 2, 1876, he was captured shortly thereafter in Deadwood. Brought to trial the following day, he was acquitted. Immediately after, he left town and headed for Colorado. A friend of Wild Bill's, Colonel George May, pursued McCall and had him arrested in Laramie on August 29. From there, McCall was taken to Yankton in the Dakota Territory. He was finally brought to trial before Justice P. C. Shannon, on December 4, and found guilty by the jury two days later. Sentence was passed on January 3, 1877. McCall was hung on a scaffold two miles out of town, on March 1. Joseph G. Rosa, *They Called Him Wild Bill: The Life and Adventures of James Butler Hickok* (Rev. ed.; Norman, Okla., 1974), pp. 296–298, 312–337.

"Wild Bill" Hickok's Grave, Deadwood
Courtesy Adams Memorial Hall Museum, Deadwood, South Dakota

hole through the center of the back of the hatband.

Bailey decided he wanted a husky partner, so he began to tempt me to join him.

I finally accepted Bailey's proposition to close my office and prospect for gold, and he formally transferred a half interest in his Chicago contract to me. I outfitted with blue flannel shirts, corduroy trousers, miners' boots, pick, shovel, and gold pan, and the hunt was on.

We traveled over a good portion of the Black Hills, finding plenty of low-grade quartz deposits, but nothing near our limit. One day we climbed to the summit of Custer's Peak, one of the highest of the hills, and while resting, enjoyed the wonderful vista in every direction. Many had preceded us, as was shown by initials, names, etc., carved on rocks and the trunks of beautiful pine trees all about us.

From the foot of the peak on one side there stretched out an extensive natural basin, probably a mile in diameter and almost as symmetrical as one of our modern stadia.

Clouds began to gather, and in a short time we witnessed a phenomenon of nature that I have never seen duplicated. A fierce electric storm came up, thunder, lightning, and a heavy rain, all *below* us, while above was beautiful sunshine. It did not last very long, and at the end, a rainbow appeared, one end extending right into the center of the basin, so low down that it seemed to touch the tops of the pines with which the valley was densely covered.

We joked about the traditional pot of gold at the end of the rainbow, shouldered our equipment, and started for camp, which, as it happened, was on the other side of this basin, our trail leading directly across it.

When part way over, Bailey, who was behind me, called in an excited tone for me to come back. He had in his hand a piece of float about the size of a hen's egg and declared it to be very richly mineralized, asserting that if we could find its source our quest was over.

It was getting late, so we stripped the bark from one of the pines, wrote our location notice on its surface, and named it the 'Rainbow Mine.'

The next day that piece of float was assayed in Deadwood and it ran about fifteen thousand dollars to the ton in silver. In mining terms it was called almost pure horn silver.

The find leaked from the assay office and we were shadowed by quite a mob of miners for some time, but by a little strategy we sidetracked them and for the next few weeks we concentrated on this basin. While from the top of Custer's Peak it appeared very symmetrical, it was really rugged and very much broken and hard to prospect. We carefully scouted over its entire surface and rim without discovering the slightest trace of the origin of our wonderful sample of float. There is no question in my mind but that there is a remarkably rich lode of silver in that vicinity and some time it may be discovered. Perhaps by now it has already been found.

By this time I was tired of prospecting and, being seized with an attack of wanderlust, I began to plan to work my way toward South America. I severed my partnership with Bailey and returned to Deadwood, now a wild and woolly town. Seldom a day or night passed without a brawl or shooting affair. Gambling dens, dance halls, and sporting houses were wide open in every direction.

Miners came in in droves on Saturday nights, and surely made the *dust* fly. One night I heard a commotion and down the street came a woman on a horse at full gallop. She had a Colt's forty-five in each hand, and both were in action, the bullets flying in every direction, while the rider emitted a good imitation of an Indian war-whoop at every jump of her mount. This was my first closeup of that well-known figure of the pioneer West, Calamity Jane. She was dressed in soldier's uniform and was the first female I had ever seen riding astride.

She and a 'Madam Moustache,' a little Frenchwoman with quite a shadow on her upper lip, who dealt at a 'Twenty-One' table in one of the gambling halls, and one other, whose name I cannot remember, were very much in the limelight in those days.

Madam Moustache was one of the most popular women of her class in Deadwood. She could speak five languages, was always polite and well gowned, and her table was always the center of a crowd.

Rarely without a smile, her voice low and musical, she presented a very attractive picture as she would call out her game, with a very charming accent, 'Gentlemans, I haf twenty-von, vat haf you?,' a phrase that was heard so often that it almost became a byword in Deadwood.

VII

Over the Trail to Santa Fé

Early in September, 1877, with Hugh B. McCune and two Germans, I left Deadwood for the South. Our equipment consisted of a covered wagon, a span of mules and three saddle horses, and a camp outfit with plenty of provisions and ammunition. We were all well armed. I carried an octagon-barreled Ballard rifle as well as a Colt's forty-five revolver, since the Sioux were still on the warpath.

Following the trail used by the Gilmer-Salisbury stage line from Deadwood to Cheyenne, we averaged about twenty-five miles a day, taking turns standing guard at night till we neared Fort Laramie.[1] From there on, until we reached New Mexico, there was no more danger from Indians.

Shortly before we left Deadwood the Gilmer-Salisbury stages had been held up and robbed by four men not very far from that city. The trail ran down a deep cut in the high banks of a dry stream and here the stage had been held up several times. The robbers concealed themselves under the bank

[1]This was the Gilmer, Salisbury and Patrick Stage Line, opened in 1877 by the three partners—John T. Gilmer, Monroe Salisbury, and Colonel Mathewson T. Patrick. Agnes W. Spring, *The Cheyenne and Black Hills State and Express Routes* (Glendale, Calif., 1929), p. 13.

on both sides and as the leaders arrived at the bottom of the cut, they would step into sight and turn their trick. Mute evidence of their work still showed in the way of all kinds of articles, bits of paper, etc., scattered through the sand from baggage and mail sacks that had been overhauled.

A bunch of cowboys had driven a herd of cattle from Texas to the Black Hills, sold them, gambled and frittered away the proceeds in the underworld of Deadwood, and, becoming desperate, had adopted this method of recouping their finances in order to report to the owners of the herd in Texas. The notorious Sam Bass was a member of this gang and the robbing of these stages is supposed to have been his maiden effort as an outlaw.

As we pitched camp the evening after passing this dry stream, four men rode up, mounted on splendid horses and armed to the teeth, and asked us all kinds of questions. They were invited to dismount and take pot-luck with us, which they finally did. We intuitively knew they were the outlaws the moment they appeared, and if they had sized us up as a party going home loaded with dust from the Black Hills, there is no telling what might have happened.

Right then there was a large reward for the capture of these men, dead or alive, and had we been expecting them and planned accordingly, there were several times after they dismounted when we might have captured them, but their appearance was too unexpected for anything punitive on our part.

While they were eating they gave us a lot of information about trails and good camps, after they learned we were headed for New Mexico. About bedtime they rode away and we saw them no more.

One evening we camped at Telegraph Springs Ranch just twenty-five miles from Fort Laramie. It was owned and managed by the widow of a physician, formerly one of the faculty of a St. Louis medical college. In addition to caring for a bunch of cattle and horses, she had a small store and kept feed and hay for the stage line and passers-by. Hay was cut from the vast prairie in the vicinity and she only asked ten cents a pound for it.

Coming from the north we crossed a bit of high land, a short half-mile from the ranch, with a down grade in the trail. Just before sundown, hearing a commotion outside, we rushed from the camphouse to investigate and saw a sight not to be forgotten. Silhouetted against the sky along the top of this ridge were at least fifty Indians, mounted on prancing horses, flourishing their rifles, gesticulating with their arms, altogether a very warlike picture. The ranch had no doubt come unexpectedly into view upon their gaining the summit of the ridge and they had halted to confer as to their next move.

Our hostess, the first woman I had ever seen wearing bloomers, was apparently cool and mistress of the situation. She had eight men on the ranch, and with the reenforcement of our party of four, there was little danger, as all the buildings were of good-sized logs built and arranged for defense purposes. She quietly directed how her little force should be posted to the best advantage and then suggested a volley or two just to let the enemy know there was somebody at home.

When we opened fire, the picture on the hill vanished almost as quickly as it had appeared, and we saw no more Indians.

In the morning the wearer of the bloomers told us of a large body of mineralized rock in the mountains some ten miles west of her ranch, and learning we had prospected in the Black Hills, she offered to guide us, bring in samples, and have them assayed at Cheyenne. If the assay was favorable, she wanted to go fifty-fifty on the deal.

I was elected to go after the specimens, and on the way was entertained by my guide with countless stories of how many times she had taken hunters after big game only to see them miss the mark when the opportunity came. As I had never killed anything in the way of game larger than a wild goose, I offered a silent prayer that we would meet no game that day.

We reached the rock ledge, got a fine lot of specimens, and started back home. Thus far my prayers had been answered, but when we were within about a mile of the ranch the tide turned. We were ambling single file along an old buffalo trail, and I was in the lead with my Ballard rifle balanced on the pommel of my saddle, when I glanced to the right and saw, not over one hundred yards away, a big blacktailed buck deer standing broadside on with his head turned toward us. I shall never forget my sensations at that moment. Instead of having a violent case of the buck ague that I always understood attacked a tyro at such a moment, I was never more composed or self-possessed in my life. Had that deer been on my left, I should have shot from the saddle, but now I quickly slid from my horse, dropped on one knee, drew a bead just behind the fore shoulder, and pulled the trigger. The big buck reared on his hind legs, whirled, and darted away. My gun was a single shot and I was reloading as rapidly as possible, but, before I had slipped the cartridge in, my quarry reared again on his hind legs and fell over backward, dead.

I actually believe my guide was even more pleased than I was. It seemed she was a dead shot herself, as was evidenced by some target shooting that was indulged in next morning. She was also a remarkable horsewoman and was riding a beautiful Kentucky thoroughbred that was her favorite mount. During the mountain part of our trip she led me through places where had I been alone I think I should have dismounted and hoofed it.

We lived high on venison for several days, but the assays at Cheyenne failed to pan out—another golden bubble busted!

At the Chug Water, a small stream a short distance north of Cheyenne, we met a large herd of cattle from Texas with a convoy of cowboys, the first of the kind I had ever seen out this way.

Traveling south along the east slope of the Rockies, we passed Denver, Colorado, and camped one night near the home of a rancher by the name of Jones. McCune had a violin on which he and I could play any old tune by ear and main strength. We would aim to go into camp as near some ranch as possible and fiddle a few tunes. Almost invariably visitors would appear and get acquainted, and in a short time one would think we were stockholders in the ranch, judging by the dividends of vegetables, fruit, melons, milk, butter, and eggs that would roll in.

Rancher Jones had several daughters, a charming schoolma'am was boarding there, other neighbors were near, so an impromptu dance was started and everybody had a fine time. Mr. Jones had a large field of wheat in the shock and was short of hands. As we bade him good-night, he asked us to mention that fact to any men we might meet on the road.

It seemed they had taken us for fortunate gold-diggers from the Black Hills and never dreamed that we might help them. When we reached camp, I suggested that we offer our services in the morning to help stack the grain, as we were below par financially and he paid four dollars a day and board.

My companions were willing, but none could stack grain. Fortunately I was familiar with farm work and as any one could pitch the bundles, the next forenoon found us all in the field. Mr. Jones, more than happy at our *condescension*, treated us like princes. At the end of four days he had as fine a bunch of wheat stacked as one would wish. We went on our way well satisfied with the adventure.

Pueblo and Trinidad were in the throes of a smallpox epidemic. It seemed as if a yellow flag, the sign of quarantine, was upon almost every other house. Leaving Trinidad, Colorado, we crossed the Raton Mountains, following the old historic Dick Whooten toll road and the Old Santa Fé Trail, exactly the same route taken later by the Atchison, Topeka & Santa Fé Railway.[2]

We followed the Old Sante Fé Trail through Las Vegas and on to Santa Fé. Shortly before reaching Santa Fé we heard of a fine game country north of the Trail, so we struck off into the mountains and made camp on the Pecos River, where a small mountain stream flowed into it. Just above us was a deer-lick—a small deposit of salt in the rocks near the stream where deer could be found almost any night.

Wild turkey were abundant, plenty of trout were in the stream, and we were in clover. I had been trading, and now carried a Sharp's carbine in the place of my Ballard rifle. It had twice the range of the rifle and carried a larger bullet.

The mountains in the vicinity were plentifully timbered with pine, spruce, and cedar, and with

[2]Dick Wootten, not Whooten, is the correct spelling.

an occasional grove of a sort of dwarf oak with very large acorns in abundance.

One day I struck out alone and tramped for hours without a sight of game, which was quite unusual. Growing weary, I sat down under a shady pine, resting my back against its trunk. The view was superb. A few feet in front was the edge of a precipice of rock that dropped down for about one hundred feet and then gradually sloped off at an angle of about forty-five degrees, the surface of the slope almost covered with a heavy growth of dwarf oak. I could see for miles in every direction and the scenery was wild, rugged, and picturesque.

I was almost dozing, when I heard a very peculiar noise. Listening intently, I finally located it as coming from the oak grove. It seemed to be moving toward me. It was a sort of grunting noise, sounding as if an animal was rooting in the ground. I decided it came from some stray hogs and paid no attention to it.

Suddenly something moving caught my eye, and to my astonishment, there at the edge of the grove, were three huge cinnamon bears, grunting and rooting industriously in the leaves and earth after acorns. The wind was from them, so they did not scent me, and as I was so far above them and sat perfectly still, they did not see me, and for the next few minutes I had a very novel spectacle of bear on their native heath. It was murder pure and simple, but I was young then, a hunter, and I decided to get all three. The largest was farthest from me, so I decided to take him first, with the idea that the others would then run toward me. I dropped him in his tracks with a shot just behind the ear, and exactly as I expected, the other two dashed toward the foot of the precipice as I threw out the shell and started to push in a fresh cartridge.

I had a belt around my waist holding sixty cartridges and the one I grabbed to reload with *stuck* as I tried to push it home and I could get it neither in nor out for some time, time enough for the two lucky ones to make a perfect getaway. That was the only misfit cartridge in the belt.

Making a détour, in order to get around the precipice, I bled my trophy and made tracks for camp, where I found nobody at home. Saddling one of the mules, I galloped to the home of some nearby Mexicans, commandeered two of them, and by their help, after blindfolding my mule, succeeded in reaching camp with by far the biggest bag of game I had ever chalked to my credit. After we skinned the animal, it was divided between the Mexicans and ourselves, and everybody was happy.

VIII

Searching for John Chisum

AFTER reaching Santa Fé our quartet broke up, the Germans deciding to go to Arizona, while McCune and I struck out in a southeasterly direction toward Anton Chico on the Pecos River. My companion had what would be called at this period a cow-complex, and he had it bad. He learned at Santa Fé there was a man down the Pecos Valley, John Chisum by name, commonly known there as 'The Cattle King of New Mexico,' who would round up nearly one hundred thousand head. It was reported that he would let out cattle on shares to a reliable man, so John Chisum was McCune's objective. Mine was a promising location to begin again the practice of medicine.

I had disposed of my mount and McCune and I were both traveling in the covered wagon. The route lay through a perfectly wild country with only an occasional habitation, many times without even a trail. In several instances the grade was so steep that we were compelled to tie up all four of the wagon's wheels.

At night the mules were hobbled and turned loose to graze. One morning they were missing. Finding their trail, we soon discovered they were being driven by some one on foot. With our weapons ready, we trailed them for about two miles to a small clearing where stood an adobe house on the edge of a small patch of growing corn in which our mules were busy at breakfast.

We removed the hobbles, which had rubbed the mules' legs until they were bleeding. We were just starting back bareback for camp when five Mexicans rushed from the shack and halted us. All were very much excited, evidently making some demand, but as we did not understand Spanish, there was a deadlock. Two, who seemed to be leaders, were armed and handled their guns rather carelessly, or so it appeared to us. The sign language was resorted to, and they showed where the mules had eaten their corn for which they demanded money.

We, in turn, showed that they had driven the mules in themselves, pointed to the bloody fetlocks, pretended to be as angry as they were, showed our weapons, and plainly gave them to understand that they could get nothing from us but a fight. Then we started for camp, leading the animals until we got out of sight, when we mounted and the incident was closed.

There was game in abundance throughout this journey, and as we had both become first-class camp cooks, we lived like epicures.

Arriving at the Pecos River near Anton Chico, we forded it, finding a very good trail on the east bank, which we then followed to Fort Sumner, also called

'Bosque Redondo' (Round Grove). Going south, about four miles from the post we entered a beautiful wide avenue of majestic cottonwoods which we traveled along till we reached the post.

Bordering on this avenue were orchards of peaches and apricots loaded with luscious fruit, and vineyards with an abundance of the famous Mission grapes—all going to waste as there was no market. There was no railway south of Trinidad, Colorado, and, except for what the people at Fort Sumner ate, the only use made of all this fine fruit was to fatten hogs.

Ten years earlier this had been an important post, with a large garrison and over nine thousand Navajo and Apache Indians, who were being fed by the Government. Later the post was abandoned and sold to Lucien B. Maxwell, of Maxwell Land Grant fame, who had moved his family here from Cimarron, New Mexico. It was now their home.

The Maxwell family occupied buildings that had formerly been officers' quarters, a short distance from and facing the Pecos River, on the bank of which we made camp. In a short time we had a visitor, a little old wrinkled chap with a sharp Roman nose, who was curious to know who we were, for passing travelers were rare. He was William Betts, called 'Old Betts,' and turned out to be quite a character. He had been a noted rider and was Mr. Maxwell's chief jockey when that gentleman kept an extensive racing stable during his palmy days.

Old Betts was one of the few old retainers left and was treated almost as one of the family.

Learning that I was a physician, he made a bee-line for the house, and in a few minutes I received a call and was ushered into the bedroom of William Maxwell, the eldest son of the family and my first patient in New Mexico. I found him dying with a severe case of malignant smallpox for which nothing could be done. He was beyond help. Incidentally, however, I did some vaccinating while at Fort Sumner.

One relic of former magnificence here was the remains of a splendid coach made to order in St. Louis and used in the old days to transport, with an armed and mounted escort, the Maxwell daughters to and from the Eastern convents where they were being educated. It was now parked by the stables and utilized as a favorite roosting place for poultry.

We rested here for a few days, meeting most of the people in the vicinity, one of the most interesting being a very beautiful señorita, Lolita by name, who was about fifteen and as bright and charming as she was beautiful. She will appear later.

McCune was impatient to get on, so we bade farewell to the hospitality of Fort Sumner and followed the Pecos River Valley for about one hundred miles south. Two days after leaving the post we met the first bad weather of the trip. We had just baked a kettle of beans in a 'bean hole' full of live coals, when it began to rain. This rain kept up for exactly four days. But for those beans we should have had a sorry time, as the wind was high and a fire was impossible. I have never been able to get up much enthusiasm for baked beans since.

It finally cleared, the earth dried rapidly, and we again hit the trail. We were not far from where Roswell is now built, when one day, late in the afternoon, a great cloud of dust appeared, rolling toward us from the valley. Comanches were known to be on the war path and our first thought was Indians. This was apparently confirmed when a puff of wind blew the dust aside, revealing a band of mounted men driving a herd of horses. Indian horse thieves of course! The way that mule team split air for shelter was no bother to them. We landed in a washout, one side of which we occupied as a breastwork, and being well armed and good shots, we decided to fight to the last.

As the cavalcade approached, however, the *Indians* vanished, as the riders were seen to be white men. You can imagine the revulsion of feeling in the washout when it developed that our supposed deadly enemies were John Chisum himself and a bunch of cowboys, rounding up a herd of cattle to drive to Arizona to fill an Indian contract.

They showed us typical Texan hospitality, invited us to camp with them, and gave us a very enjoyable evening. In Santa Fé and at Fort Sumner we heard vague rumors of trouble in Lincoln County, but in the Chisum camp we were virtually at the seat of war.[1] Being strangers we knew nothing of the persons who were freely discussed, including 'Billy the Kid,' who at that time was leader of the Chisum fighting men. We listened to many bloody tales and hairbreadth escapes, so wild and woolly that we both had a suspicion that we were sized up as tenderfeet and a lot was being rehearsed for our special benefit. Later we learned better.[2]

[1]Trouble was not new to Lincoln County. Sparsely populated, poorly policed by civilian or military personnel, with grazing cattle in the thousands ranging far and wide over the open lands, thievery and rustling were hardly stranger to John Chisum. As the largest stockman in the county, he was the most frequent victim of petty and large scale thefts. Indeed, "1877 was the most demanding year of Chisum's ranching life." In January and March two of his foremen were killed. By April open conflict between a band of Chisum's Jinglebob cowboys and a local rancher sparked a succession of events. Many threats were heard from all sides. Although conditions were ripe for an explosion, bloodshed was held in abeyance. A strong show on the part of the law in early summer, coupled with Chisum's sense of organization and calm, order prevailed. Such would not be the case in 1878, the year the Lincoln County War exploded in all its fury. Harwood P. Hinton, "John Simpson Chisum," *New Mexico Historical Review*, xxxi (July 1956), 196-205.

[2]Chisum reputedly met Billy the Kid in the fall of 1877. It is generally believed he employed him for a short time, although there is contradictory evidence on this point. At the age of eighteen, Billy would hardly have been appointed leader of Chisum's fighting men. Besides, in the fall of 1877, he had yet to win his bloody reputation. It was not until March 1878 that he began his gunman career. There is no doubt: Hoyt, the tenderfoot, was being treated to fanciful yarns. *Ibid.*, pp. 315-316; Florencio Chavez, "Fought With Billy the Kid," *Frontier Times*, ix (March 1932), 243.

John Chisum

John Chisum's Home Ranch, Pecos Valley, New Mexico

McCune was most disappointed. Chisum was short-handed and offered him a job as cowboy, but there was nothing doing in letting cattle on shares. After learning of my own objective, he pointed in a north-easterly direction, saying, 'Doc, over yonder is the Panhandle of Texas, a big country, full of people, an epidemic of smallpox, and no doctor. There's the place you're looking for.'

Mac and I conferred the most of the night and decided to stick together, cross the plains, and in-vestigate the Panhandle.

Next morning John Chisum gave us some good advice, had his boys throw a fresh quarter of beef into our wagon and a ten-gallon keg of water, as there was one stretch of eighty miles without water, investigated our supply of ammunition which he considerably increased, after cautioning us that the Comanches were then on the warpath, and wished us good luck as we pulled out.

IX

Into the Panhandle

IT WAS now late in November, 1877. Our route ran in a northeasterly direction through a perfectly wild country, known on the maps as the 'Llano Estacado' (Staked Plain). There was no sign of a trail. The landscape was rough and broken with stretches of sand and large tracts of mesquite. For probably half the distance there was gently rolling plain covered with grama and buffalo grass with an occasional lake of fresh water containing no alkali.

This part of the country was an ideal grazing district and we were seldom out of sight of either buffalo, antelope, or wild horses. The dry eighty miles we made at night, guided by the north star, or a compass if the sky was clouded. In fact, on account of Indians, this was our habitual procedure during the entire journey. At daybreak we camped in as secluded a spot as possible. Buffalo chips everywhere made splendid fuel with a minimum of smoke to betray us. Rattlers were not scarce, but as we always slept in the wagon, there was no danger from that source. The Canadian River drains the Panhandle from west to east near its middle. On this river, about fifty miles from the New Mexican line, was the village of Tascosa, the only American settlement then in the Panhandle west of Fort Elliott. In 1877 there was no law or order, no organization whatever, not even a mail service, the only government being the gun which every one carried day and night.

There were only three American women in the Panhandle west of Fort Elliott—Mrs. Tom Bugby, Mrs. Charles Goodnight, and Miss Lizzie Rinehart.

We reached the Canadian River at a sheep ranch owned by James Campbell, some distance above Tascosa, and were made welcome. Campbell was then arranging to go on a buffalo hunt and invited me to join him—an invitation that I accepted with alacrity.

About this time McCune felt that he had had his fill of 'roughing it' and left in the covered wagon for his old home in Iowa.

I needed a pair of boots by this time, but my financial resources were very low. When I spoke to Campbell about it, he at once took me to the little store he kept for his employees, fitted me out with a pair, with the remark, 'The valley is full of smallpox and you will soon have all the money you want.'

With an outfit we traveled south fifty miles or so, making camp near the head of a brake with a fine spring for water. Hunting buffalo I found to be wonderful sport. Campbell loaned me a fine horse and, although I have hunted all kinds of game since in different parts of the world, I have never quite

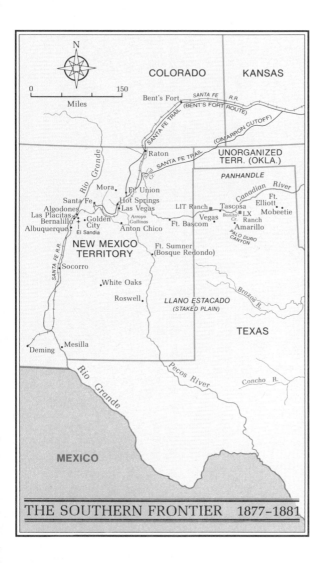

THE SOUTHERN FRONTIER 1877–1881

equaled the thrills that I experienced in the midst of a great herd of buffalo, mounted on a good horse and with a good gun in my hands.

Campbell's men were Mexicans. He and I would bring down the game and the employees would do the rest. After they had skinned and quartered the animal, it would be brought to camp in a wagon and divided. All the meat was given to the Mexicans, except the hump and hind quarters, which Campbell retained. Two quarters were impaled on a gambrel and suspended from a cut-off limb of a tree above the ground. Fresh meat could be preserved for some time in that way. When enough to fill a wagon accumulated, it would be sent to the ranch.

In loading these quarters into a wagon it took at least two, and sometimes three, Mexicans to a quarter. I was a six-footer and at this time a powerful and athletic man, and I ventured some caustic remark as to the efficiency of the Mexicans, which Campbell at once resented. I came back with 'I can put any two quarters you have into the wagon alone,' whereupon Campbell was at once ready to wager that I could not.

My new boots flashed into my mind and I quickly bet to double my debt for them if I lost or have Campbell square it if I won. Done! Stepping up to the two largest quarters that he indicated, I put an arm around each, lifted them from the limb, toted them to the wagon, and threw them in, much to the astonishment of all, including myself, as this happened to be a new stunt for me. But the boots were mine!

Campbell was considered a good sport, but for some reason he never liked me afterward.

We had a wonderful Thanksgiving dinner at this camp, with buffalo, antelope, and wild turkey served in different ways on the bill of fare.

Just before sundown a Mexican rode into camp leading a saddled mustang. Word had gone down the river that a *medico* was in the country. Señorita Piedad Romero, called the 'Belle of the Panhandle,' the fifteen-year-old foster daughter of Don Casimiro Romero, wealthiest Mexican in the Panhandle, was very ill with smallpox and this *mozo* had been sent to find and bring the doctor as soon as possible.

Don Casimiro's *hacienda* was at Tascosa, just one hundred miles away, so we pulled out at sundown, rode all night, and after a short rest in the morning, we kept on till we reached the Canadian River, opposite Tascosa, late in the afternoon. There was an adobe shack at the ford, and as we rode up, some Mexicans came out. After they talked with my guide, he dismounted and motioned to me to follow him into the shack. I did so and found a man on his back in great pain, which I soon discovered was due to a dislocated shoulder sustained while hunting buffalo. Having no anaesthetic, I pulled off one of my boots, used my heel as a fulcrum, and by main strength reduced the dislocation. Fastening his arm to his body with an improvised bandage, I ordered him to keep quiet and come to me in Tascosa in three days. All this was done by signs, as I could not speak or understand Spanish at that time.

Next morning he grew curious, slipped off the bandage to see if his arm was all right, and at the first motion, out it popped again, so he had the pleasure of operation number two. His curiosity was satisfied.

I crossed the river to Tascosa and found the young beauty, Señorita Piedad, a most loathsome object. There was not a spot on her body without a pustule. One of the torments of smallpox at a certain stage is intolerable itching. I racked my brain for something to allay that. There was no drug store in the country, of course, and my stock of medicines was very limited. One thing that was plentiful was gunpowder, and knowing it consisted of charcoal, saltpeter, and sulphur, I tried an experiment. I added water, made a paste, and had it spread over the entire body. It was a decided success. Señorita Piedad, my first patient in the Panhandle, recovered. Later she married a fine young American, and at last accounts, they are still living and enjoying life.

Her foster mother, Doña Solome Romero, a beautiful woman of the pure Castilian type from one of the best families in New Mexico, was especially grateful at the recovery of Piedad, who was her niece as well as her adopted daughter.

On Christmas a dinner and *baile* were given by

the Romeros at their commodious *hacienda* and Señorita Piedad, now fully recovered, made her debut
in Panhandle society. I participated as a guest of
honor. James Kennedy, son of the junior partner of
King & Kennedy, 'The Cattle Kings of Texas,' was
also a guest.[1] His mother was Spanish, and with his
athletic physique, dark hair and eyes, he was about
the handsomest bachelor in the Panhandle. He was
a wild one, so his father put him in charge of two
thousand head of cattle with a complete outfit and
sent him from the home ranch in southern Texas to
the Panhandle with the hope of making a man of
him.

Jim Kennedy and I became very good friends and
were together so much that we were dubbed by a
facetious cowboy 'the roulette twins,' *red* and *black*.
Both he and Doña Solome were teaching me Spanish, as practicing medicine through an interpreter
was rather unsatisfactory, and I was also adding to
my 'bag o' tricks' by taking guitar lessons from Miss
Lizzie Rinehart.

At first Kennedy conducted himself in an exemplary manner, became very popular, and his father's
expectations seemed about to be fulfilled. But, in
the course of time, he drove a herd of beef cattle to
Dodge City, Kansas, sold them and, unable to with-
stand the temptations of the underworld there, he
'stepped out' and was brought back home with a

[1] Hoyt's spelling of Kennedy is incorrect; it should be
Kenedy. See entry in *Biographical Notes*.

Casimero Romero Home, Tascosa
Courtesy The John L. McCarthy Collection, Amarillo Public Library

shoulder and one arm all shot to pieces. He never recovered from these wounds, although I think he lived for a year or two.

The plaza at Tascosa was about one hundred yards square and all the buildings were of adobe, or sun-dried brick. The plaza was bounded on the north by the store of Howard & McMasters; on the east by the house of Pedro Romero, a nephew of Don Casimiro; on the south by a blacksmith shop owned by Henry Kimball, assisted by a character known as 'Bronco Jack,' who had at some time met a bullet which crippled one of his legs; and on the west by the store of Mr. Rinehart, who had formerly been a sheriff in New Mexico.[2]

One day 'Bronco Jack' and Benito, a Mexican, had been playing monte, when a dispute occurred and they quit and Jack went back to his work. I

[2]Supposedly the first white to settle permanently in Tascosa, Henry M. Kimball, "a carpenter and buffalo hunter, and later, at Channing, Texas, a blacksmith and wheelwright," arrived on July 4, 1876. He planted a garden and continued to hunt buffalo in the vicinity, while doing carpentry work for the small local Mexican population. Edward M. Dealey, "The Story of Old Tascosa," *Frontier Times*, 4 (October 1926), 40.

Shortly after his arrival and that of Casimero Romero, two merchant partners from Elizabethtown, New Mexico, reached Tascosa, George J. Howard and Ira Rinehart. The latter had served as sheriff of Elizabethtown. The Howard-Rinehart partnership was short-lived, but ended amicably with Rinehart buying out Howard. In the spring of 1877 James E. McMasters arrived and entered into a partnership with Howard. John McCarty, *Maverick Town, The Story of Old Tascosa* (Norman, Okla., 1946), pp. 53-54.

stood leaning against the door jamb at Howard &
McMasters' store, lazily watching Bronco Jack in the
shop opposite where he was repairing a covered
buggy. Something caught my eye and I saw Benito
stealthily gliding diagonally across the plaza toward
the blacksmith shop, a long bowie knife glittering
in his hand.

I whistled. Jack looked up and I signaled with my
hand. Scenting danger, he jerked out his gun and
limped toward the door. Benito was but a few paces
from Jack when he came in view. Jack threw down
on him ordering him to stop, but instead Benito
sprang at him like a wildcat. Jack's gun barked, the
bullet passing through the chest muscles of Benito's
left side and then between my head and the door-
post, burying itself in the wall behind the counter
exactly on a level with my ear.

The warriors clinched in a deadly embrace. Bang
went the gun again, and between powder, smoke,
and dust raised from the dirt floor by their strug-
gles, they were soon half hidden from view. The
gun cracked four more times. Then Benito was seen
staggering from a side door, and collapsed on the
ground a few paces away. All this took but a few
seconds. I ran across, calling to Jack, 'Are you
hurt?'

'Hell, no,' he replied, 'but I put six bullets
through that greaser all right. You had better look
after *him*.'

Examination, however, revealed nothing to verify

this but a flesh wound from the first bullet. Benito had fainted from excitement and the loss of blood from a small severed artery. In a few minutes he was made comfortable on a *colchon* (wool mattress) on the floor in front of a bedstead in Pedro Romero's house.

Later it developed that the last five bullets from Jack's gun had pierced the top buggy from five different angles. It was a long long time before Bronco Jack heard the last of 'How about them ar' six holes through that greaser?'

There had been bad blood between the Americans and the Mexicans—the sporting element—for some time and this affair came near being a cause of war between the two factions. Almost before the dust had settled in the blacksmith shop, word went like wildfire through the Mexican settlement that Bronco Jack had murdered Benito. In less time than it takes to write about it, the Mexicans began to assemble, armed to the teeth. They only lacked a leader to begin a slaughter of the Americans, which looked to them an apparently easy matter, as they greatly outnumbered us.

The gravity of the situation was evident, and knowing that they had nothing personal against me, I took a hand. Assuring Benito and his friends that his wound was a simple affair and not dangerous, I succeeded in arranging a meeting between the combatants and led Jack into the room, crowded mostly with Mexicans, to shake hands with Benito and bury the hatchet. According to the understanding, Jack came unarmed. I was sitting on the bed just behind Benito's *colchon*, when Jack limped over to it and leaned over to grasp Benito's hand. Just then a villainous-looking Mexican, full of whiskey, pulled his gun and fired point-blank at Jack's back. Fortunately an American cowboy behind the Mexican jerked his gun simultaneously, and using it as a club, laid about six inches of the Mexican's scalp open so that he sank insensible to the floor.

This lucky blow came at the right instant to deflect the gun of the would-be assassin, the bullet passing just under Bronco Jack's right elbow between my knees and into the *colchon* on the bed where I was sitting. Two rather narrow escapes within thirty minutes!

I then had another pleasant job, sewing up the villain's scalp!

From the west, two Americans with one horse drifted in, and after a few days, continued their journey down the valley. The fact that they had but one horse excited more or less comment, as a man afoot in that country at that period was either a curiosity or a suspicious character. Moreover, while they were in town, they were rather exclusive and gave little information regarding themselves.

They had been gone but a few days when one of them returned alone with the horse, making camp at the river close by. The L I T Ranch was in the valley just west of Tascosa, and Superintendent

McCarty and a number of his men had noticed the two men when they first came through. They all happened to be at Tascosa when the lone man returned with the horse, and at once 'spotted' him.

My headquarters at that time were at the store of Howard & McMasters where I had a room. That evening McCarty, who was a friend of mine, came in and told me this story: They had seen this man come back alone, which looked very suspicious, so they put him through a sort of 'third degree,' and as his answers were contradictory and unsatisfactory, they called in a number of men in town and had a regular trial, found him guilty of murdering his companion, and decided to hang him.

The man's defense was that two or three days after leaving Tascosa his comrade was taken very sick and became delirious. When the man who had returned awaked from a sleep of exhaustion, his partner had disappeared and he was unable to find him. He also claimed to be sick himself, and for this reason McCarty, a level-headed and considerate man, decided to have me examine him. He urged haste, as the men were preparing for the execution.

We were just in time, as the party was starting for a nearby grove of cottonwoods. I examined the prisoner, confirmed his claim that he was a sick man, and suggested that instead of the 'necktie social,' he should be taken to the spot where he said his comrade had disappeared and see what could be found, volunteering to be one of the party myself.

My plan was approved and we started at daylight next morning. Besides myself, McCarty took two of his cowboys, one of whom was part Indian and an expert trailer, and the poor prisoner, who was so ill that he had to be tied to the saddle and often supported by a cowboy on each side. He succeeded, however, in guiding us to the camp where we found conditions about as he described. It was too late to do any trailing, so we slept under the stars and at daylight I found the victim all broken out with confluent smallpox.

Meanwhile our Indian made a détour around the vicinity and in a very short time signaled to us he had found a trail. To me it was marvelous how he could follow it, as he was most of the time on horseback, and at intervals would break into a trot.

The trail was a zigzag one which finally entered the mouth of a canyon that was recognized as the property of an eccentric American, Mitchell by name, a sort of recluse, who had married a Mexican woman and had been living here for some years. He was rarely seen and it was generally believed that he was a fugitive from justice.

This canyon was unusual from the fact that although at least a mile wide at its mouth, it gradually narrowed toward its head, with steep, precipitous rocky walls on each side, until it was only a few rods in width. Then it turned to the right, and after a short distance it suddenly widened out again and formed an immense natural corral.

This canyon was used by Mitchell to trap wild horses, which were numerous on the plains above. I have seen as many as one hundred and fifty in one herd in the Panhandle. Mitchell and a few Mexicans would find a band, spend from four to six weeks in walking them down, when they could easily be driven to his canyon and into the corral where the old stallions would be shot and the rest broken in by his *vaqueros*.

We reached Mitchell's *hacienda*, where we were noisily welcomed by Mitchell's youngsters and a pack of dogs, and on entering found our quest over. The murdered (?) man was there in bed with small-pox. He, in a delirious condition, had been found somewhere in the canyon by one of Mitchell's sheep-herders. He was brought in and tenderly cared for by Mitchell and his wife. They no doubt saved his life, and all this automatically pardoned our prisoner. The unfortunates both remained with the Mitchells and recovered.

Returning one day from a call a short distance down the valley, as I passed the home of Pedro Romero, I was startled by piercing shrieks, evidently a woman's. Springing from my horse I rushed into the house only to see Don Pedro dragging his wife, Doña Refugia, around the floor by her thick braided hair and at the same time taking his 'daily dozen' by kicking her ribs. I was carrying a heavy quirt with a loaded handle, and having first ordered him to let up, to which he paid no attention, and thinking that he had possibly gone insane, I struck him over the head with the heavy end of my whip and knocked him to the floor insensible.

I realized that I had struck a hard blow, and as Romero lay quite still, I was afraid that I might have killed him. As I knelt to examine his pulse and heart, I heard a rustle, and glancing up saw the Doña, a ferocious expression on her face and a knife in her hand, the blade, seemingly, about three feet long. If I hadn't seen her first, in another second I should have been slashed into ribbons. I had always been considered a sprinter, but I am quite positive I broke all my previous records as I sailed through her front door and onto my horse. This door will be in the limelight later, as Billy the Kid flashed through it, head on, during a foot race.

That incident was fifty years ago and I can assure my readers it was my last offense as an intermeddler between a man and his wife.

Pedro fully recovered, mutual friends brought us together, explanations were made and a truce declared; but I was careful never to allow him to get behind me.

X

The Doctor Turns Cowboy

JOHN CHISUM'S statement that the Panhandle was 'full of people' was a mistake. Smallpox soon faded away and there was little for me to do. There were all kinds of hunting, plenty of adventure and excitement, and I was enjoying life, but my income diminished, and it was not long until a debonair young *medico*, distinguished as the first to locate and practice medicine and surgery in the Texas Panhandle, was in that financial condition commonly known as flat broke.

I was too proud to send home for funds, which would not have been an easy matter anyway as the nearest post office was Dodge City, Kansas, several hundred miles away, and the only communication with it an occasional bull train with freight or Old Dad Barnes, an antiquated old-time cowboy who, about every three months, ambled up and down the valley on a has-been mustang, picking up letters for Dodge City at fifty cents a letter and retrieving answers at the same price. As a solution, I applied to W. C. (Bill) Moore, superintendent of the LX Ranch, the largest in the valley, for a job.

Moore was short-handed and took me on. He had a staff of about fifty men, a good part of whom were refugees, many under an alias and a few with rewards for their apprehension hanging over them. This latter class even included Moore, but this was not known until later.

Bill Moore, a Californian and raised on a cattle ranch, was one of the best *vaqueros* I ever saw. The riata of that day was made of rawhide, and in California, where the ranges were then in the 'wide-open spaces,' a sixty-foot riata was used. In Texas the ranges were broken by patches of brush, mesquite, and timber, and a forty-five-foot rope was employed.

During round-ups Moore would sit back and watch some wild and exceptionally unruly steer baffle every cowboy who was trying to rope him for branding purposes, and after all had failed, Bill would put spurs to his mount and dash in. And I never saw him miss.

Later it transpired that Moore had killed some member of his family in California, and fled to Wyoming, where he became manager of a large cattle ranch, and after a time became incensed at a Negro employee and killed him. He then escaped to the Panhandle of Texas, where the Bates & Beals Company had recently established the LX Ranch, and after a short period of probation they made him superintendent.

During my sojourn of about a year in that section, Moore was probably the most popular and highly esteemed cowman there. Although most reserved and

LX Ranch Headquarters
Courtesy The John L. McCarthy Collection, Amarillo Public Library

dignified with outsiders, he was very cordial and
courteous with his own crew. A few years later he
moved to New Mexico, west of the Rio Grande, and
started a ranch for himself. There were two brothers
owning land adjoining his. This land had a fine
spring of water that Moore wanted. They refused to
sell, and after sending them word he was coming
after them, he rode up to their home and shot them
both down in cold blood.

He again made his escape and was not heard of
again. Many years afterwards one of Moore's two
foremen from the LX Ranch, Charles A. Siringo,
had become a detective, and while tracking down
a criminal in Alaska, met and instantly recognized
him, although he denied his identity. Siringo, who
knew him quite well, was certain he was the man,
as Moore had a peculiar cast in one eye which could
not be readily disguised and which can be seen in the
picture in this book.[1]

My first duty as a cowboy was with a bunch of the
boys assigned to construct a large corral. Cedar
posts were cut down, hauled from the brakes and
planted in a deep ditch which we had dug around
the outer edge of the corral. I was raised on a farm,
where I had done my bit in both digging and chop-
ping, but my hands were now soft and this sort of

[1]A picture of Moore appears in the original edition of
Hoyt's book, opposite p. 64, taken from Siringo's *Riata and
Spurs*, but efforts to locate the original for reproduction
proved unsuccessful.

job produced quite a crop of blisters, the last I have ever raised by engaging in manual labor.

Will Rogers, our humorist cowboy, in a letter to a friend, writes of a recent visit to the Panhandle and says that 'while at the old corral on the LX Ranch I saw a flock of oil derricks instead of snubbing posts.' If I had only foreseen!

Instead of putting me through the usual initiation handed to a tenderfoot, such as putting burrs under my saddle, sniping me, etc., I was treated royally, doubtless because of the fact that I had treated some of the boys for smallpox and did not kill them.

The senior foreman, Charles A. Siringo, then one of the most expert cowboy riders, ropers, and gunmen in the Panhandle, taught me the tricks of the trade, and a friendship was then formed that was continued to the day of his death in 1928.

Every cowboy is supposed to supply his own outfit. I had practically everything but a riata, and with Siringo as teacher, I 'rolled my own.' We took a large cowhide that had been stretched and dried, trimmed off legs and corners until it was circular in shape, and then with a sharp knife cut it into a long strip one half-inch wide, by going around its circumference. After it had been cut into four equal lengths, this strip of rawhide was fastened to a convenient tree or post. The hair was scraped off with a knife and then the strips were rubbed very thoroughly with tallow or brains until they were quite soft. Finally the four strands were braided together in a certain way, one end made into a *hondo* (loop), and the riata was ready for business.

Siringo then taught me how to throw it, an accomplishment I have not entirely forgotten to this day. During the Filipino Insurrection in Luzon, Philippine Islands, in 1900, I was Chief Surgeon on the staff of the late Major-General Frederick Dent Grant.[2] Desiring to mount a force of his troops, he asked for four hundred American horses and that number of wild broncos from Oregon was shipped to his command. A number of ex-cowboys and men familiar with horses were detailed from the different units, a typical western corral was constructed, and the breaking of these beasts begun.

One day General Grant and I were sitting on our horses, interested spectators of the performance. An officer taking a fancy to one of the horses had pointed him out to the man in the corral, who had already made several unsuccessful attempts to put the rope over his head. There was a large bunch of horses milling round and round toward the right. The one wanted kept in the middle of the pack and when the rope was thrown, he would duck his head and escape.

After several misses, I made a facetious remark about the roper, and another officer hearing me came back with something like ''Tis much easier to criticize than to do.'

[2]Hoyt's Philippine service is the subject of the last ten chapters.

I was nettled by the tone of his remark. Intensely interested in the scene before me, my memory flashed back over twenty years and I felt an uncontrollable urge to get hold of that rope. Turning to the General, I asked permission to enter the corral and try my luck.

He gave me an astonished look, but seeing I was in earnest, consented. All this was done on the spur of the moment, and my idea was to ride into the corral, get the rope, and follow my prey on horseback. Being above him I thought I could easily put the loop over his head, quickly wind my end of the riata around my saddle horn, and secure the horse just as I used to do in Texas.

But I had another think coming! As I spurred my mount through the milling circle, it flashed through my mind that I was on a Whitman saddle with no more horn than a muley cow and my entire plan of campaign was changed in an instant. Instead of a thrill I had a decided chill.

Dismounting, I directed the man to hold my horse and reached for the rope. The moment I touched it I had chill number two, and I hardly know to this day just what kept me from throwing up the sponge. I had not touched a riata since I left Texas in 1878, and all my experience there had been with a rawhide, while this rope was *hemp*. At that instant a typhoon or an earthquake would have been welcome to me, but none came.

The rope felt so different from a rawhide that I

knew I should fail, and what little courage I had was fast oozing. But there I was, a rope in my hands and the horses still milling to the right, round and round. I coiled the hemp in my left hand and with my right began opening up the loop, and to my great surprise it responded, so in a moment my confidence returned.

I stepped about, throwing the loop around my head and backward and forward on the ground a moment, and then began to walk toward the herd. The horse, a fine-looking animal, had kept well in the center in an almost uncanny way all the time, but during the last round he had in some way been forced to the inside and came from my left in full gallop, and as he flew past I gave the twist of the wrist that turned it up and under him in such a way that it caught both hind legs. The next instant I had my hemp around the snubbing post and the chase was over. It was one of the easiest and simplest things I ever did, but it was all due to my streak of luck in his coming as he did from the left *on the inside*. I owe an apology to my readers, but that incident flashed back from memories of long ago, seems apropos, and is therefore introduced here.

When we had completed our corral, selecting six horses from our *remuda de caballos*,[3] I became a range rider, being paired with 'Latigo Jim'—the only name I ever knew him by—and located in a small log cabin on Bonita Creek, just south of the

[3] A *remuda de caballos* is a relay of horses.

Canadian and about the middle of the south edge of the LX Ranch, which had an area of forty square miles. Range riding means patrolling the boundaries daily, and if any trails are found leading from the ranch, the rider must follow them and bring back the strays.

Our beat consisted of twenty miles, ten east and ten west from our cabin. Our 'chuck' was bacon, sourdough bread, black coffee with sugar, potatoes, and jerked or fresh beef, the meat being alternated at our pleasure with the abundant game. Deer, wild turkey, quail, antelope, and buffalo were all nearby. We were both good camp cooks, so we fared rather sumptuously. From the home ranch was issued green coffee. When we had roasted this in a skillet, ground it at the bottom of a tin can by pounding it with the end of a hammer handle, and brought it to a boil in a quart tin pail, we had as fine coffee as I have ever tasted.

Jim had never seen a doughnut. So we saved bacon grease, I mixed the dough as I had seen Mother do, and while I worked in the sour for raising, Jim poured in the right quantity of sugar. When it had risen, I rolled out the mass with an empty quart bottle, sliced it in strips, dropped them in the hot grease, and in a few minutes had as nice-looking a batch of browned doughnuts as one could wish.

They looked so good that Jim could not wait till all were fried, so grabbed one and began. In a moment I heard vehement expressions of disgust as he spat his mouthful into the fireplace. In fact he was quite profane. 'If that's a doughnut, excuse me,' he said. I registered astonishment and tried one myself, only to discover that in his haste to help me, Jim had picked up the salt can instead of the sugar.

Twice during my tour of range riding we were visited with a severe Norther, each one starting just after dark, and in a short time bunches of cattle all along the line were drifting south with the storm. Each cowboy on the ranch was out on the south boundary doing his utmost to stem the tide and bring back the stragglers, but a good many got away and kept on going.

At night those wild Texas cattle will stampede at the drop of a hat and there are few more dangerous adventures than trying to stop or head them off. The Texas cow-horse is a remarkable animal, sometimes more intelligent than his rider in doing the right thing at the right time in emergencies. During these night stampedes in a Norther, when it is dark as pitch, the wind howling, wild cattle dashing here and there over broken and rough terrain, the way your horse will carry you at full speed, without stumbling or falling, sometimes for hours, is little short of marvelous.

XI

At the Palo Duro Ranch with Colonel Goodnight

WHEN the grass sprouted in the spring of 1878, Moore sent a party of eight men, including Latigo Jim and myself, a cook and 'chuck' wagon, in charge of Jack Ryan, south across the Staked Plain to gather up strays that had drifted with the storms. Ryan was the junior foreman of the ranch, a first-class cowman, genial and cheerful in disposition, a good mixer, and just the man for the place.

Going south as far as the headwaters of the Brazos and Concho Rivers, we picked up quite a herd and began gradually to work homewards. After a while we struck a tough bit of country, and while scouting around, picked up the fresh trail of a bunch of horses. We followed this trail, which led into a secluded camp, in which, upon turning a point of rocks, we ran into a camp of four men and saw just beyond about twenty-five horses. Both parties saluted. We dismounted and each began to size up the other. After talking a moment, Ryan recognized the leader of the four, introductions followed, and all of us were soon chatting and very much at home. They claimed to be on the same errand as we, except they were after stray horses.

As soon as we pulled out, Ryan told us, what we

had already surmised, that they were horse and cattle rustlers. The leader was William Nickel, alias Slap Jack Bill, a young man, quite handsome and, according to Jack, from a fine family in the States, but the black sheep of that family. We shall meet him again.

Some of our supplies were getting low, so Jack sent me ahead to the Charles Goodnight Ranch in the Palo Duro Canyon for the needed articles and told me to meet him at the head of the canyon as he came up with the herd.

I was instructed to ride straight north and told that my destination was just one day's ride. So I started right after breakfast without any provisions, expecting to run into the ranch by sundown. But someone blundered, as it took me just three days to reach the ranch. I did not mind it the first day. At night I picketed my horse, and with blanket and saddle for a bed, I slept under the stars. But about noon the second day, my appetite began a hailing sign of distress.

There were plenty of buffalo and antelope, but my horse was not fast enough for me to kill one with a Colt's forty-five, which was the only weapon I had carried on this trip. Passing a big mesquite I heard a *whiz-z-z*, and as my horse jumped sidewise about six feet, I caught sight of an enormous rattlesnake and quickly shot its head off. I sat on my horse looking at that reptile for some time. I had been told by old hunters they were good meat. I was *hungry*. I picketed my horse, started a fire of buffalo chips, and after skinning and cutting up my game, roasted a portion on the end of a mesquite branch spit, and was agreeably surprised to find that the meat greatly resembled chicken or rabbit and was very palatable. I satisfied my hunger and had enough for a couple of meals next day.

For relish there were frequent beds of prickly pear, rather young yet, but juicy and of good flavor. At that time there were fresh-water lakes at intervals along the plains that quenched thirst, and, take it all in all, it was not so bad.

Just before sundown the third day, I sighted the walls of the Palo Duro Canyon, and before dark I was made quite comfortable by Colonel Charles Goodnight and his good wife and was treated to one of the most enjoyable meals at their ranch home that I can remember.

When I rejoined our outfit, I got a cordial welcome, as Ryan had discovered his mistake in directing me and, to make amends, cut my night watch from then on. When we reached the head of the brakes leading to the Canadian River, we found an ideal spot for a camp. There was a fine spring at the bottom of a steep bank, from the crest of which there lay unfolded before us a magnificent panorama of the entire surrounding country, both plain and valley. The stream flowing from this spring supplied abundant water for our animals.

Here Ryan decided to leave the herd until he

reported to headquarters and learned what Moore wished to have done with them. So, leaving Latigo Jim and me in charge, supplied with fifteen horses and a chuck wagon, with instructions to hold the cattle until relieved from the home ranch, he started home with the rest of the party.

Jim and I had taken a tarpaulin and our blankets to the ridge above the spring and there pitched our camp. We had been in this spot one week when a horseman came in from the east with the information that he was a Ranger, that the Comanches were out, and that he had been sent up the valley to spread the alarm.

We found a shovel in the wagon and on this ridge dug a hole about six feet long, four wide, and four deep, filling a bunch of gunny sacks with the earth and placing them all around the edge of our fort. After digging a winding tunnel through which to crawl in or out, we were ready for any hostile outfit that might show up. Ryan had left us two Sharp's carbines with plenty of ammunition, in addition to our revolvers. There was a hole in the tarpaulin big enough to run a fist through, about halfway between its center and edge. So we doubled it over with the hole underneath, and spread it over our fort as a roof, holding it down by placing on top of the gunny sacks a lot of large stones from near the spring. With our blankets inside, we slept there as soon it was completed. Looking up, we could see the hole about the middle of the ceiling.

We waited about two weeks, and as no word came from the home ranch, we decided to make a move. Drawing lots to see which one would go in to headquarters, Jim won. Promising that someone would be out within three or four days, he promptly departed.

I had a big bunch of cattle and fourteen horses to look after, but as the grazing was fine, they made very little trouble. The cattle would scatter and graze most of the day, never straying more than a short distance from the little stream, and before sundown I would round them up not far from camp, where they would bed down for the night.

I kept one horse picketed at camp, saddled and ready for use day and night, while the others were hobbled and never strayed very far, except on one occasion. The picketed horse also acted to a certain extent as a sentinel. As a rule, if a strange horse approaches, either day or night, the picket horse will whinny.

I crawled from the fort one morning to find not a hobbled horse in sight. I was a light sleeper, but I had not heard a sound. There were the cattle all right and I could discover no reason for the absence of the horses. Putting some corn in one saddle-bag and bread and jerked meat in the other, I soon found the trail. The direction was south. The horses kept well together and seemed to be traveling rapidly. Thereupon I concluded they had been stampeded, but by whom or what was beyond me.

The trail finally led by the bed of a shallow, recently dried-up lake, where the earth was soft and almost muddy in spots and there the mystery was solved. Tracks of wolves were plainly to be seen and I hurried along.

About midday my horse began to tire. I stopped, gave him some corn and, after a brief rest, went on again.

About two hours before sundown I saw a dark spot on the horizon which grew larger as I approached. I was soon near enough to witness a strange sight.

There were my poor horses lined up in a formation almost as symmetrical as that of a cavalry squad. They were fighting off with their hobbled forefeet two large gray wolves which, snapping and snarling, were doing their best to get a big meal after their long chase. Their appetites were whetted by the smell of blood which the friction of the hobbles had drawn. The wolves were so intent on their prey that I rode within fifty yards without being seen. Then I dismounted and prepared to attempt some killing myself. I was a trifle unsteady after my long ride, the targets were bounding here and there, and, as I did not want to score a miss, I took my time, but it was only a moment before I saw my chance and brought down one of the beasts with a shot through his spine. His mate instantly fled, but I had taken an extra cartridge from my belt before I shot and was holding it with my teeth, so was able quickly to send a bullet after number two. I hit him, but did not bring him down. He was running from me and I think the ball went through the muscles of his back, as he wheeled around twice, biting and snapping at himself near the hip. I fired again, but it was a long shot and I think it was a miss.

The horses were in a sad plight. Their fetlocks were a sight where the hobbles had worn through the flesh. Removing the hobbles, I started for camp and, strange to say, they followed me like a pack of hounds, instead of having to be driven.

It was nearly daybreak when I reached camp and, fastening the horses to a rope attached to the wagon, I crawled into the fort and was dead to the world until nearly noon. Something wakened me then, and glancing at the canvas ceiling of my dugout, brightly illuminated by the sunshine, I saw projecting from that hole in the under half of the tarpaulin at least a foot and a half of the business end of a snake as large as my arm. It was sinuously weaving about as if looking for a soft spot to drop on. Through the semi-transparent ceiling the rest of its body could be traced from the hole to the gunny sack. Its length seemed to be unlimited.

Harry Houdini in his best days never put over a vanishing act that compared with mine as I fled through that tunnel, nor was any previous training necessary. When I got out, I found the snake had got in, so I stripped off the tarpaulin and shot it. It was about ten feet long, but of what variety, or whether it was poisonous or not, I never did know.

As my blankets had been in the dugout for several days, I took them out to air and had another surprise. What I found under those blankets would have gladdened the heart of a Smithsonian entomologist—tarantula, scorpion, centipede, and a reptile resembling a horned toad—quite a happy family, including several other species strangers to me. From then on the fort was 'to let.' Comanches were conspicuous by their absence and I never entered the stronghold again.

It had been a long time since I had seen a newspaper or printed matter of any kind. Rummaging through the chuck wagon, where I now bunked, I found a well-worn copy of Shakespeare in small print and during the rest of my enforced hermit life I consoled myself with it.

After being alone for exactly thirty days, I was finally relieved by Moore himself with an outfit. He gave a number of reasons for the delay, but I was so pleased to see people again I paid little attention to them.

Moore was well satisfied with my care of everything, and when we reached the home ranch, gave me a week's vacation which I put in at Tascosa. I then took part in the big round-up in which most of the ranchers on that section of the Panhandle participated. The work was hard and exciting, but uneventful, and after returning to range riding a short time, I found I had recouped my funds sufficiently to return to civilization. Therefore I quit the cow-boy life, an experience I have never regretted, and returning to Tascosa, made my home at Howard & McMasters as before, pending the passing of some party with which I might travel to New Mexico, where I had decided to locate.

XII

Back in Tascosa

JAMES CAMPBELL, my first acquaintance in the Panhandle, came in one day with a small bunch of wild mustangs his party had rounded up, and turned them into the corral back of the store. I had that morning lent my horse to a friend who had a saddle, and while I was chatting with Campbell, a Mexican rode up on a burro to get me to go down the river a few miles to aid a man who had just been shot.

It just happened that there was not an available horse to be found anywhere and Campbell offered me one of his mustangs. He had not forgotten the boot incident, and I instantly realized he hoped to get even by seeing me spilled. Nevertheless, I accepted his offer.

Henry Kimball, the blacksmith, had recently made for me a fine wrought-iron Spanish bit for a new horsehair bridle that had been given me. Taking my equipment to the corral, I soon had a handsome white mustang roped, snubbed, blindfolded, saddled and bridled, and let out in front of the store. One end of my riata was round his neck, the rest of it was looped in my left hand.

Removing my saddle-bags containing my drugs

and instruments, I pointed him toward the east where there was a strip of small sand hills, figuring on a soft spot to land if I were thrown.

I sprang on the mustang's back, and jerking the handkerchief from his eyes, gave him the spurs. He pitched his best, but I kept my balance, giving him both spurs and quirt at every jump, and almost before we were through the sand hills, he quieted down and became apparently as meek as Moses. To make sure, I put him through at a stiff gallop for several miles until he was reeking with lather and then returned for my saddle-bags. There was no one outside, so I rode up to the hitching rail to dismount. After the mustang had quieted down, I hung the riata to the saddle horn in the usual way, and when I returned to town, he was so docile that I let the riata remain where it was, and as I dismounted simply carried the bridle rein over his head to fasten it to the rail.

But the instant my feet touched the ground, he threw a vicious kick at me with his left hind foot and did his best to grab me with his teeth at the same time. My activity saved me from the kick and the Spanish bit from his teeth. I had a firm hold of the bridle rein, and as he then reared up on his hind feet, I sprang back and with all my strength undertook to pull him over on his back where I could easily control him.

But alas, my made-to-order nice new Spanish bit broke in two in the middle, the bridle peeled from his head, and away he went at full speed down the valley out of sight. Along with him went my beautiful California full-rigged saddle, a fine Mexican saddle blanket, and my rawhide riata.

The principal topic at the store that afternoon was who was the goat, Campbell or the Red Doctor. Word was passed down the valley, and just one week later the mustang, saddle, and riata were brought in by a cowboy from a ranch fifty miles below. My saddle blanket, a present, was the only loss I had.

One day later on, a big broad-shouldered man, with a very forbidding countenance, arrived at Tascosa afoot from the west. He claimed to be a sailor and very athletic. He announced he had been told there was a runner there and he was the man he was looking for, as he was fully prepared to run a foot race, one hundred and fifty yards, with anybody, and would back himself for all he had, about one hundred dollars.

The boys came for me, and after sizing him up, I accepted his challenge. The course was measured off, judges and all preliminaries arranged for, and we were off. I was surprised to find myself winning with but little exertion, as from his talk I expected a close race. I could never understand why he classed himself as a runner.

He was very ugly after his defeat and began to 'licker' up. In preparing for the race I had stripped down to trousers, shirt, and my old running shoes, a present from Ned Moulton during my University days, leaving my belongings, including my forty-five, in my room at Howard & McMasters. Clad as I was, I strolled into Rinehart's store and was watching a poker game between a couple of cowboys. A dry-goods box was the table and smaller boxes were used as seats, all in front of the fireplace at the rear of the long store room. I stood with my back to the fire, facing the front and only door.

One of the players was quite a wag and we were all laughing at his wit when in stalked the sailor. It seemed to me he was trying to conceal the fact that he had been drinking. When about halfway across the room toward us, he suddenly pulled a gun and began whirling it around his finger. About every other whirl he would throw the muzzle in our direction. My first thought was that he had taken a few drinks and was 'showing off,' but a look at his face, which was demoniacal in its expression, quickly changed my mind.

Involuntarily my hand went like a flash for my gun—and to my horror *it was gone*. He saw my motion and fired at me point-blank at a distance of not over six feet. What saved me I have no idea. I thought I was a goner and at that instant my life seemed to float before me as I had always heard it does when one is drowning. My thoughts were, 'What a horrible way to die! Without a show on earth! If I only had my gun,' etc.

As quickly as he could, the sailor fired again, after

Howard & McMasters' Store, Tascosa
Courtesy The John L. McCarthy Collection, Amarillo Public Library

which nothing could be seen, as that end of the room was dense with powder smoke. I was experiencing a feeling that was new and one that I can truthfully say I have never experienced since, that of *abject fear*.

As the man fired the third shot, I realized I was not dead and decided to make an effort to escape. I saw the flash of the third shot through the smoke and it was not directed toward me. Crouching as low as I could, I started with a sort of weaving motion toward the door. September 22, 1927, at the Soldiers' Field in Chicago, I saw Jack Dempsey do the identical stunt, except he crouched and weaved *toward* Tunney, whilst I was hotfooting *away* from my man, a move that saved my life.

As I passed him, he fired the fourth time, and as I flew across the plaza—in my opinion making the best sprinting time in my career—I heard two more shots. I jumped over the counter in Howard & McMasters' store in a short cut to get to my room, grabbed my gun, and came back over the counter to the door just in time to see my man on horseback disappearing around the rear corner of Rinehart's store. I fired twice before he was entirely out of sight, but I never knew whether the shots had any effect. It was at long range for a forty-five, he was crouching low, and his horse fairly flying.

My escape was nothing short of miraculous, but the affair was tragic after all. There were two Mexicans standing at my right also watching the game.

When the smoke cleared, one of them was found mortally wounded by the last two shots and he died in a few minutes. Strange coincidence, the two cowboys were also unarmed. They escaped by throwing themselves on the floor and staying there. Rinehart, formerly a sheriff with a reputation as a 'two-gun' man, was behind the counter when the sailor entered and he took refuge on the floor at the first shot, although he had a double-barreled shotgun loaded with buckshot under the counter for just such emergencies.

There was another strange thing about the incident. There happened to be only one horse in Tascosa at the time. He was tied in front of Rinehart's store and was stolen by the sailor as he made his getaway. As soon as possible a party of Americans and Mexicans were in pursuit—I among them—but we never found the slightest trace of the fugitive. He evidently escaped by way of the Canadian River which was but a short distance from Rinehart's and had high banks that would conceal him for some distance up or down. With a start of over an hour and a very good horse under him, he had every advantage in the world.

At another time I had occasion to visit the Bugby Ranch.[1] I had never been there and asked for directions. I was told to follow the trail on the north side of the Canadian River east until I came to a sandy-bottomed creek, dry most of the year; to cross it and

[1] Thomas S. Bugbee, not Bugby, is correct.

turn to the left upon reaching the first arroyo and
follow this arroyo to the head where I would find
the ranch.

I reached the creek—it was called Sand Creek—
late in the afternoon, found it apparently dry, and
started across. About a dozen yards from the farther
bank my horse suddenly began to sink. Instantly I
realized we were in quicksand and that my horse,
already weary, would not be able to carry me
through. Quickly loosening my riata from the saddle horn, I sprang from his back, throwing myself
full length on the sand, and rolled over and over to
shore leaving a trail of water behind me. My clothing was soaked. My horse was now down almost to
his withers, struggling frantically, and but for the
riata around his neck would have perished. There
was a log embedded in the sand at the shore, and
bracing my feet against it, with the riata wound
about my shoulders, I was able to help him in such
a way that he finally slowly struggled out. His trembling began to disappear and we started for the arroyo. At first I led him to give myself a chance to
warm up, as it was near sundown and quite cold.
We soon reached the arroyo and, finding a good
trail, I hoped to strike a place soon where I could
make both myself and my horse comfortable.

There were many large cottonwood trees along
the arroyo and in most of them were numbers of
wild turkeys going to roost. They were plentiful all
along the Canadian Valley. It was now quite dark

and the stars were shining when we reached the head of the arroyo. It proved to be also the end of the trail, which had gradually been growing dimmer for some time. It was a beautiful night, clear and cold, but no ranch was in sight—nothing but plains as far as I could see. Evidently there was a mistake somewhere. My horse was exhausted, I was wet to the skin, and, as the last drop in our bucket of woe, my matches were soaked!

I picketed my horse, and as the grazing was good, he was all right. The night was very cold and I was compelled to prance about most of the time to keep from actually freezing. I thought many times of my friend Paist in the blinding blizzard on the Northern Boundary.

Just as the eastern horizon began to get gray, I detected in the distance a wisp of smoke curling heavenward and there was no delay in the way I split the air in that direction. The smoke came from the Bugby Ranch, where I arrived just in time for breakfast. Hot biscuit, honey, plum preserves, fried chicken, butter, and cream—the first time I had seen any of the last three articles since arriving in the Panhandle! Years passed, Mr. Bugby retired, and I was once entertained at a dinner in his beautiful home in Kansas City. Although it was a sumptuous affair, I felt constrained to say to Mrs. Bugby that it did not compare with that, to me, memorable breakfast in the old Panhandle.

At this period, when I was riding I carried, in

addition to my forty-five, a Winchester repeating rifle in a saddle boot. Returning to Tascosa I avoided the Sand Creek crossing by leaving the trail and skirting the heads of the brakes with the idea of picking up some game. Not far from the home cabin of the LX Ranch, I came to the summit of a slight ridge where a small natural basin could be seen, perhaps fifty feet deep and one hundred yards in diameter. Right in its bottom was a large flock of wild turkeys. They sighted me the moment I appeared and scattered in every direction but mine, running like greyhounds to get out of the basin and take flight. A wild turkey has the same trouble in taking off that airplanes have. They both must run on the level a short distance before they can rise into the air.

The instant I saw them I pulled my rifle, sprang to the ground and opened up. Being somewhat conceited about my marksmanship I aimed my first shot at the head of the bird, but I scored a miss. I then changed my tactics, and aiming at their bodies, brought down eight fine gobblers before the rest disappeared over the edge of the basin. With my mustang almost covered with turkey, I visited the LX Ranch where both I and the birds were welcome. Moore had a fine cook who rose to the occasion ably. Part of the game I took home and the feast continued there.

As my little room back of the counter was poorly ventilated, I would bring my *colchon* and blankets and make my bed on the floor in the store beside Jim McMasters, with our feet toward the front door. Jule Howard had married a Mexican woman and lived in another part of the building.

One night we were awakened by a pounding on the door and by voices ordering the doors to be opened or they would be shot to splinters. This was mixed with much profanity and we could hear horses prancing about. Grabbing our guns we sprang from our beds, Jim going to the right and I to the left. We were none too soon, as four bullets came crashing through the doors and the counters just above where he had been lying, my second narrow escape at those very doors.

Jim then did some talking himself as we both opened up with our guns, emptying them in short order through the doors, but the attackers had evidently moved from before the doors as they fired their first volley. Shouting with scorn and derision at our marksmanship, they galloped away. They fired several volleys after the first, but none of them struck the doors. Several bullets were found buried in the adobe walls on both sides of them. We never had the slightest clue as to who the night raiders were—probably cowboys we both knew, out for a lark and hunting excitement.

A young bachelor, Mr. Boggs from Boston, had appeared with three thousand head of sheep, driven from the west, and camped on a range near Tascosa where he came for supplies. He was a very friendly

Group of Texas Panhandlers in 1884
Left to right, standing: W. S. Mabry, Frank James,
C. B. Vivian, Ike P. Ryland. Sitting: James H. East,
James E. McMasters, Patrick Garrett

chap and everybody liked *him*. His sheep were another story. A sheepskin has about the same effect on a cattleman that a red flag has on a bull.

Boggs was a good mixer and soon confided his intimate personal history to the cowboys whom he met in Tascosa.

In Boston he had fallen in love with a very charming, and, according to the picture he exhibited, beautiful girl whose parents were wealthy. One day her father and he had a conference. Boggs was asked concerning his financial status, and after confessing that his bank balance would show but three thousand five hundred dollars was frankly told by the lady's father that before he could hope to become his son-in-law he must show assets of not less than twenty-five thousand dollars. He was also advised that the West was the place to make money.

This advice he took, and after investigating several propositions, finally decided on sheep. He had bought his drove in New Mexico for a dollar a head. Learning that the Texas Panhandle was a fine grazing country, that there were no laws, taxes, or expenses of any kind but the upkeep of two or three Mexican herders, he decided to become a Texan *pro tempore*, and here he was.

Personally he had the sympathy of all. But his sheep were decidedly unpopular with the cattle barons. Liking young Boggs too well to resort to force, they determined to get rid of him and his sheep by a ruse.

Boggs traded with Rinehart, and when he was in the store one day four cowboys entered and started a poker game on the old dry-goods box always there for that purpose. It was a lively game and Boggs was soon an interested spectator. He was leaning forward in an effort to see one of the hands when suddenly the player on his right sprang up filling the air with the most horrible curses, and after accusing poor Boggs of tipping off his hand, jerked out both his guns and opened fire. At the same instant, another player defended Boggs just as vehemently and opened up with his own artillery. The other two joined in and bedlam reigned supreme. Several fell dead (?), Boggs was carried out in a state of collapse, his life saved by a miracle, he was told later. This was of course a blank cartridge battle, the dead disposed of, and blood washed away long before Boggs was back to normalcy. The game was well played and I doubt if Boggs ever suspected it was anything but genuine.

Although the play had been a perfect success and was instantly followed with the most adroit propaganda, that his life was in danger every moment he remained in the Panhandle, etc., for some unknown reason it did not work and Boggs and the sheep still stuck. Another conference was held at Howard & McMasters and a new plan devised. The next time Boggs came to town a stranger to him galloped in, announced himself as a Texas Ranger sent to notify all cattlemen and sheepmen in the Panhandle that the Legislature had just levied a tax of five dollars a head on cattle and two dollars on sheep. He declared, too, that a force of Rangers would be up the valley, collecting, in a few days, and notified all owners to be prepared to pay in cash.

The next day there was an exodus of three thousand sheep toward Kansas and later word came they had crossed the line.

The Panhandle cattle barons grinned. It was a lowdown trick, but if Boggs had not been so well liked, there would have been shooting—and that would have been a good deal worse.

XIII

Billy the Kid Gives Me a Horse and a Bill of Sale

O NE MORNING a small herd of buffalo, doubtless chased from the plains by hunters, crossed the Canadian at Tascosa and stampeded past, a few passing through the outskirts of the village. Miss Lizzie Rinehart, an expert rider and a dead shot, owned a fine racing mare, Spider by name, which was saddled and in front of the Rinehart store when the buffalo appeared. One look and Miss Lizzie was in the saddle with her gun, and Spider was showing her speed. She brought down one buffalo with the first shot and wounded another before they were out of range.

Later Miss Lizzie married a very popular young cowboy, Robert Russell by name. In the course of time he and Jule Howard, of Howard & McMasters, clashed, and as Jule beat him to the draw, Bob was added to the 'Boot Hill' cemetery at Tascosa.[1]

[1]It appears that Russell took exception to George J. (Julius) Howard's interest in his young wife. In the fall of 1879 this lead to a confrontation outside Howard & McMasters' store, with Howard killing Russell. "The widow with bitter determination selected a spot in sight of Howard's store for the burial ground. Thus Boothill Cemetery was born atop one of the many knolls that reach down like fingers from a giant hand to the Canadian River." McCarty, *Maverick Town*, pp. 94–96.

E. W. Parker, manager of the Southern Division of the National Mail Company, Atchison, Kansas, now appeared on the scene, announced the establishing of a Star Route weekly horseback mail line from Fort Elliott, Texas, to Las Vegas, New Mexico, by way of Tascosa, and asked for a guide to escort him through the Panhandle.

A rumor started that Parker was a detective, and although rumor travels fast, this one was slow in comparison with the exodus of cowboys in every direction. Charles A. Siringo, who was then a cowboy on the LX Ranch, says that one even stole a horse to expedite his vanishing.

Being now quite familiar with the valley trails, I volunteered to serve as Parker's guide and in this way did my bit toward establishing the first mail route through the Panhandle of Texas.

Our trip was uneventful. Mr. Parker selected sites for stations between Tascosa and Fort Elliott. While at the Fort I was a guest at a country dance given by some settlers in the neighborhood, and although a stranger, I had a good time. One incident I have never forgotten.

We were in a good-sized adobe house which had for seats wooden benches placed against the wall. One face particularly attracted me, that of a young woman who was a real beauty, with luxuriant wavy brown hair, oval face, low forehead, big brown eyes, and complexion and teeth all that could be desired. She would have attracted attention anywhere.

Her costume of calico was simple but neat. Yet, although she seemed by all odds the prettiest girl at the ball, she was not dancing. I was told upon my arrival that no introductions were necessary, so I walked over to the bench where the beauty was sitting and politely asked for a dance. Giving me a lovely smile she remarked, in a deep contralto voice almost masculine in timbre, 'I've sot and sot til I've 'bout tuk root, guess I will'; and joined me with alacrity. She was from Arkansas and was a good partner, but when I learned that her chief amusement was dipping snuff, the flirtation quickly subsided.

As we were jogging along the trail on our return to Tascosa, Mr. Parker, after observing me very intently for a few moments, said, 'Dr. Hoyt, if I had your body with my head I would conquer the world.' Was it a compliment or otherwise? Many years after we met in El Paso, Texas, and had some very interesting reunions. His 'body' was better than he thought, as he lived to an advanced age.

Through Old Dad Barnes I had secured a new supply of vaccine, and although smallpox had disappeared, I was still vaccinating many. Superintendent McCarty of the L I T Ranch entered the store one day as I was vaccinating a Mexican and, as I finished, Mac rolled up his sleeve and took his turn. As I worked he smoked a cigarette and told a story. Just as I finished he turned to look at his arm, and seeing a tiny drop of blood oozing out, fell to the floor in a dead faint.

McCarty was a fine fellow with a high rating for nerve, and rumor said he was entitled to one notch on his gun; but you never can tell. That vaccination cost him a lot of money. The question, 'Don't you want to get vaccinated, Mac?' sprung on him where drinking was going on never failed to be answered with, 'What'll you have, fellers?'

Roy—or Rox—Copeland, a former cowboy, took the contract to carry mail on the new route between Tascosa and Fort Bascome, New Mexico, the latter point being an abandoned fort near the Texas line. After a few trips Copeland was taken ill and I volunteered to help him out. The Comanches were out again and most of this ride was made at night. Returning from Bascome, my mount, a very poor one, made slow time and at sunrise I was still about ten miles from Tascosa.

As I ambled along I met, well mounted and armed, five men whom I had never seen before. They stopped and made inquiries about the location and direction of cattle ranches in the vicinity, volunteering the information that they had heard there was a scarcity of horses in the Panhandle, so had driven a herd of about one hundred and fifty head from New Mexico to sell to the Texas cattlemen. After I told them I was carrying the mail, *adios* was said and we went our respective ways.

Later in the day this party rode into Tascosa and it soon became known that they were the gang of William H. Bonney, called 'Billy the Kid,' led by that redoubtable gunman himself. This was early in the fall of 1878 and Billy's gang consisted of Tom O'Phalliard, called 'Big Foot Tom,' Henry Brown, Fred Waite, and John Middleton, a man of middle age who had been an outlaw for some years.[2]

Billy Bonney was then eighteen years old, a handsome youth with smooth face, wavy brown hair, an athletic and symmetrical figure, and clear blue eyes that could look one through and through. Unless angry, he always seemed to have a pleasant expression with a ready smile. His head was well shaped, his features regular, his nose aquiline, his most noticeable characteristic a slight projection of his two upper front teeth.

It must not be forgotten that at this period this section was one of the really wild spots then in the Great West. As I have said before, there was not a semblance of government or law in the Panhandle, consequently it was the Mecca for the outlaw, the gunman, and his kind. Billy and his gang, with their horses, which they had *collected* in New Mexico, camped near Tascosa which, while it consisted only of two stores, a blacksmith shop, and an adobe house, was the center of supplies for the big cattle ranges in the Panhandle.

[2]For Billy the Kid, see entry for Henry McCarty in *Biographical Notes*.

McCarty has a good chapter on "Billy the Kid" in which he incorporates much of Hoyt's details in his narrative. *Ibid.*, pp. 75-93. Correctly spelled O'Folliard, the sobriquet used by Hoyt does not appear in contemporary sources.

The news of Billy's advent in the Panhandle spread like a prairie fire. His reputation, with the fact that there was a big reward offered for his capture, dead or alive, was well known, so a meeting of prominent cattlemen of that section was called and Billy sent for. He came smiling as usual, with as much poise and *sang-froid*[3] as any man there. He was asked some pertinent questions, and he told them that he had learned they were short of horses, so had gathered a bunch and was there to supply them. After some desultory talk, he was informed by the Panhandlers that they knew all about him, but were not looking for him, and so long as he behaved, they would let him alone. But he was cautioned emphatically that to transgress in any way meant a short shrift. His reply was also brief, that all he and his friends wanted was to be let alone.

Bonney's party mingled freely, sold and traded horses with anyone so inclined, varying their business dealings with drinking, gambling, horseracing, and target shooting. Billy was an expert at most Western sports, with the exception of drinking. Much has been published of his exploits during drinking bouts, but in my opinion they are mostly fiction. I never knew of his taking a drink of liquor all the time he was in the Panhandle.[4]

[3] *Sang-froid* means coolness.
[4] Charles Siringo disagrees with Hoyt. He states that Billy the Kid did drink for "sociability." *History of "Billy the Kid"* (Santa Fé, 1920), p. 71.

To tell the truth, this fact helped to make me friendly with the outlaw, for I was a teetotaler myself. Reared in strict Christian principles, I had never touched liquor.

Billy's men, however, made up for his abstinence. John Middleton was drinking heavily one day at Howard & McMasters' store and began to get ugly, evidently looking for trouble. Others present were in a similar condition and it began to look squally. At that time and place and under those conditions war was fashionable. Peace seemed to trouble men's minds. In this particular instance old John seemed to be taking the initiative, profanely and vociferously declaring to the world just what a very bad man he was.

He had his hand on his gun and during his boasts glared fiercely around hoping some one would give him the slightest excuse to begin hostilities. Just at this juncture in walked Billy the Kid.

In a mild voice that contained, however, a curious note of challenge as well as command, he said, 'John Middleton, you damned idiot, light out for camp and stay there till I come.'

Wheeling toward him, Middleton, his eyes flashing, replied, 'Billy, you'd never talk that way to me if we were alone. You think you're showing off.'

'If that's the way you think just come with me out behind the store and we *will* be alone,' was Billy's quick reply, as he backed toward the door, hand on his gun.

Middleton's face turned an ashen color, his lower lip dropped, and with a sickly grin he stuttered out, 'Aw' Billy, come off, can't you take a joke?'

'You bet I can,' said Billy, 'but this is no joke. You heard me. Git for camp and git quick.' And old John shuffled out the door like a whipped dog.

Realizing he and his men were on probation, the Kid ruled his gang with a rod of iron, so to speak, whenever they overstepped the bounds or attempted to. I saw the Middleton incident almost exactly duplicated one day in Rinehart's store when Billy found Tom O'Phalliard about to shoot down a Mexican he had been playing monte with. In spite of his discipline, however, his men fairly worshiped him and would have backed him with their lives any time it might become necessary.

There were several small Mexican settlements in the vicinity and one of the most popular diversions was a weekly *baile* at home of Don Pedro Romero— who has been introduced before—fronting the plaza at Tascosa on the east side.

There was an unwritten law that no one should attend these functions armed and all guns were usually left at Howard & McMasters' store. The Kid's party, learning of these affairs, signified a desire to join in. They were told they would be welcome so long as they complied with the regulation, which they emphatically promised to do.

On a beautiful moonlight night a Romero *baile* was in full swing. The Kid and I stepped out to

William H. Bonney alias "Billy the Kid"

enjoy it, and incidentally strolled across the plaza, about one hundred yards in width, to Rinehart's store opposite. Returning I challenged the Kid to a foot race to the dance hall. I found he could run much faster than the 'Sailor,' but I led him all the way. As we neared the door I slacked up, while Billy kept on at full speed through the door.

Mexican adobe houses, for some reason, have a threshold about a foot high, and as the Kid flew through, the heel of one of his cowboy boots caught on it, landing him at full length on the floor in the middle of the ballroom.

Quicker than a flash his prostrate body was surrounded by his four pals, back to back, with a Colt's forty-five in each hand, cocked and ready for business. The Kid's unconventional entrance was to them an indication of something wrong, and their lightning exhibition of preparedness showed wonderful efficiency of its kind. How or where their guns were concealed was never quite understood, but their owners all registered chagrin when they learned they were barred at all future Romero *bailes*.

Another diversion was draw poker which all indulged in. Some time previously I had won a very pretty ladies' gold watch which Billy admired and wished to purchase.

In a previous talk he had told me about his romance with a little New Mexican beauty, none other than Señorita Lolita whom I had met at Fort Sumner on the Pecos River, and suspecting he wanted the watch for her, I made him a present of it, which pleased him very much.

Attached to this watch was a handsome long chain of braided hair. In the picture of Billy the Kid that is shown in this volume and which was taken at Fort Sumner when he returned from the Panhandle early in 1879—or possibly late 1878—and no doubt the only one of the outlaw in existence, the two strands of this chain can plainly be seen crossing his shirt-front.

After learning his history directly from himself and recognizing his many superior natural qualifications, I often urged him, while he was free and the going good, to leave the country, settle in Mexico or South America, and begin all over again. He spoke Spanish like a native, and although only a beardless boy, was nevertheless a natural leader of men. With his poise, iron nerve, and all-round efficiency properly applied, the Kid could have made a success anywhere.

As will be shown later, no less a personage than the late General Lew Wallace thought of him as I did, and also did *his* bit in an effort to save him.

Late in October, 1878, a Mr. Teats, who had contracted to carry mail between Fort Bascome and Las Vegas, New Mexico, visited Tascosa and I decided to leave the Panhandle and return with him. The day of our departure Billy the Kid rode into Tascosa leading 'Dandy Dick,' a beautiful race-horse, by far the choicest in his entire *remuda de caballo*, and to my great surprise made me a present of him. I had ridden him several times and admired him, but as he was Billy's favorite, I never dreamed he would part with him.

At his own suggestion, in order to protect me in case my ownership was ever questioned, he stepped up to the counter in Howard & McMasters' store, picked up a piece of paper, and rapidly wrote for me a formal bill of sale, just as if it was a purchase, signed it and had it witnessed by the proprietors, probably the two best-known men in the Panhandle at that time.

This paper I have preserved all these years and until very recently claimed it was the only specimen of Billy the Kid's handwriting in existence. My mistake will be disclosed later.

The origin of 'Dandy Dick,' however, remained a mystery. Billy never said where he got the horse. 'There's a story connected with him' was as far as he would ever get. The old saw—murder will out—is apropos here. In 1921 I once more got in touch with my oldtime cowboy friend, Charles A. Siringo, then at Carrizozo, New Mexico. A correspondence followed and I sent Mr. Siringo a photostatic copy of my bill of sale, which he incidentally showed to James Brady, Court Interpreter at Carrizozo.

The moment Mr. Brady read the description of the horse and identified the writer, he exclaimed, *'My God, it was my father's horse that he was riding when killed by the Kid!'*

The horse was of Arabian stock, well known locally as a racer, and had been owned formerly by Major Murphy, of Lincoln, New Mexico, who was one of the leaders in the Lincoln County War. William Brady, 'a brave and honest man,' says Charles A. Siringo, was elected sheriff of Lincoln County and soon afterward 'Dandy Dick' was presented to him by Major Murphy.[5] James Brady had often ridden the horse when he was a small boy.

[5] Major Lawrence G. Murphy was a probate judge and political boss of Lincoln County, while Major William Brady was sheriff. The latter was killed with his deputy George Hindman on April 1, 1878. Maurice G. Fulton, *The History of the Lincoln County War*, edited by Robert N. Mullin (Tucson, 1968), pp. 26–27, 158–164.

Bill of Sale given by Billy the Kid to Dr. Henry F. Hoyt
Courtesy The Panhandle-Plains Historical Museum, Canyon, Texas

XIV

Life—and Death—in the Panhandle

WHEREVER I traveled during my pioneering days I observed as a Western characteristic a keen vein of humor, especially along the line of practical jokes. The Panhandle cowboy rarely lost an opportunity to play the 'snipe' or 'badger' game on every tenderfoot that came into the country. There were numerous other 'sells,' but those were the outstanding ones.

For those who may not know, I will briefly describe a 'sniping.' At an evening meal one cowboy will casually ask another if he is going with the bunch after 'snipe' to-night. This remark quickly grows into a general conversation about the hunt to take place. Many details are discussed, such as where would be the best place to go, where would game be the most plentiful, etc., and during all this chatter the victim is entirely ignored.

His curiosity becomes aroused, he asks some questions, and the answers result in a strong desire to go along. Objections are at once voiced that he wouldn't understand, might frighten away the snipe, might forget instructions, etc. This only makes him keener to go, and finally, after making him swear he will do everything he is told to do, consent is very reluctantly (?) given and he receives his instructions, which are very simple.

Each hunter receives a big gunny sack, its mouth held open with a barrel hoop or bent willow. The men mount and after a ride of some miles into a maze of canyons, hills, and brakes, from which the victim could not find his way back to camp in the dark to save his life, the horses are left. After silently stealing away for some distance, the leader leaves one of the men with emphatic instructions to squat behind a convenient rock or tree, hold the mouth of the bag at a certain angle near the ground, and at certain intervals emit a long low whistle.

They are very particular about the exact tone of this whistle and the victim has been practicing it during the ride until he has finally struck the right note and is praised for his efficiency in picking it up so quickly.

After placing several of his men, the leader then sets the victim down in a most inaccessible spot. He is left whistling his little solo and holding the bag, thrilled with ambition to do his part and hoping that the proverbial beginners' luck may strike him and permit him to take back the biggest kill of the party. He is instructed to hold his post at all hazard until he hears two shots, the signal the hunt is over, whereupon he must join the rest where the horses were left. If by chance he misses the way, he must then fire a few shots and they will come after him.

The jokers then return to camp and the sequel

can be easily imagined. According to Panhandle traditions, a near-tragedy was connected with the 'sniping game' in several instances.

Many years after my cowboy days I traveled forty miles in a buckboard up the Salt River valley in Arizona and during the entire ride was never out of sight of a covey of quail in one direction or another. We put up for the night at a large cattle ranch and during supper the cowboys—about a dozen in number—began to talk about going on a *quail hunt* that night, just exactly as we used to begin to work the snipe game in Texas.

I was a stranger to all, dressed in city clothes, and it was plain to me that I was sized up as a tenderfoot, and that a game was being put up on me, especially after I had butted in and some reluctance was shown in taking me along.

This opinion of mine was further clinched when the method of the hunt was described: A large plateau some miles away was covered with the Chola cactus, which is marked by its dense growth of thorns. I was told the quail from every direction roosted there at night because the thorns protected them from their many predatory enemies.

Holding in one hand an improvised lantern—a tin can with a hole cut on one side, a lighted candle stuck in its bottom and a piece of wire as a handle—the hunter, by throwing the reflected light into the cactus can blind the quail and approach near enough to knock it from its perch with a small iron rod three feet long, held in the other hand. After this explanation I was more than satisfied it was a frame-up pure and simple and decided to turn the tables by a ruse. I happened to be armed, a fact that was unknown to the cowboys.

It was not a very dark night and as I have a well-developed bump of location it was an easy matter to plan for my *coup*. The moment I was left alone, with my iron poker and tin can, I intended to sneak out 'Injun' fashion up a draw I had located while coming out, that would land me between the ranch and the boys as they returned, turn my coat inside out and, with a handkerchief mask over my face, step out at the psychological moment and treat them to an old-fashioned 'hold-up.' After disarming them and collecting their valuables I intended to compel them to tie each other up with articles of their clothing and return to the ranch, my fun to materialize when they arrived with the story of their terrible experience.

But, to my intense surprise and, I must confess, to my disgust, the joke was on me after all. We entered the Chola tract, a beautiful sight in the night as it glistens like a veritable lake of silver under the stars, and there, exactly as had been described, were the little birds perched among the branches of the cactus in about every fourth bush. There was little sportsmanship in this method of getting them, except that more birds were missed than hit. We had a wonderful breakfast next morning and the story of my aborted joke they thought one of the best ever.

About the time I left Tascosa many settlers were drifting into the Panhandle. The town began to grow, and in 1879 one John Cone and a man named Duran opened another store, making three altogether.[1] Surveyors also came; Oldham County was organized with Tascosa as the first county seat.[2]

James McMasters, of Howard & McMasters, was the first county judge, Bull Vivian the first county and district clerk, C. B. (Cape) Willingham the first sheriff and tax collector. Willis was the first district judge and J. N. Browning (afterwards Lieutenant Governor of Texas) was the first district attorney.[3]

Tascosa was first named 'Atascosa'—Spanish for boggy—because of the treacherous quicksands of

[1] John W. Cone operated a mercantile store in partnership with Dolores Duran. McCarty, *Maverick Town*, p. 192.

[2] Oldham County was established August 31, 1876, and was named for William S. Oldham (1813–1866), a political figure prominent first in Arkansas, then Texas, particularly during the Civil War when he served as a senator in the Confederate States congress. It was formally organized on December 8, 1880. Joseph N. Kane, *The American Counties* (3rd ed.; Metuchen, N.J., 1972), p. 276.

[3] Hoyt's memory is a bit spotty here. Correct names are: C. B. Vivian, Cape B. Willingham, and Frank Willis. The first Oldham County district attorney was Temple Houston. James N. Browning, a lawyer in Tascosa, was not admitted to the bar until 1881. He later served four terms in the state legislature and was lieutenant governor of Texas, 1898–1903. McCarty, *Maverick Town*, pp. 66, 177; Walter P. Webb, ed., *Handbook of Texas*, 3 vols. (Austin, 1952), I: 228.

the Canadian River bed, but when it was learned there was already an Atascosa County and River in Texas, the 'A' was dropped.

Next came the inevitable saloon, started by Jack Ryan, my former boss on the LX Ranch, and one Frank James, no kin to Jesse! Among their early customers was an unknown drifter, who after a few drinks became ugly and was taken in hand by the sheriff. No jail had yet been built, so the prisoner was chained to a pillar supporting a cottonwood beam in the ceiling of the saloon and left there to spend the rest of the night.

He became thirsty and as the chain was too short for him to get to the bar, he tore up one of his blankets, and after weaving it into a lariat, successfully 'roped' one of a number of bottles of brandy standing on the floor at the end of the bar.

Much encouraged, when the first bottle was emptied he persevered, and, when the proprietors arrived in the 'cold gray dawn' of the next morning, they found him peacefully wrapped in the arms of Bacchus, corralled in a circle of empty bottles!

Tascosa was fast becoming a 'wild and woolly' town in every sense of the word. Saloons increased until there were five, and there were several dance halls, the most popular ones being in 'Hogtown,' the sporting suburb of this embryo metropolis of the Panhandle, where 'Sally,' 'Frenchy,' and 'Rocking-Chair Emma' were the reigning belles.

Tascosa now had about everything belonging to a

C. B. "Cape" Willingham and Jack Ryan

wild west community but a 'Boot Hill' cemetery. Her nearest competitor, Dodge City, Kansas, three hundred miles away, could boast of having planted over eighty victims with their boots on before *their* 'Boot Hill' cemetery was a full-fledged yearling.

Tascosaites were chagrined over this sad and evidently hopeless situation. Early in 1877 a plot of ground had been selected and fenced in as a cemetery on one of the sand hills near-by, but it remained untenanted.

There were strong hopes when the sailor killed the poor Mexican in Rinehart's store, as I have told, but his friends spirited his body away to some place of their own. Some then had an eye on me to help out, having heard that doctors took life so easily, but I disappointed them all by departing for New Mexico, and gloom prevailed.

But at last a ray of light flashed across the dismal scene. A group of drunken cowboys galloped into Tascosa, yelling and shooting. One saw a woman in her yard feeding some tame ducks, took a shot at one of the birds and blew its head off, whereupon the woman fainted. Rumor flashed through the town that she was shot. Sheriff Willingham, armed with a shotgun, went after the gang, meeting them as they rode up to Jack Ryan's saloon for a bit of refreshment.

The Sheriff ordered them to dismount, telling them they were under arrest. All obeyed except the cowboy who had shot the duck. He reached for his gun, but before he could get it into action Sheriff Willingham bored him through with a load of buckshot, and the 'Boot Hill' cemetery of Tascosa at last had a tenant.[4]

The ice was now broken and it was not long until more than twenty-five were laid away on the sand hill, and a Tascosaite could meet and face a resident of Dodge City without blushing.

But by and by a railroad was built through the Panhandle, Amarillo was started—I have actually killed buffalo where Amarillo is now built—the county seat was moved to Vega, and Tascosa's doom was sealed.[5] Where formerly the main street and plaza of this cow city stretched their lurid way, today only a dim outline can be traced through the scrubby underbrush. Of two solidly built lines of adobe buildings not even a vestige remains. The only human being left amidst this solitude is a little old lady with a history.

[4]Hoyt's account of the beginning of Tascosa's Boothill Cemetery parallels that given in Dealey, "The Story of Old Tascosa," p. 40, and in Charles Siringo, *A Lone Star Cowboy* (Santa Fe, 1919), pp. 129-130. A contrary view is expressed in McCarty, *Maverick Town*, pp. 94-96. It appears that Hoyt's story relates to the second man to be buried in Tascosa's Boot Hill, Fred Leigh. His encounter with Sheriff Cape Willingham is ably recounted by McCarty, pp. 96-99.

[5]The Fort Worth & Denver Railroad came through Tascosa in 1887 and produced a short-lived boom. With the incorporation of Amarillo and Channing, Tascosa began its rapid decline. In 1915 Vega was chosen by the electorate as the county seat. Dealey, "The Story of Old Tascosa," p. 41; McCarty, *Maverick Town*, pp. 254-255.

She is Mrs. Mickie McCormick, all that is left of 'Frenchy,' one of the belles of the old days. Her 'man,' Mickie McCormick, who owned *the* livery stable of Tascosa, became broken in health and died after spending all they had in trying to get well. According to old-timers, Mickie 'was as foine a little Irishman as ever drank a toddy.' 'Frenchy' was an eye-witness of many of the incidents that built up—or rather down—the population of 'Boot Hill,' including what is known as the 'Big Fight at Tascosa,' started by Len Woodruff, formerly a cowboy on the LX Ranch, who finally escaped death after being literally shot to pieces. The row began over 'Sally' and 'Rocking-Chair Emma,' and when it was over 'Boot Hill' added four new names to its directory—Ed King, Frank Valley, Fred Chilton, and Jesse Sheets, all killed by Woodruff—in self-defense of course.

James H. East—once a cowboy on the LX Ranch, now, in 1927, a retired and highly respected citizen of Douglas, Arizona—was the sheriff at the time of the 'Big Fight,' which took place after midnight, March 23, 1886, and was all over before East knew of it. The men engaged in the affair were widely known and had many friends. Before afternoon a crowd of over five hundred armed men assembled at Tascosa, all siding with one faction or the other. But for the strategy and cool nerve of Sheriff East, backed by his able deputy, L. C. Pierce, a war would certainly have started that would have resulted in a great deal of bloodshed and many more casualties.

Woodruff had been arrested by Sheriff East; the friends of the slain men wanted him lynched, and it took a great deal of nerve and diplomacy to prevent it. Later on Sheriff East took Woodruff to Mobeetie, where he was tried and acquitted. He lived for some years after, but never recovered entirely from his wounds.[6]

In those good old days there were two other young 'soldiers of fortune' drifting about in that part of the world, whose early careers were in many respects similar to my own. These were Emerson Hough and Randall Parrish, both of whom later became noted for their writings about the life of the West. Although we crossed each other's trails, we did not happen to meet until many years afterward, when a friendship was established that continued up to the time of their deaths. All of Mr. Hough's experiences of the old times, Lincoln County War, Billy the Kid, etc., were imparted to me in conversation as we chanced to meet in Chicago and elsewhere, and I cannot remember them in detail.

In response to a note from me during the World

[6]Hoyt's narrative follows closely that of Dealey, "The Story of Old Tascosa," pp. 34–36, which originally appeared in the *Dallas News* in 1916 and reprinted in 1926, with one important exception: the date of the Tascosa "Big Fight" was March 21, 1886, not March 23. Dealey's narrative fleshes out the story in more detail. However, the most accurate account appears in McCarty, *Maverick Town*, pp. 140–155.

"Frenchy" and Mickie McCormick's Home, Tascosa
Courtesy The John L. McCarthy Collection, Amarillo Public Library

War, Mr. Parrish jotted down some experiences that so nearly parallel many of my own that I cannot refrain from including them.

'My first appearance in that land of young men,' wrote Parrish, 'occurred about the time you pulled out, but it was still sufficiently lively down there in spots. I was educated for the bar, being admitted to practice before I was of age, and settled temporarily in Kansas, at Wichita, when that city had four thousand inhabitants, with an open prairie all around it. As I remember now there were forty lawyers and near-lawyers in the town when I joined the colony. Stood the strain as long as I could, and then joined up with a cattle party at Medicine Lodge bound for Santa Fé, but left them at Tascosa, and took up cow-punching as a diversion, landing a job with the Merill & Cassett outfit, either 1879 or 1880. Do I remember Tascosa? I'll say I do—you could smell the town four miles away when the wind was right, and when we first rode in we were behind a big cattle party who had cleaned the place entirely out of grub. All we could buy was whiskey and sardines. The next time I was there I came in strapped on a bronc from a cow camp forty miles below where I had been accidentally shot. Every time that bronc got scared and jumped sideways I fainted, but the boys had heard there was a doctor—doubtless you—and were bound to get me there. He was there all right, but was a horse doctor, and he did a rotten job, but got the ball out after a fashion.

After I got up I and another fellow started for Las Vegas, by way of Fort Union.

'Got there broke flat, and took the first job that opened—washing dishes in a restaurant of rather unsavory reputation. Confess I did not last long, but began an upward career which included helping to lay the first streetcar track in the place, wiping nights in the round house, operating a high-ball game at Raton, and finally landed a fireman's job on the Santa Fé, with a freight-train run from Vegas to Albuquerque. Say, that was a hard one, but I stuck for quite a while, finally leaving to join a bunch of sheepmen, who were intending to buy in southern New Mexico, and drive through to Colorado. That was what brought me to Fort Sumner, and gave me a very slight acquaintance with the Kid. One of our fellows went crazy—very common with sheep-herding—on the trail going down, and tried his best to kill me—would have succeeded if his gun hadn't jammed. We overpowered him, strapped him into a buckboard with the mail carrier, and sent him back to be looked after. Then we went into Sumner along that wonderful avenue of cottonwoods. Where I saw Billy was in the big general store beside the river. It was three days before he was shot, and he sure did give us the look over proper. I didn't know who he was at the time, not until I saw him lying dead later. The night he was killed we were camped seven miles out, but the news reached us. Sumner was very interesting to me, and has always remained clear in my memory. Many of the old post buildings were still standing, and had their old signs up, "Adjutant's Office," etc.

'Our sheep mission failed and I was then cast adrift, finding my way to White Oaks, Socorro, Deming, and finally to Silver City, working at various jobs, until I joined a party of prospectors. We had all degrees of luck, mostly bad, tramping across most of southern Arizona, and down into northern Sonora.

'It was rather unhealthy there at that time, as Geronimo was on the run, killing anything he found in his way. We had one set-to with him, and lost a pal, and found many a burned ranch home, and several dead bodies. For about two months it was hell in that country. I ended up with mountain fever, and only pulled through by accident. The boys managed to get me into Tombstone, where the Locomotive Fireman's Union took care of me, and when I got well enough they passed me through up the line to Denver. I worked awhile as rodman on the ditch survey between Greeley and Loveland; then drifted into newspaper work in Denver. Stuck to this line for years in Denver, San Francisco, Omaha, and Chicago, until I began writing and publishing books. Am now writing my thirtieth volume, with nothing very much to complain about. All I got out of the southwest was experience, but I got plenty of that, and have found it valuable.

'A few years ago down in the Ozarks in Missouri I

ran across Bill Young, who was night marshal in Deming, New Mexico, when I was there. I remembered him very well, as he had thrown me out of a dance hall on at least two occasions, and we had a nice visit. He is a typical hill-billy, now back on his native heath, and perfectly contented. I asked him what he liked to do best in the world, and he said, "Fish," which explains everything. However, he was some marshal in his day, I'll tell the world.

'I was mighty glad to hear from you and wish I had time to write you more at length, and gossip a bit about those old days. Every old-timer is a friend to me—they are getting scarce.'

XV

*I Become a Bartender and
Eat with Jesse James*

I BADE farewell to my friends in Tascosa, where I
had enjoyed many good times and adventures,
exciting and otherwise, and where I had also en-
dured at times many hardships and experiences that
were far from pleasant. With Mr. Teats I had a
pleasant, uneventful ride to Las Vegas, New Mexico, where I put up at the Exchange Hotel on a corner of the plaza, and began to plan for my future.

The Atchison, Topeka & Santa Fé Railway had
almost reached the town, which was both wild and
wide open.[1] Strangers were pouring in by hundreds,
anticipating a boom upon completion of the railway; many were of the sporting and criminal types.

I could find no opening in my line. The town
was full of doctors, and but two, Dr. Shout, of the
regular school, and Dr. Cunningham, a homeopath,
seemed to be at all busy.[2] The clerk at the hotel

[1] The Santa Fe entered Las Vegas on July 2, but the official celebration took place on July 4, 1879. Milton W. Cal-
lon, *Las Vegas, New Mexico—The Town That Wouldn't
Gamble* (Las Vegas, 1962), p. 92.

[2] Dr. Stout, not Shout, had settled in Las Vegas in 1859.
Dr. J. M. Cunningham later became the owner of the hotel
at nearby Hot Springs, which Hoyt alludes to further on in
this chapter. F. Stanley [*pseud.*], *The Las Vegas Story* (Denver, 1951), pp. 180, 295–296.

became very friendly and began urging me to join with him and a friend, a man of some prominence, in financing a faro game. Las Vegas had been for some time very quiet from a sporting point of view, but the advent of the railroad had put new life into the town and, according to my two new friends, now was the time to reap a harvest.

The plan was for each to put fifteen hundred dollars into the 'bank-roll,' lease an apartment adjoining the barroom that had formerly been used for the same purpose, and engage a professional dealer and lookout, whom they had already selected. The rest would take care of itself.

Although there was a wide spread between this proposition and the Christian training of my early home, I had for two years been in almost daily contact with gambling. I was anxious to make money enough to complete my medical course, and in the end, casting all scruples aside, I 'signed on the dotted line.' The 'roll' I brought from the Panhandle was not enough and I was compelled to sell Dandy Dick and another horse I owned to Mr. Teats, who put them on one of his mail routes and I saw them no more.

For thirty nights our dealer, Scudder, never quit loser and it began to look as if we might rival Monte Carlo. But from the thirtieth night we began to use red ink and we did this steadily until the bank-roll and all winnings we had not spent had vanished. I was again broke. Doubtless it served me right!

Sophisticated readers at this point will exclaim 'Huh! both whipsawed and double crossed,' but they are mistaken. It was a square deal, on both sides of the table. The real cause of the failure was insufficient capital for the size of the game we were compelled to play. We should have had not less than twenty-five to thirty thousand dollars in the bank-roll to make a success. Although I was hard hit at the time, it was doubtless one of the very best things that could have happened to me. Had we won, the chances are I might soon have blossomed out as a professional gambler.

I had formed a friendship with a young civil engineer, Joel Huntoon, a good fellow from a fine family in Topeka, Kansas, and like myself, in financial difficulty. To reduce expenses we roomed together at the Exchange Hotel. One day he got a small job as a surveyor and hot-footed it to our room to get me to help him on a fifty-fifty basis, as he knew of my former experience in surveying. The job was subdividing a small ranch a short distance east of *Arroyo Gallinas* (sounds nice, but in plain English is 'Chicken Creek') and now a part of the new town of Las Vegas. We were offered a small bunch of lots in payment for our services, but we insisted on cash. Eventually the lots became very valuable, but we had more need of a little money then than we did of a bigger sum later.

The fee I got was small and did not last long. The hotel proprietor, a German by the name of

Weschle, knowing my financial situation, came in one day and offered me the job of bartender, on the watch from noon till midnight, at seventy-five dollars a month and board.[3] When I consulted Joel, who knew I had never tasted liquor and did not know one drink from another, he advised me to take it by all means.

'I'll post you all right so you will have no trouble,' he said.

Whereupon he told me I would never be called upon for more than four mixed drinks in that country, viz., whiskey toddy, cocktail, gin-fizz, and sherry cobbler, and wrote out full directions for the concoction of these.

I committed the rules to memory, tucked the paper up my sleeve for a sly consultation should I forget, and tackled the job. I got on far better than I expected, my only worry being a feeling that I might be recognized by some visitor from my old home. I would sooner have faced death any time.

I began work some time before Christmas, 1878. On Christmas Eve a grand ball was given at the hotel and guests came from hither and yon, among them a stageload from Sante Fé. There was a large crowd in the hotel and I was more than busy. It was the first Christmas in my life that I was not a free

[3]Charles Emil Wesche (not Weschle) was proprietor of the Exchange Hotel as well as being a dealer in dry goods and groceries. *Las Vegas Daily Optic*, November 7, 1879; March 16, 1880.

agent and I began fairly to hate myself. Glancing up I saw several army officers in full dress, evidently a part of the Santa Fé visitors, enter the room and approach the bar.

As they neared I almost collapsed, for one of the party was Captain Gregory, my commander for seven months on the Northern Boundary Survey in 1873. I did some quick thinking. Under the bar was a pot of blacking for marking purposes and stooping over I grabbed the brush and quickly blacked my red mustache, a successful move, as I could see when I straightened up facing the mirror back of the bar. Some other accomplishments in my bag o' tricks were being able to twitch my ears and scalp at will, and to look at one with a pair of crossed eyes that would have turned Ben Turpin of the movies green. With all these rearrangements of my countenance I faced my customers.

Recognized? Hardly. My own mother would have promptly disowned me had she happened along. I had a good laugh from those who *did* know me, thinking it was my way of putting over a Christmas joke, and I was glad to let it go at that.

Shortly after I arrived at Las Vegas letters and newspapers from home told me some interesting news. The reader will recall my disposition of the bones of the outlaw Charley Pitts in Lake Como, St. Paul, Minnesota. The lake had frozen over early and a neighbor, as well as lifelong friend of mine, August Robertson, sallied forth after muskrats with spear and hatchet. As he was crossing the lake over the clear ice, a corner of a box projecting through aroused his curiosity. Smashing it open with his hatchet, he found it was full of bones.

A favorite dog had recently disappeared and by his process of deduction August decided he had learned its fate and passed on. After reaching home he reported the incident to his father who, deducing from another angle, decided it was something besides dog and proceeded to investigate. Cutting into the ice and knocking off the entire end of the box, out rolled a human skull! Sheriff and coroner were notified and an inquest was on. Big headlines and newspaper articles speculated about the horrible murder that had been committed. The bones full of bullet holes—Pitts was shot through the body in five different places —pointed toward a dastardly crime. The police and detective departments were criticized and urged to clear it up and apprehend the culprit. The incident was spread through the entire country by the Associated Press. My brother did not learn of it until the inquest was in full sway, but he then hastened to my uncle, Dr. Murphy, gave him the facts, whereupon he quickly burst the murder bubble and took charge of the bones. As I did not return home when expected, he presented them to a young physician in Chicago, who, if still living, doubtless has a fine skeleton on display in his office.

The publicity attending this reached Missouri,

and my father forwarded a letter addressed to me at St. Paul condemning me in unmeasured terms for my brutal treatment of 'pore charley pitts,' winding up with 'I'll git yu yit.' The writing was almost unintelligible and the letter unsigned.

There was a famous Hot Springs six miles from Las Vegas, equipped with an old-time adobe line of bathhouses and a hotel. Scott Moore and his good wife were proprietors. Their cuisine was noted all through New Mexico and as they always had an extra fine dinner Sundays, there was, as a rule, a big crowd on that day.

I rode out one Sunday and found at a corner table the only vacant seat in the room. Glancing at the three guests already there, I was simply amazed to recognize the one on my left as Billy the Kid, urbane and smiling as ever. We shook hands, but neither mentioned a name.

We were chatting away of old times in Texas as if we were a couple of cowboy friends, when the man on Bonney's left made a comment on something he said. Whereupon Billy said, 'Hoyt, meet my friend Mr. Howard from Tennessee.'

The fourth man had nearly finished his meal when I sat down, and soon retired. Mr. Howard had noticeable characteristics. He had piercing steely blue eyes with a peculiar blink, and the tip of a finger on his left hand was missing. I mentally classed him as a railroad man. He proved to be most congenial, was a good talker, had evidently traveled quite a bit, and the meal passed pleasantly. After dinner we separated and Billy, taking me to his room, gave me, after pledging me to secrecy, one of the surprises of my life. Mr. Howard was no other than the bandit and train robber, Jesse James.[4] I was skeptical, but Billy soon convinced me it was true. Jesse James had been in seclusion for some time; Mr. and Mrs. Moore were former friends whom he could trust, so he came out to size up the situation in a new territory. Billy also knew the Moores, and as he had not seen a passenger train since he was a youngster, he had slipped into Las Vegas, discarded his cowboy togs for an entire new city outfit of clothing, and was having the time of his life for a few days at the Hot Springs. He made his purchases at the store of Charley Ilfelt, who also knew him and who still remembers the incident. Mr. Ilfelt spent the winter of 1928–29 at the Hotel Virginia, Long Beach, California, and verified my recollection in regard to several incidents of the old days.

The Moores, finding themselves hosts of two of the most conspicuous outlaws the West has ever known, brought them together, and they apparently became friends.

Jesse James was prospecting and preparing to

[4]Because of the controversial nature of Hoyt's brief encounter with Jesse James and James' reputed meeting with Billy the Kid, the reader will find an extensive discussion in "Comments on Jesse James and Billy the Kid," pp. 479–486, *post.*

make a move, and after meeting Billy and sizing him up, made him a tentative proposition that they join forces and hit the trail together. Although both were outlaws with standing rewards out for their capture, their lives and activities were entirely different. Billy was never a train or bank robber nor a hold-up man in any sense of the word. His only peculations had been rounding up cattle and horses carrying some one else's brand, a diversion more or less popular among many old-time cattlemen, and at that period not considered a crime—if one could get away with it. It was very much the same as bootlegging today.

His offenses, for which he was now an outcast, were entirely traceable to the now historic Lincoln County War. General Lew Wallace knew this or he certainly would never have made Billy the offer that will appear later.

On account of the difference in their status, and of the fact that a union with Jesse James would carry him away from the magnet at Fort Sumner, Billy turned down his proposal.

We all met again that evening and had quite a visit, 'Mr. Howard' little dreaming I knew his identity. Billy had said I was a doctor who had befriended him in the Panhandle. In discussing different parts of the country I could not resist the temptation to ask Mr. Howard if he had ever been at my old home, St. Paul, Minnesota. He replied in the negative, in the most nonchalant manner, and changed the subject. It was no doubt lucky for me that he was not a mind-reader. He evidently did not know of the recent publicity that had been given his former pal, Charley Pitts, and myself. It was a case of, 'where ignorance is bliss, 'twere folly to be wise.'

When I was alone with Billy, he gave me a brief account of his adventures after I left Tascosa. He had soon disposed of the few horses he had left, and with two of his party had returned to Lincoln County, by way of Bosque Redondo, of course, and found the war still on. If my memory is correct, Henry Brown and Fred Waite left him at Tascosa and traveled east. While at the Bosque, Billy had his picture taken and afterward made his Lolita a present of the watch and chain I had given him. He also told me that he had greatly improved his skill with a gun.

In Tascosa the rear of the store was a veritable graveyard for empty quart beer-bottles, and one of the outstanding sports of the cowboys was to set up six in a row and at a range of fifty yards shoot for the drinks, or whatever they might fancy, with their forty-fives. Here Billy was champion. He could pull his gun and demolish the six bottles in just one half the time of any one else. He and I exchanged weapons to see if there was any special magic in his, but it made no difference. He was also a marvelous shot with a Winchester.

In the picture of Billy the Kid can be seen the handle of his forty-five with which he had shot his way into fame—of a certain kind. The entire gun is shown in another picture with the profile of its present owner, that celebrated delineator of the old two-gun man of the Wild West, William S. Hart, of Newhall, California.[5]

[5]Hoyt's first reference is to the photograph of Billy the Kid which is reproduced on p.151. The second photograph alluded to does not appear in the first edition—an editorial oversight by the original publisher. According to the curator of the ranch house at the William S. Hart County Park, Newhall, California, the gun in question was purchased by Hart from Bat Masterson. It subsequently proved a forgery; Hart was "taken."

XVI

The Correspondence between Governor Wallace and Billy the Kid

THE FACT of the Kid's return to the seat of war was soon known, and General Lew Wallace, then Governor of the Territory of New Mexico, determined to take a hand himself and see if he could not bring about peace. To this end he made a visit to Lincoln, at the risk of his life, and sent word inviting Billy to a conference; object, a peace talk. Billy came and they had a long conference alone, during which he imparted to the Governor some very important and valuable information about a number of men more or less prominent in the war.[1]

Governor Wallace then made Billy the following proposition: That Billy allow himself to be arrested, the Governor giving his word that if, at the

[1] Governor Wallace came to Lincoln on March 5, 1879, for the purpose of undertaking a complete investigation into the death of Houston I. Chapman, intent on arresting suspects to the slaying. He quickly learned that Billy the Kid was on his way out of the territory and was resting his horses at a friendly rancher's. Wallace ordered the military to intercept and arrest him. However, before that could be done, the governor received a letter from Billy, undated but probably March 12 or 13, telling him he was present when Chapman was killed and knew who did it. It was conciliatory and indirectly asked for a meeting to explain. The meeting was arranged by the two letters which follow in Hoyt's narrative. Fulton, *The Lincoln County War*, pp. 331-337.

ensuing trial, the Kid would testify exactly to the facts as he had done at that meeting, he (the Governor) would not only see that Billy's life was saved, but that he would also be set at liberty.

That was Billy's story to me during our visit. He frankly stated that at first he fully intended to carry out this plan. The men separated with the understanding that the Governor would make all arrangements and mail to the Kid his final instructions. This he did under date of March 15, 1879, giving the most implicit instructions as to just how Bonney should come in. The Governor's letter and the Kid's reply follow:

Letter from Governor Lew Wallace to Billy the Kid

Lincoln, March 15, 1879

W. H. Bonney,

Come to the house of Old Squire Wilson (not the lawyer) at nine (9) o'clock Monday night alone. I don't mean his office but his residence. Follow along the foot of the mountain south of town, come in on that side, and knock at the east door.

I have authority to exempt you from prosecution if you will testify to what you say you know.

The object of the meeting at Squire Wilson's is to arrange the matter in a way to make your life safe. To do that the utmost secrecy is to be used. *So come alone.* Don't tell anybody—not a living soul—where you are coming or the object. If you could trust Jesse Evans, you could trust me.

Lew Wallace

Billy the Kid's Reply to Governor Wallace

> San Patricio
> Lincoln County,
> Thursday, (March) 20, 1879

General Wallace,

Sir, I will keep the appointment I made but be sure and have men come that you can depend on. I am not afraid to die like a man fighting but I would not like to die like a dog unarmed. Tell Kimbrell to let his men be placed around the house and for him to come in alone; and he can arrest us. All I am afraid of is that in the Fort we might be poniarded or killed through a window at night but you can arrange that all right. Tell the commanding officer to watch Lt. Goodwin, he would not hesitate to do anything. There will be danger on the road of somebody waylaying us to kill us on the road to the Fort. You will never catch those fellows on the road. Watch Fritzes, Captain Baca's ranch, and the brewery. They will either go to Seven Rivers or the Jacarilla Mountains. They will stay close until the scouting parties come in. Give a spy a pair of glasses and let him get on the mountain back of Fritzes and watch, and if they are there, there will be provisions carried to them. It is not my place to advise you, but I am anxious to have them caught, and perhaps know how men hide from soldiers better than you. Excuse me for having so much to say and I still remain,

> Yours truly,
> W. H. Bonney

P.S. I have changed my mind. Send Kimbrell to Guiterez' just below San Patricio one mile because Sanger and Ballard are or were great friends of Campbell's. Ballard told me yesterday to leave for you was doing everything to catch me. It was a blind to get me to leave. Tell Kimbrell not to come before three o'clock for I may not be there before.

By the courtesy of Maurice G. Fulton, of Roswell, New Mexico, and Mr. Lew Wallace, Jr., I am enabled to present photostatic copies of this remarkable correspondence.[2]

One letter is written by a cultured scholar and gentleman, well versed in political and military science and governor of a vast domain. The other is from the hand of a beardless boy, yet in his teens, who had not seen the inside of a schoolroom since he was eleven years old, who for five years had lived in close comradeship with many of the most brutal, bloodthirsty, and hardened criminals in the West, and who had become an outlaw himself with a price on his head.

Visualize these two human beings, contrast them, and read carefully the letter from each.

Billy's reply to Governor Wallace speaks for itself in unmistakable terms. As will be seen later, he replied in good faith, arranging details and anticipating contingencies like a trained soldier.

As Billy himself explained to me, this correspondence was carried by special messengers and there

[2] Fulton's *The Lincoln County War* notes the role of George Kimbrell, Lieutenant Millard F. Goodwin, Celsa Gutierrez, Bill Campbell, Charles Fritz, and Captain Saturnino Baca, but there is no mention of Ballard or Sanger. The original letters are the property of the Indiana State Historical Society, Indianapolis.

Lincoln, March 15. 1879.

W. H. Bonney.

Come to the house of old Squire Wilson (not the lawyer) at nine (9) o'clock next Monday night alone. I don't mean his office, but his residence. Follow along the foot of the mountain south of the town, come in on that side, and knock at the east door. I have authority to exempt you from prosecution, if you will testify to what you say you know.

The object of the meeting at Squire Wilson's is to arrange the matter in a way to make your life safe. To do that the utmost secrecy is to be used. _So come alone._ Don't tell anybody — not a living soul — where you are coming or the object. If you could trust Jesse Evans, you can trust me.

Lew. Wallace.

Letter from Governor Lew Wallace to Billy the Kid
Courtesy Indiana Historical Society, Indianapolis

San Patricio Lincoln County
Thursday 20th 1 8 7

General Lew Wallace;

Sir I will keep
the appointment I made.
but be sure and have men come
that You can depend on I am not
afraid to die like a man fighting
but I would not like to be killed
like a dog unarmed. tell Kimbal
to let his men be placed around
the house. and for him to come in
alone; and he can arrest us. all I am
afraid of is that in the Fort we
Might be poinied, or killed through
a Window at night. but You can
arrange that all right. Tell the
Commanding Officer to Watch) Let Goodwin
he would not hesitate to do anything
there Will be danger on the road of
Somebody Waylaying us to kill us on the
road to the Fort,

Billy the Kid's reply to Governor Wallace
Courtesy Indiana Historical Society, Indianapolis

You Will never Catch those
fellows on the road Watch
Fritzes. Captain Becas. ranch
and the Brewerys they Will either
go to Seven Rivers or to Picarillo
Mountains they Will stay around close
untill the Scouting parties come in,
give a Spy a pair of Glasses and let
him get on the Mountain back of Fritzes and
Watch and if they are there their will be provisions
carried to them, it is not My place
to advise you, but I am anxious
to have them caught, and perhaps
know how men hide from soldiers, better
than you, please Excuse me for having so much to say
and I still remain Yours Truly

tell Kimbal not to come before dayl008 for I may not leave before

P.S. —————— W. H. Bonney
I have changed my mind send Kimbal to
Gutierres just below San Patricio one mile. because
Sanger and Ballard are or were great friends of Conects
; Ballard told me yesterday to leave for you were doing
every thing to catch me. it was a blind to get me to leave

was a delay in getting off his reply to Governor Wallace. During this delay Billy's friend Ballard came and told him that the Governor was laying a trap to catch him. Billy, with the idea that the plan for him to come unarmed and alone was an absolute secret between him and the Governor, naturally became suspicious at once. He had had much experience in treachery and false promises and this seemed to be 'the last drop in the bucket.' Instantly changing his mind, he *then* added the postscript which is, as he intended it should be, ambiguous, as can be seen. But he did not keep that, or any other, appointment with Governor Wallace.[3]

At this time I had never met General Wallace, but when I heard the story in detail I was firmly

[3]Hoyt's memory has confused the sequence of events. The Kid initially wrote to Wallace, hinting at a meeting. The governor replied with instructions for the meeting on March 15, the text being quoted by Hoyt. The Kid kept the appointed time as stated in Wallace's letter, Monday night (which was March 17) at nine o'clock. Following that meeting, he then wrote Wallace the March 20 letter quoted in full by Hoyt. As a result of that letter, Sheriff George Kimbrell and a posse made the "voluntary arrest" of the Kid and O'Folliard "about a mile below San Patricio" and brought them to Lincoln on March 21.

While in jail, Wallace visited the Kid to get better acquainted with him. The Kid kept his promise: he appeared before the grand jury and testified on the Chapman killing during the spring district court session. However, when a change of venue to Doña Ana County for his trial was approved, the Kid became apprehensive and made good his escape "in the latter part of June, 1879 . . ." Fulton, *The Lincoln County War*, pp. 336–348.

convinced that Billy had made the mistake of his life in turning down this opportunity and strongly urged him to make another attempt to get in touch with the Governor. His mind was made up, however, and he would not consent to do anything more.

Later I learned from General Wallace himself that I was right. Many destinies in this world are guided or changed by trifles. If Ballard had not come, if the letter had been sent without a postscript, and if Billy had kept the appointment, it is virtually certain his life would have been saved and he might have become one of the useful and respectable men of that country. Many stranger things than this have happened in our history.

When the Kid left Las Vegas, with his usual generosity he presented Mrs. Scott Moore with a beautiful saddle horse. Whether he gave her a bill of sale or not is not known. The chances are he did.[4] I will refer to 'Mr. Howard' later.

The 'Jesse Evans' referred to in General Wallace's note to the Kid was originally a tough youngster, slightly older than Billy, from Silver City, New

---

[4]The *Las Vegas Daily Optic*, January 4, 1881, reported that Mrs. Minnie Moore, who was an excellent rider, was given Billy the Kid's horse by Frank Stewart, one of his captors. When captured at Stinking Springs by Pat Garrett, December 21, 1880, the Kid gave his favorite bay mare to Stewart, "perhaps realizing that she would go to him anyhow as booty." At Las Vegas, Stewart exchanged the animal with W. Scott Moore for a $60 revolver. Fulton, *The Lincoln County War*, p. 391. This would appear to be the correct version of Hoyt's story.

General Lew Wallace
Governor of The Territory of New Mexico, 1878–1881
Courtesy General Lew Wallace Study, Crawfordsville, Indiana

Mexico, where Billy lived from the age of eight to twelve and where they became chums. Later they became outlaws together and had many adventures. They once met a party of emigrants who fed and treated them well, and later when the emigrants were attacked by a band of Apaches, the two boys came to the rescue with a gallant charge, using both Winchesters and Colts, and doubtless saved the travelers' lives. The affair resulted in eight dead Indians, four wounded emigrants, two dangerously so. Billy came out with a slight wound in his left hand and his partner Jesse with a bullet through his hat.

During the Lincoln County War the two pals split and became deadly enemies for a time, but they finally met and made up. Jesse Evans, however, was fated to die with his boots on, the usual wind-up of men of his class.[5] Billy the Kid lost out on this terminal point by a scratch! He had pulled off his boots on that fatal night, July 14, 1881, when he entered the bedroom of his friend Pete Maxwell, at

---

[5]There is no evidence to sustain the view that Billy and Jesse Evans became chums in Silver City. Nor did Billy live in Silver City between the age of eight to twelve. Nor is there any record that the two "became outlaws together."

This story of Billy and Jesse first surfaced in Pat F. Garrett, *The Authentic Life of Billy the Kid, the Noted Desperado of the Southwest* (Santa Fe, 1882), and its authenticity is highly questionable. See reprint edition (Albuquerque, 1964), p. 9.

Fulton, *The Lincoln County War*, p. 67, records that "legend, one of questionable credibility," says that Evans was responsible for Billy the Kid's arrival in Lincoln County.

Fort Sumner, New Mexico, and was cut down by the bullet from Sheriff Garrett's unerring Colt's forty-five. When killed, Billy was twenty-one years, seven months, and twenty-one days old and had the reputation of having killed twenty-one men, not counting Indians.[6]

During my stay of about five years in the Southwest I met many men who knew Billy the Kid and had seen him in action, and they were unanimous in classing him as a man to whom fear was unknown, and in time of danger or under fire, as cool and composed as if he was attending a social gathering. There were different opinions as to his marksmanship and dexterity in handling guns. The majority seemed to think that Billy's perfect poise and self-possession had more to do with his so-called success than his marksmanship. Even Pat Garrett told me in El Paso, Texas, many years after, that one of

[6]The Kid was felled with a single shot which hit him in the left breast. "He never spoke, but died in a minute." The circumstances and details surrounding his death at the hands of Pat Garrett, sheriff-elect of Lincoln County, is recounted in full in *Ibid.*, pp. 398–402.

Hoyt is repeating one of the myths that have been spun concerning the life of Billy the Kid. Emerson Hough in *The Story of the Cowboy* (New York, 1897), laid the foundation for this myth writing that Billy died at age twenty-three, having killed twenty-three men. John Lord, *Frontier Dust* (Hartford, Conn., 1926), uses the figure twenty-four. See Jeff Dykes, *Billy the Kid, the Bibliography of a Legend* (Santa Fe, 1952), pp. 25, 56. Frankly, no one knows for sure the number of men Bonney killed, nor is his birthplace known for certain.

Billy's gang, John Middleton, was his superior in every way with a gun. This I doubt, as Middleton would never have suffered the humiliation I saw, during the incident I have noted, in Tascosa.

My first meeting with Pat Garrett was in the office of the 'Optic'—the Las Vegas, New Mexico, newspaper—while I was bartender at the Exchange Hotel. He was up on a flying visit from Lincoln and was there but a day.

During a hark-back in El Paso, about a year before he was murdered, he told me the following: The late Theodore Roosevelt was President and Garrett had made an application for the position of Internal Revenue Collector at El Paso. Some political enemies sent in a protest containing three specific charges, viz., 'That he could neither read nor write and that he was a drunkard.'

Pat got wind of this and entrained for Washington. He sent his card into the White House and was ushered into the presence of the President. After a pleasant chat, Mr. Roosevelt turned to his desk, wrote something on a piece of paper, and handing it to Pat said, 'Mr. Garrett, kindly read this aloud, and if it suits you, sign it.' Garrett complied, and with the remark, 'Mr. President, it suits me exactly,' attached his signature.

The paper was as follows: 'I, the undersigned, Patrick F. Garrett, hereby give my word of honor, that if I am appointed Collector of Internal Revenue at El Paso, Texas, I will totally abstain from the use of intoxicating liquors during my term of office.'

Wise Mr. Roosevelt. The three charges went into the discard, just like that, and the next day Garrett received the appointment.

XVII

The Assistant Postmaster Joins the Vigilantes

TENDING BAR was becoming irksome, but nothing better seemed to turn up until one day Postmaster T. F. Chapman, to my great surprise, offered me the post of his assistant, at a salary of one hundred and fifty dollars a month.

As the Santa Fé Railway neared Las Vegas, the company secured the right to erect an imposing new hotel and bathhouse at the Hot Springs, and this was now completed. Mr. Chapman had leased the property, was going to manage it in person, and as this would need all his time, he came to me to help him out. The advent of the railway had tremendously increased the business of the post office, which was now doing a money-order business alone of over one thousand dollars a day.

I accepted his offer with alacrity, shed my long white apron for good, threw a kiss at the old bar, and fairly sprinted to the office to resign.

'Vy you quvit,' exclaimed mine host Weschle; and when I explained, he inquired, 'Vat you git mit de new yob?'

I told him, and he exclaimed, 'You stay mit me. I gif you two hundred dollars by de mont.'

I thanked him, glad to know my services were so

satisfactory, but explaining that bartending was not exactly my game, I quit.

I was at a loss to understand why Mr. Chapman selected me. To him I was a man from behind a bar, which from the point of view of my upbringing was about as low down as one could get in the social scale. I was a perfect stranger to him; he knew nothing of my antecedents; in fact, he did not even know whether or not I was under an assumed name. In spite of all this, however, he placed me into a position of marked responsibility and trust without requiring bonds or other security. It all seemed a marvel to me.

Some months later the mystery was explained. It seems that after I had been behind the bar for a month or so, Mr. Chapman overheard Landlord Weschle boasting in Jeff Reynolds's bank one day that he had a new bartender and was now obtaining about four times as much revenue from his bar as he ever had before.[1] Evidently Joel Huntoon, when he coached me, overlooked one item in the usual education of a bartender, the art of 'knocking down.' It was this that put me in the post office.

One day late in the afternoon Huntoon and I sauntered up a narrow street leading from a corner of the plaza toward a section known as 'the hill.'

[1] Jefferson Raynolds (not Reynolds) and his brothers, Joshua and Frederick were Las Vegas' pioneer bankers. Ralph E. Twitchell, *The Leading Facts of New Mexico History*, 5 vols. (Cedar Rapids, Iowa, 1911-1917), 5: 262-263 and *note*.

We had gone but a short distance when we met two Mexicans, one of them dressed in a typical Spanish costume, flare-bottomed trousers, buttons on the side, a short jacket with gilt trimmings, all topped off with a very splendid sombrero.

He was a small man, and as he and his companion passed, he gave us a vicious and ugly look, so that I kept my eyes on him, and, partially turning, called Huntoon's attention to him by remarking, 'That chap is certainly looking for trouble.' I had noticed the muzzle of a gun projecting below his short jacket.

On account of an epidemic of crime that followed the influx of toughs and criminals arriving daily on the new railway, a Vigilante Committee had been organized, of which T. F. Chapman was the leader and to which both Huntoon and I belonged. At the same time strict regulations had been issued making it a crime for any one but an officer to carry arms.

Huntoon and I both noticed the gun, and as the Mexican walked with a slight stagger we decided to turn back, overtake, and disarm him, and, as he seemed to be of the better class, escort him home or to his hotel as might be. He seemed to be slated for trouble if let alone.

Just as we started after them, they met an old Mexican stone mason, Patricio Ortega, well and favorably known in the community, coming quietly along with his empty tin lunch box on his way home from work. As they met, the Mexican with the gun staggered against the old man, cursed him for getting in his way, and shot him dead in his tracks. Almost on the crack of the pistol, an American sprang forth from a door at the side of the narrow street with an old-fashioned musket in his hands, which he used as a club. With a terrific blow over the head, he knocked the murderer insensible. Hardly two minutes had elapsed since our meeting with the Mexicans.

An officer in the plaza, hearing the shot, was on the spot in a moment and took charge of the situation. With the help of the prisoner's companion, they dragged him to the jail but a short distance away. The doors were hardly locked behind them before a crowd filled the street in front of the building yelling, '*Hang him! Hang him!*'

In order to see better, Huntoon and I climbed on top of a high adobe wall at the side of the street. This position gave us a fine close-up view of the affair, and from this vantage we observed an exhibition of sheer nerve not often seen. Don Desiderio Romero was sheriff of San Miguel County. Word reached him of the riot at the jail, and not waiting for a posse that he ordered to assemble and follow him, he came dashing in at full speed, mounted on a superb stallion which he guided with his knees, a forty-five in each hand. He plunged through the crowd until he reached the center of the street in front of the jail doors. Here he stopped, and using his guns as clubs, backed his steed through the mob until he was against the jail doors. Now he threw his guns down at full cock on the crowd, ordering them back and swearing he would shoot the first man that touched him or his horse or did not put up his gun quick—and guns were not scarce in spite of the regulations. It was certainly a rare exhibition of pure nerve. His voice and face, as well as his action, indicated that he meant business; the guns in the crowd vanished, and little by little the mob faded away. When the posse arrived, they found him practically alone, but complete master of the situation.

Huntoon and I went to our belated meal with a-plenty to talk about and were not surprised to get the tip that a Committee meeting was on at midnight. We were on time and, being eye-witnesses, gave our testimony. The murderer's fate was quickly sealed. The meeting disclosed the fact that he was the scion of a wealthy and influential Spanish family of Mesilla, New Mexico, and that his name was Don Manuel Barela. He had come from home after merchandise with five large freight wagons drawn by mules. He had completed his purchases; his wagons were loaded and in camp ready to start south the following morning. He had then decided to go into Las Vegas to do a little 'stepping-out' as a farewell.

At midnight the Committee quietly assembled near the jail, proceeded to the door, and knocked. It was opened a little and the jailer asked what was wanted. Mr. Chapman put his foot into the crack, followed it with the muzzle of a forty-five, and in a low tone ordered the keeper to stand back and deliver the keys. I do not know, but I have always felt that the sheriff, knowing the Committee was composed of many of the leading citizens, kept out of the way that night. At any rate, he was conspicuous by his absence. The jailer, realizing resistance was useless and recognizing Mr. Chapman—no one was masked—led the procession to the cell and unlocked it.

Barela had been put in a cell with another murderer, an Italian by the name of Louis Torbillo, who had recently been caught red-handed after killing a Mexican woman, Señora Tomasita. Barela had become conscious, was sober, quickly sensed his visitors' purpose, and began to beg. As his victim was well known to most of the members of the Committee, his pleadings fell on deaf ears. He was taken from the cell, a rope was ready, the noose was put around his neck, and he 'stepped-out' for the last time. A big burly chap—I did not know him—grabbed the rope, jerked Barela from his feet, and began kicking him. Chapman threw his gun down on the big fellow and sternly ordered the brutality stopped. The order was quickly obeyed and the man slunk away under the jeers of the rest.

There was an old unused windmill in the middle of the plaza. Barela was taken there and quickly hanged on one of the wings. After a brief conference, it was decided to save a lot of money to the county by serving the Italian murderer in the same manner, and this was at once done.[2]

To Charles Ilfelt, a leading merchant and member of the Committee, whom I have mentioned before, I am indebted for the following further details: Mr. Ilfelt had not been notified of the meeting and was asleep, his bedroom facing the plaza, but he was awakened and through his window saw what was going on. The Barela family were good customers of his and much of the freight then ready to go south was purchased from him. The bodies were taken down the next morning by order of the sheriff. Mr. Ilfelt wired Don Mariano Barela, a brother of the victim, telling him what had happened. Don Mariano telegraphed back to 'have good care taken of the remains, buy a good casket, and ship body to Mesilla,' all of which was carried out by Mr. Ilfelt.

[2]There is conflicting evidence on these hangings described by Hoyt. The *Weekly New Mexican* (Santa Fe), June 14, 1879, copying the story from the *Las Vegas Gazette,* reported the hanging of Manuel Barela and Giovanni Dugi on June 4 from the windmill in the Las Vegas plaza. Stanley, *The Las Vegas Story,* p. 73, repeats this same story, but on p. 127 changes Dugi's first name to Guillermo. It seems Dugi killed Tomas Gallegos and a French Canadian, Pierre Brisson, while Barela "had committed a cold-blooded murder."

XVIII

Days of Violence

Pending the completion of the railroad, the Barlow & Sanderson Stage Line still carried passengers and mail daily from Santa Fé. Twice, with but a few days intervening, the stage was held up a short distance from Las Vegas and both passengers and mail robbed. The mail as brought in after these affairs was in a terrible mess. Bags were slashed and all letters which looked as if worthwhile were cut open. A deputy United States marshal was put on the case after the first hold-up, but accomplished nothing.

After the second hold-up a conference was held at the post office. Mr. Chapman came from the Springs and the marshal reported with a Mr. Parker, a clerical-looking man with a dark complexion and long black beard, who owned and ran a hotel and livery stable in Las Vegas. Parker stated that four young men—the number that robbed the stage— came to his hotel, rented a two-horse platform spring wagon on each day of the robbery, and drove into the country, returning with the team in a lather and tired out. They had left his hotel, but he was confident they were still in town and was absolutely positive he could identify any one or all of them.

Four men together would attract attention, so it was decided to pair off, and go the rounds of the dance halls, gambling houses, and saloons, meeting and reporting progress at regular intervals. Chapman and the marshal took the lead and were followed by Parker and myself, each with a couple of Colt's forty-fives concealed on his person.

We entered one of the largest gambling resorts on the plaza, and sauntered casually from table to table, Parker apparently carefully scrutinizing every face. At the rear of this long room was a game run by a young man of the 'tin-horn' class, by the name of Webb. I knew him well, as my acquaintance with people had become quite extensive after I went into the post office.

After sizing everybody up, Parker would join me and give the signal, 'They are not here,' and we would pass on to the next joint. This programme we kept up all night long, during which we visited the Webb place a number of times, always leaving with Parker's signal, 'They are not here.'

The next night and for several following, this procedure was kept up by Parker and the marshal, until Parker finally gave his opinion that the birds had flown, and the hunt was abandoned. There were large rewards offered for the capture of these robbers. Mr. Parker will be heard from later.

The arrival of every train from the north meant recruits for the underworld and crime still flourished. Page B. Otero, a scion of one of the most prominent families of New Mexico, now a resident of Los Angeles, California, contributes the following account of one incident:

'Four men, known as Tom (sometimes called 'Dutch') Henry, John Dorsey, Jim West, and Bill Randall, came into New Mexico from Texas. They took possession of a cabin in the hills near Mora, county seat of Mora County, and began to live off the country. They made many raids on the near-by settlements, taking by force whatever objects they wanted. The gang once entered the old town of Las Vegas and drove off with a new buggy and team of horses, leaving word that if the owner wanted them he should come to their headquarters and get them. This sort of thing kept up for quite some time, but no one seemed particularly anxious to go after the gang.

'One day about noon they rode into town, tied their horses in front of the Ward & Tamme Saloon, and entering, started drinking. They were heavily armed and strutted around the streets, virtually daring anyone to interfere. Joe Carson was City Marshal at this time. The principal dance hall was owned by George Close, and when it opened that evening the four men entered, walked up to the bar, and asked for drinks. They had been drinking more or less all afternoon and were in an ugly mood. Just at this time Marshal Carson entered the hall and approaching them asked, politely enough, that they hand over their artillery to the bartender while they remained in the city, saying that it would be returned to them when they were ready to leave.

'This started the fireworks, and when the smoke cleared, Marshal Carson was lying dead in the doorway of the dance hall with seven bullet holes in his body; Bill Randall was on his hands and knees on the sidewalk shot through the abdomen and died that night; Jim West was lying in the street shot through the liver and yelling like a coyote; Tom Henry was unhurt, and John Dorsey caught a bullet through the calf of one leg. Both Henry and Dorsey were captured as they were attempting to escape and, along with West, were locked up in the old town jail.

'A few nights later the three were taken out by the Vigilantes and strung up on the windmill in the middle of the old town plaza. Bonfires were lighted and most of the population of both Old and New Towns were present.'

It was in the summertime—1879—and the weather was hot. Mr. Otero, himself a member of the Vigilantes, with several others, was sleeping out on top of the porch at the warehouse of Otero, Sellers & Company—Mr. Otero's father being senior member of the firm—and from there they could look directly into the door of the George Close dance hall and see the shooting.

Now comes Mr. Lute Wilcox, then owner of the 'Optic,' the leading newspaper in that section, and now a citizen of Denver, Colorado, who gives his picturesque account of the wild incident as follows:[1]

'During the summer of 1879, at Las Vegas, Dutch Henry's gang of five arrived from the Panhandle to get Joe Carson, the town marshal, against whom they had an old grudge, originating at Fort Worth. Joe told them to lay aside their arms in accordance with the rule. They said they could manage their own guns and needed no advice.

'That night Joe went to George Close's dance hall to enforce the order. The gang was dancing with the 'fairies' and there was a hot gunplay.

'At the "Optic" office I was sitting at my work of getting up a copy book. Mrs. Carson, living overhead in the Gard Building, came running down, stuck her head in the door at the rear, and cried that Joe had been killed, speaking intuitively from telepathic sense. I arose quickly, realizing that something unusual had happened. Halfway across the space to the rear of the dance hall we stumbled upon an object on the trail. I struck a match and Mrs. Carson fell upon the prostrate form of her husband, while I hurried on to get help.

'A large crowd of refugees had assembled, scared out of their wits, huddling in the alleyway and also in an open space between the Close place and Mrs. McDonald's restaurant.

[1]After it moved to Las Vegas, where it began publication on November 4, 1879, the *Daily Optic's* proprietor and editor was Russell A. Kistler. Wilcox later became the owner. James Marshall, *Santa Fe, The Railroad That Built an Empire* (New York, 1945), pp. 99–100.

'We packed Joe into Dr. Severson's drug store on Sixth Street, but the man was dead, of course, with so many shots. The Mrs. was hysterical and carried on frantically, but eloped a few weeks later with the Justice of the Peace, Hoodoo Brown, to Vinita, Indian Territory.

'Mysterious Dave Matthews and Dave Rudebaugh were in the mêlée and did much of the return damage to the gang, one of whom had been left outside to hold the horses. His name was unknown to us and he evidently escaped in the darkness. A telegraph operator named Costello, an innocent bystander, was killed and a number wounded, without discommoding the girls other than to give them the customary jolt, which was a part of their business, as Lady Maud and Cockeyed Liz declared. The glass front of the dance hall was demolished in the crush.

'A few minutes later, when we had caught our second wind, with more or less bravado and combat, Colonel James A. Lockhart, now a grocer at Miami, Florida, mounted a box at Houghton's corner near the scene of the ruckus, and proclaimed the spirit of indignation, incidentally a reward of ten thousand dollars in the name of the town for the capture of the outlaws, who sloped away *poco pronto*,[2] as you can imagine. We all struck out on horses, but the most of us were back empty-handed at daylight. Captain Barney was so eager for that reward that he got away on a short spurt riding a

[2] *Poco pronto* translates "a little quickly."

Las Vegas, about 1879
Courtesy Western History Department, Denver Public Library

burro borrowed from the Blake kids. The two Daves and the two Pinkertons, Lee and Muldoon, were old-time man-hunters, knew their onions, and kept on going. They found their game ensconced in a vacant *jacal*[3] below Cherry Valley in Mora Canyon, twenty-five miles or so north of town. The officers were under the cover of an arroyo and threw pebbles against the door of the hut to notify the quartette of their presence. The gang finally surrendered under truce with the promise of safe conduct to the county jail, but nothing more. The officers got back to New Town about 4 P.M. and the news created such a hubbub that we had to get out an extra.

'That night, about ten, seventy-nine of us squeezed one by one into Talbot's darkened barn and held a short consultation, while the livery stock stood by and offered no protest.

'The sheriff was Desiderio Romero, living in an adobe *casita* on Halfway Hill. We sent our leader, Bob (Red) Old, with two other men, one of whom was Arthur Jilson, and the other an interpreter, to Red's house, a few rods distant, while we remained at the *acequia*[4] under the hill. Desiderio was wise and showed no resentment, but dressed quickly and was brought into camp. He marched in front on our way over to the hoosegow back of the plaza.

[3] A *jacal* is an Indian hut.
[4] A *casita* is a small house or cabin; *acequia* is a trench or drain.

'There was a grape arbor leading from the street to the jail door, as you may remember, and Tio Desiderio was given the honor first to enter the narrow trail. He was much perturbed and called excitedly to the captain of the guard of his *muscaderos* inside to open the *puerta*, 'and be damned quick about it.' The coverts swarmed in like a pack of hungry *chinos* at meal call. Doc Ames, dentist, got the keys from Pine without resistance and opened the door to the farthermost cell. The boys soon had the bandits out into the *placeta*. I had been appointed sergeant of a squad of *bravatinos* to pack out West, who had been wounded in the hips and was unable to navigate.[5] I had my compatriot right there, but we had some delay in getting out, as our man with the others had been chained to the floor. We made a sort of cat's-cradle with our hands and came tagging along with our poor fellow moaning piteously and protesting that he should not be strangled because he was injured. He subsided, however, at the scaffold, when Henry commanded him to 'shut up and die like a man.' Father Coudert from the priory appeared from a side street and making the sign of the cross, pleaded with us as Christian gentlemen to spare the lives of our four victims. No heed was paid to the padre's entreaties.

[5] Hoyt has coined two Spanish words—*muscaderos* and *bravatinos*, no doubt meaning musketeers and brave ones. His use of *chinos* (*chinas* is correct) is meant to be derogatory—meaning mixed bloods. A *placeta* is a small square.

'You will recall that after the noose committee had done its damndest, and the jerk crew was in action, a shot was fired, as the beginning of a fusillade that followed. This shot was traced to Mrs. Carson, but was not authorized, as it had not been prearranged at the livery, as were all the other details. You will remember also how the stiffs were the next day placed one by one in wheelbarrows and toted off to the *cárcel*[6] after Doc Shout had pronounced them dead. I presume the remains were hid away in the Campos Santos out on the Hot Springs Camino.[7]

'I have only to recite the joke that went with the affair. The merchants on the plaza were somewhat put out by such a bold ceremony right out in front of their stores and held a meeting to declare their objections to such unholy doings. They reported that their well and windmill had cost them six hundred dollars. And now just think of it—they would have to dig up sixty dollars more to remove the infernal thing as a nuisance incompatible with the peace and dignity of the dear old plaza.'

Mr. Otero says the party of two-gun men from Texas that 'started something' in George Close's dance hall that memorable night consisted of *four*, while Mr. Wilcox writes that there were *five*. Next we have the story from Charles Ilfelt, still living, who was one of the Committee, was there in person,

[6] *Cárcel* is jail.
[7] Campos Santos is a cemetery.

and well remembers that the number of victims of that whooper-up windmill party were *four*. I was there through it all and saw the bodies hanging from the windmill next morning as the bus came in from the morning train, and *my* recollection has always been that there were *four*.

Naturally, it was a very exciting time. Hundreds of people, men and women, old and young, milled around that ghastly group most of the night, and anything like an adequate description would be hard to give. I have made an effort to get an official report of the details of this affair, but so far have not succeeded. Chances are that records that far back are lost. A few years after it occurred, the 'Optic' offices and all their files were entirely destroyed by fire. Taking everything into consideration, it is no wonder after a lapse of forty-nine years that memory might slip a cog in some detail.

The vagaries of memory under excitement were illustrated in quite a remarkable manner in a noted murder case that occurred in St. Paul, Minnesota, many years ago.

A traveling man by the name of Farnsworth was in the lobby of the Merchants' Hotel when a prominent newspaper man, Frank Meade, entered in a somewhat intoxicated condition. They were casual acquaintances, they met and in a few minutes quarreled. The lobby was crowded. Farnsworth was the larger of the two and unarmed.

Meade pulled a gun, a shot was fired, and Farns-

worth sank to the floor mortally wounded.[8] I attended him while Meade was jailed without bail. The
case was discussed pro and con, and it was learned
that at least a half-dozen reputable citizens were
ready to testify positively that the two men were
only from six to ten feet apart when the shot was
fired, which fact meant murder if the wound proved
fatal.

I notified the county attorney there was no hope
of Farnsworth's recovery, so he placed in the next
room a deputy, Thompson by name, and instructed
me to call him in just before the end and have him
take Farnsworth's dying statement.

When the time came, Mr. Thompson sat by the
bedside and listened to the story of the tragedy.
Farnsworth was weak and spoke very slowly. I am
methodical by nature, so taking out my prescription
book I wrote in it, word for word, his 'dying statement,' in part as follows: 'He was drunk. We quarreled. I saw him pull a gun. We clinched. I grabbed
the gun by the barrel trying to wrest it from him.
We struggled and as I had hold of the gun he fired.'

[8]Frank Mead, not Meade, former mayor of Mandan, shot
Frank Farnsworth, also from Mandan, on the night of September 7. Farnsworth died two nights later with Hoyt in
attendance. The local paper reported the death bed statement taken down by Hoyt. Charges against Mead were filed
on September 13, 1886. He was tried on April 25-26, 1887,
with the jury verdict of not guilty. *St. Paul Dispatch*, September 8, 9, 10, 1886, carried full details of the affair. The
trial proceedings are in District Court File, Criminal 1683,
Ramsey County Records Center, Minneapolis.

Mr. Thompson, *the next morning*, dictated to his stenographer from memory the 'dying statement.'

Frank Meade was indicted for murder and was defended by Davis, Kellogg & Severance. Davis was an ex-Governor of Minnesota, and later United States Senator, and Frank B. Kellogg retired in 1929 from the office of Secretary of State.

Several prominent men, eye-witnesses of the affair, testified positively that the two men were some distance apart when the fatal shot was fired. Thompson was called, but before he got to the dying statement, the manner in which he obtained and *recorded* it was brought out. Whereupon the Judge promptly sustained the objection of Meade's attorneys, and it was thrown out.

It seems that, for some unknown reason, neither the County Attorney nor Meade's lawyers knew just what the 'dying statement' contained. Both thought it was unfavorable to the defendant Meade. The instant it was thrown out, I realized what it meant to Meade and at once showed and explained my notes to his attorneys. Mr. Davis then took it up with the Judge, I was put on the stand, verified my notes, they were then accepted as testimony, and Meade was cleared.

The decision matters not. I am presenting this incident to illustrate how little dependence can often be placed upon memory under intense excitement. This Las Vegas quartet who had paid the penalty were still at the end of their respective ropes as the bus rolled in, full of passengers from the morning train from the north. I was sitting on the veranda in front of the Exchange Hotel gazing at the gruesome spectacle and wondering what might have been the men's thoughts after they realized their fate. As the bus passed the old windmill on the way to the hotel, my reverie was cut short by a series of shrieks, evidently feminine, from one of the passengers. The driver plied his whip and the bus dashed up to the curb with a woman struggling with a man and screaming, 'Let me go!—Take me home!—Take me home!—I will never live in this God-forsaken country!'

I stepped to the bus, introducing myself to her companion as a physician, and together we carried the woman into the hotel, where I soon quieted her with an opiate. They were a Mr. and Mrs. A. M. Conklin from Arkansas, who, hearing of the new railroad and the rapid development in New Mexico, had followed the crowd. They were a remarkably fine Christian couple, the husband a newspaper man, and one can imagine the shock they both received as they entered the plaza and saw the figures swinging from the old mill. Mrs. Conklin could not overcome the impression the terrible sight had given her and kept begging Mr. Conklin to return to the old home. But being a man of strong character and visioning a bright future for the Territory, he decided to remain. After a short stay in Las Vegas, they settled in Albuquerque. The railroad finally was completed to that point and a great celebration was held in honor of that fact, Mr. Conklin taking a prominent part. This occurred April 22, 1880, and as I was a visitor there, I met the Conklins again.

Mr. Conklin had not found just the opening he was seeking, and told me frankly that if he did not succeed very soon he would yield to his wife's entreaties and return to Arkansas. But fate decided otherwise. A short time afterward, the opening he was hoping for materialized and he became the editor of 'The Socorro Sun' at Socorro, New Mexico, and one of the leading citizens of that place.

The Americans had built a church there and the Conklins were welcomed into the congregation. A Christmas festival was held on Christmas Eve, 1881, and Mr. Conklin was master of ceremonies. When the gayety was at its height, in walked two well-known Mexicans, Abran and Enofrio Baca, brothers. Both were intoxicated. They at once started a disturbance and became very ugly, so Mr. Conklin approached them and requested them to be quiet. He told them they were quite welcome, but that this was a church and if they wished to remain they must act in a suitable way. They became more violent than ever and dared Mr. Conklin to fight. He reiterated what he had already said and told them they must behave or leave. They finally left the church.

After the festival was over and all had started home, as Mr. Conklin with his wife by his side passed out the door, Abran Baca caught Mrs. Conklin by one arm and jerked her away from her husband and the same instant Enofrio put a bullet through the editor's heart and he fell dead on the church steps.[9]

Although avengers were close after them, the Bacas escaped into Old Mexico. Indignation in New Mexico rose to high pitch; Governor Lionel A. Sheldon, who had succeeded General Lew Wallace, offered a reward of five hundred dollars, and the citizens of Socorro a like amount, for the capture of the murderers, dead or alive.

Months passed without results, although a proclamation of the reward and complete descriptions of the murderers were broadcast everywhere.[10] Finally

[9] For a discussion of the circumstances surrounding Conklin's death, see the entry for A. M. Conklin in the *Biographical Notes.*

[10] Charles D. Potter in his "Reminiscences of Socorro Vigilantes," edited by Paige W. Christiansen, *New Mexico Historical Review*, XL (January 1967), 30, disputes Dr. Hoyt's version. He notes that warrants for the Bacas arrest were refused by the local Mexican alcalde and Sheriff Juan María Garcia. With that refusal, the vigilantes were quickly formed by Colonel Ethan W. Eaton. Shortly after its organization, on December 28, Antonio María Baca "was captured and placed under guard in the Park Hotel corral." The next day a gun was smuggled to him; that night he shot and wounded one of his guards, Jack Ketchum. In the return fire, Baca was killed instantly. *The Albuquerque Daily Journal*, December 30, 1880, commented: "Last night, one man, a prisoner named Antonio María Baca, shot the guard who was stationed over him; the prisoner was then knocked down and killed."

in April, 1882, a copy fell into the hand of that fearless and resourceful Texas Ranger, James B. Gillett, who was stationed near the Mexico border in El Paso County. The two criminals wanted were prominent citizens of Socorro and belonged to one of the best families in New Mexico. In the spring of 1882 an uncle of theirs, Don José Baca, was the judge of El Paso County, Texas.

The story of how the Ranger captured the two fugitives and landed them both in the Socorro jail is full of thrills from start to finish. It is splendidly told in Mr. Gillett's book, 'Six Years With the Texas Rangers.' Abran was captured at the home of his uncle, Judge Baca, and Enofrio at Saragosa, a town in the State of Chihuahua, Mexico, about five miles south of the border. The captures were about a month apart, and the second one came within an ace of stirring up some very serious international complications.[11]

A brother of mine, George L. Hoyt, had settled in Socorro about the same time as the Conklins. One of our sisters, who is the wife of George R. Harvey, Judge of the Court of First Instance at Manila, Philippine Islands, was visiting him. When this atrocious crime was committed, a Vigilante Committee of which my brother was a member was at once organized.

There was little delay in the justice that was

[11] For the role played by James B. Gillett in the Baca case, see Conklin's entry in the *Biographical Notes*.

handed to this pair as they were successively landed in the Socorro jail. The Vigilantes promptly took care of that detail with precision and dispatch, although I think it was their first experience in Socorro. One of the brothers was hanged quite near my brother's home, and our sister has never forgotten the shock she received at the sight she beheld upon opening the door the next morning.

XIX

Humors of Practice in Bernalillo

A MAN NAMED McDonald from Covington, Kentucky, called one day and informed me of an opening for a doctor at Bernalillo, New Mexico, a prosperous town in the Rio Grande Valley, a short distance above Albuquerque. There was no drugstore and my only competitor was a Dr. Carroll, aged and ready to retire. I decided to go, and after giving my good friend and employer due notice, I began to plan for the new move. I had become friendly with Mr. Herbert, the proprietor of the largest drug business in Las Vegas, so I told him of this opportunity and made him a proposition for him to 'grubstake' me to a stock of goods for a drugstore on a fifty-fifty basis. He consented at once. I selected a bill of goods amounting to two thousand dollars and arranged to ship them to Bernalillo by bull-train. As they pulled out, Herbert said, 'How are you fixed, Doc?' I told him. 'Not enough, my boy,' and out came a roll from which he peeled off two hundred dollars and handed it to me. That was the West fifty years ago!

In this transaction there wasn't a scratch of a pen between us—simply a gentlemen's agreement. Moreover, do not forget that my first introduction to Mr.

Herbert was when I was bartender at the Exchange Hotel, where he was *not* a customer!

As bull-trains were somewhat slower than the present-day air-freights, I decided to take my time in starting for Bernalillo by stage. In the meantime my friend Mr. McDonald offered me a seat in his buckboard, behind a span of Kentucky trotters with which he was going to Albuquerque.

Bernalillo in 1879 was a residence town of practically one street on the east bank of the Rio Grande. Its leading citizen, Don José Leandro Perea, was rated not only the wealthiest, but was considered the most influential person in New Mexico. He was a man of strong character, yet ruled over his vast domain with moderation and good judgment. He had lost his first wife, who had presented him with a number of children, the youngest a daughter of about fifteen. The children were all married but the two youngest, and the old Don had recently taken a rather young woman for his second wife.

Some of the Perea women were beautiful, and all were fine-looking, educated, and accomplished. The men were of medium size, very agreeable, and with courteous manners. In addition to the Pereas, Bernalillo was also the home of branches of the Armijos, Oteros, Montoyas, Castillos, and other old families, all of whom prided themselves on their pure Castilian ancestors. Although brunettes predominated, I remember seeing blue eyes and brown hair among both the Perea and Otero families. With few exceptions, they all spoke English as fluently as Spanish, having received their educations mostly at Eastern colleges and convents. I lived and practiced my profession among these people until the fall of 1881, and from a world-wide experience since, can truthfully affirm that I never have practiced among a finer or more honorable clientèle.

After a pleasant trip over the Old Santa Fé Trail, a part of which I was already acquainted with, Mr. McDonald put me in Bernalillo some time in advance of my stock of goods. I leased a two-room adobe building on the main street about the center of the town, and proceeded to form a 'Get Acquainted Club' of one member.

That club became quite active, when I was suddenly stricken with some kind of fever, was put to bed, and old Dr. Carroll was called in.

He at once confided in me that he was not a physician; that all he ever gave was quinine, castor oil, and native wine. This wine, of very fine quality, was made each year by most of the families, from the famous Mission grapes that are found everywhere in the Rio Grande Valley.

Although the good old doctor's drug supply was limited, I found him to be a splendid nurse and I was well cared for. My goods arrived about the second week of my illness, and as I had been delirious for some days, Dr. Carroll had them stored in my adobe.

Judge McCutchin, his wife, son, and daughter

from Washington, D. C., had come to Bernalillo for the Judge's health. Hearing of my illness, they kept me supplied with all kinds of suitable dainties as soon as I began to convalesce, and it was not long before I was in the adobe rooms unpacking and fitting up the new drugstore.

My first professional call came one midnight. The wife of one of the most prominent families had been in agony for twenty-four hours. Dr. Carroll had attended them for years, was called, gave her a liberal potion of each of his 'sheet-anchors' without results and a family consultation resulted in their deciding to try out the new *medico*. I soon discovered the agony was due to an acute bladder trouble and relieved it instantly by a catheterization, a procedure unheard of among these people at that time. The reputation of the '*medico colorado*'—the cognomen given me by the Mexicans on account of my red hair—was on a very firm basis in Bernalillo from that night.

Don José Antonio Montoya was ill with pneumonia. Dr. Carroll informed the family it was a hopeless case and left for Santa Fé to be gone a week. A son-in-law of the patient came and asked me to come and stay at the house and let them know just before the end came, that they might have the priest perform the last rites.

I went to the house, and after carefully examining the old gentleman, informed the relatives I would stay provided the case was turned over to me professionally. This they quickly consented to do. This was about five o'clock in the afternoon.

I do not remember ever stepping into a Mexican sickroom fifty years ago without finding every window and door closed as tight as wax. Fresh air, especially night air, for the sick meant to them death. If you ever 'step-out' in the City of Mexico after night, one of the first sights you notice is a white covering of cloths over the mouth of every policeman and any passer-by who may be feeling poorly. Another custom in a serious illness was a gathering of the entire clan in the sickroom around the patient; the nearest female relative sitting tailor-fashion where the pillow belongs, with the head of the stricken one in her lap.

The Montoya clan was a large one, and as I entered the room I think they were all there. In the face of strong protests, I threw open all windows, put on extra blankets, and had the bed moved where the head was near the window with the most air. Don José's wife took the pillow part and a daughter acted as nurse in applying the remedies I had ordered.

Don José had been ill just ten days when a typical crisis occurred. His pneumonia was double and the outcome doubtful. Resolution had begun, and as the temperature dropped, his throat began to fill up with the exudate. Being too weak to raise and expel it, he began to choke and get black in the face. His wife screamed '*El es muerto*' (he is dead) and fell in a dead faint, as did two other women in the room.

Throwing aside the women who had fainted, I quickly rolled the old man on his stomach, pulled his head back by grabbing a handful of hair with my right hand, then with my left hand and a handkerchief I jerked his lower jaw open, pulled his tongue out, and as I shook his head vigorously with my right, a cupful of exudate was expelled and he gasped. This treatment I kept up in a modified degree for a minute or two, the breathing returned, as did the color, and in a short time Don José was resting easily and eventually he recovered. There was great rejoicing among the clan, the only fly in the ointment being, I strongly suspect, with all due respect to the cloth, a little disappointment on the part of the good little French priest, who had patiently been waiting in an adjoining room all night for that last call.

My reason for this suspicion is that when Don José, after his complete recovery, called to pay my fee of five hundred dollars, he mentioned that just before he left home His Reverence dropped in as they were counting out the gold—there was no bank in Bernalillo—and my fee was discussed.

'You are paying him too much,' remarked His Reverence.

'He saved my life,' replied the Don. 'I would have gladly paid him twice as much if he had asked it.'

An epidemic of mumps was especially prevalent

in the lower town where lived the families of the poorer classes, most of them retainers of the *gente fino* of the upper town.[1] There is little to be done for mumps except care and nursing, but the patients wanted something done in the way of medical treatment. Every Mexican has a garden, and all raise *frijoles* (beans), so they can be found in every home. So I emphatically ordered a bean poultice for each and every case downtown. In a few days I had numerous calls and reports of 'no better.' I started out and found — — ? A nice little flat bag of *raw beans* fastened to each jaw!

It was not uncommon to take a long ride to some outlying ranch, sheep or cow camp, and find a fractured arm or leg, with absolutely none of the ordinary materials available that I could use as splints. So I would order a panful of adobe mud and use it exactly as we use plaster of Paris and had fine results with it.

My medical practice as well as the drug business was increasing daily. I secured the services of Jack McCutchin, son of the lady who had been so kind to me in my sickness, to tend the store during my absence. After I had been in Bernalillo a couple of months, I was offered, and accepted, the position of postmaster, which went along very nicely with the drug business.

It was about this time that I sent for my brother,

[1] *Gente fino* should read *gente fina*, meaning well-educated people.

George L. Hoyt, to come out from St. Paul and help me. After three months I made my quarterly report to my friend Herbert at Las Vegas and sent him fifty per cent of the net profits. At the same time I made him an offer to buy the entire stock, pay him all the cash I had, and give my notes for the balance, in three equal amounts, payable in thirty, sixty, and ninety days, with interest at twelve per cent per annum, the regular rate then. He accepted my offer by return mail, and I took up each of those notes on the dates they were due. Also, as Herbert did a jobbing business, I purchased most of my supplies from him from then on, so the deal was not a bad one for either of us.

One day in walked a party of railway officials, ex-Governor Anthony from Kansas, A. A. Robinson, William B. Strong, and two others whose names I have forgotten. They asked for information as to who were the leading citizens that they could meet for a conference. I suggested Don José Leandro Perea and offered to go with them to his home. We went, and after a conference or two, they secured the right of way to build the Atchison, Topeka & Santa Fé Railroad down the Rio Grande Valley. The railway officials showed their appreciation of the courtesy I had extended them by referring me to Contractors Perkins and Somers, who were to build six miles of the new railway through and past Bernalillo; the call resulted in my services being retained to attend their employees when needed.

They employed a large force of workers, and as sanitation, germs, and infections were largely unknown at that time, this contract proved very lucrative to me.

XX

Men of Different Kinds Come to My Store

SOME MILES east of Bernalillo rises from the valley
a majestic mountain called El Sandia (the water-
melon) and about twenty-five miles east of it is a
district that contains in places paying percentages
of placer gold. An abundance of water is required
to secure gold in this form. For years Mexicans had
packed pay dirt on burros from this district to the
Rio Grande, the nearest water supply, and made
wages.

A mining engineer had examined this property
and decided that a feasible process to secure this
gold was to dam up one of the big canyons on the
east slope of El Sandia Mountain, pipe the water to
the placers, and wash out the gold by the hydraulic
method—the simplest, most economical and successful method then known when all the necessary conditions were present. This plan was adopted by a
Boston syndicate which organized the San Pedro
Mining Company and sent out General Ruger—a
former army man—as general manager to develop
the proposition.

The railway was completed beyond Bernalillo
and I had been appointed division surgeon from
Lamy Junction to Albuquerque. I was once again

remembered by the company when General Ruger stopped at their general offices at Topeka, Kansas, on his way out, to arrange for shipping twenty-five miles of iron pipe from Pittsburgh, Pennsylvania, to his mine, and at their suggestion I was appointed surgeon for his company.[1]

With a large force of men General Ruger built an enormous dam and connected it with the placers twenty-five miles away by an iron pipe, ten to fifteen inches in diameter and with a pressure test of eight hundred pounds to the square inch. This was considered quite an engineering feat in those days.

During this construction there was an epidemic of pneumonia among the men, and after losing several cases at the company hospital situated at the dam, I decided that the altitude had something to do with it. From that time I had all patients brought down to the valley, a drop of about five thousand feet. After this change I did not lose a case.

The project was apparently going to succeed and

[1] The San Pedro and Cañon del Agua Company was founded by a group of Boston and New York businessmen under the presidency of George William Ballow, a Boston banker. The company's operations were placed under the direction of a superintendent named Colonel M. G. Gillette. A lengthy description of the mine and its operations is given in *The Weekly New Mexican* (Santa Fe), July 19, 1880. The name of "General Ruger" is nowhere mentioned. (It could be that General Ruger may well have launched the initial operations. If so, most likely this was Thomas Howard Ruger, a West Point graduate, Class of 1850.)

*Building the Atchison, Topeka & Santa Fe Railroad
through New Mexico*

Courtesy Santa Fe Railway by Western History Department,
Denver Public Library

the presidency of the company was tendered to General U. S. Grant, who visited the property to investigate. He and his party were taken from Lamy Junction in Government ambulances to the placers and thence to the dam and reservoir. After completing his examination, the General decided to take the train at Bernalillo, where they arrived about three hours before the departure of the daily train for the north. Hotel accommodations at Bernalillo were meager and, as my office adjacent to the drugstore was comfortable, the party became my guests until train time.

This was the second time I had met the great soldier. Soon after the close of the Civil War, General Grant with his wife and two of their children, Frederick and Nellie, visited St. Paul. My uncle, Dr. J. H. Murphy, had served as surgeon with General Grant at Vicksburg. When he called to pay his respects to his former commander, I went with him and was presented to the General and family. I had a short but pleasant visit with Fred, who was four years my senior. This must have been in 1865 or 1866, and fate threw us together again in 1898 in the Spanish-American War, where he was a Major-General and I was Chief Surgeon of his commands for more than two years.

But I have drifted from Bernalillo. The General was very sociable, and frankly told me that his opinion of the mining property was very favorable and all it needed for success was the necessary snow and rain to fill up the big reservoir. His party left on the northbound train.

The next and last time I met the General was as a guest at a memorable banquet given at the Hotel Lafayette, Lake Minnetonka, Minnesota, by Henry Villard, president of the Northern Pacific Railway, in honor of the completion of that road, in 1883. Besides General U. S. Grant, President Arthur and Generals Sherman and Phil Sheridan were also guests at this dinner. Mr. James J. Hill, president of the Great Northern Railway Lines, made one of his first public speeches that evening.

Soon after inspecting the property General Grant accepted the presidency of the San Pedro Mining Company. At once the stock of his company was kited sky high, due chiefly to his name. The moment he learned of this, he resigned and, as a result, the price of the stock dropped almost to zero. Eventually this costly enterprise ended as a complete failure. I never knew why, as I left New Mexico in the fall of 1881, but many years later I was told that co-incident with the completion of the dam, there were a number of years of almost total drought. No water, no gold.

A young bachelor, Billy Graves, opened the first hardware store in Bernalillo during the railway construction. He was a New-Yorker, a nephew of ex-Governor Horatio Seymour and of Senator Roscoe Conkling, from the same State, and as he had a winning personality, he soon became popular.

Exposed to a rainstorm one day, Graves came home drenched to the skin and developed pneumonia. He recovered, and while convalescing came into the drugstore one day just as I had received an emergency call. I was alone and, instead of locking up, suggested that he make himself at home and take charge during my absence. Knowing the town was full of tough characters, brought by the railway, Billy replied that he would gladly stay if I would lend him a gun. My only weapon was my old Colt's forty-five that I had carried since I left the Black Hills, and turning it over to him I rode away. No one came into the store. A comfortable couch against the wall, the head near an open window, looked most inviting, so Billy stretched himself out, and when I returned later, I found him fast asleep. He had put my gun under the pillow as he lay down and when he reached for it to return it to me, it was gone, evidently taken from the outside through the open window.

I felt lost without it, but regrets were useless. A few days after, a traveling man from the Simmons Hardware Company of St. Louis came through town and Billy presented me with a double-action Colt's thirty-eight, with a short barrel. It was a new model that had not been out very long and, as a matter of fact, it was far more suitable for me than my big forty-five. That gun has been over most of the world with me and I still have it, apparently as serviceable as ever.

I had among my patients Don Panteleon Miera, who, as I learned from others later, was a man with a history. Both he and his wife were among the *gente fino* and he seemed to be respected and in perfectly good standing everywhere. He was a quiet, reserved person, but if he liked one, he could be very gracious and entertaining. He had a strong face, but his eyes were a trifle shifty.

It seemed that in the early sixties there was an almost continual procession of 'covered wagons' wending their way westward over the 'Old Santa Fé Trail' toward the Pacific Coast, and many who started were never heard from again. After months had elapsed friends or relatives often started in search of the missing, and after a long time it gradually became known that many had been traced as far as Algodones, Sandoval County, New Mexico, a small village a few miles north of Bernalillo. Two strangers appeared one day in Bernalillo and aroused a good deal of curiosity. A rumor was started that they were detectives. Don Panteleon Miera suddenly disappeared, the two strangers proved to be detectives, as rumored, and Bernalillo had the most startling surprise in its history.

It soon became known that Don Panteleon was the leader of a gang of murderers who made a business of enticing travelers into a house at Algodones and, after killing and robbing them, buried their bodies in a deep pit under the building. It was a plan of systematic murder similar to the one carried on by the infamous Bender family in Kansas, led by the daughter Kate.[2]

A year or two passed. Mrs. Miera received word that her husband had escaped and, after many hardships, had crossed the desert through the Indian country, and finally had reached California. He vowed he had reformed and was now a respected citizen, under an assumed name, of course, but was homesick and lonesome for wife and children and begged to be forgiven and allowed to return. This state of affairs existed for many years, but as time passes people forget, hearts relent and soften. Finally, after many vows and promises, mingled with the tears and prayers of his family, the good people of Bernalillo relented and Panteleon Miera came home. All this happened before my coming to Bernalillo: I knew nothing about it, and in the meantime had become physician for the Miera family.

One day a stranger, superbly mounted, rode into

[2]The allusion is to the Bender family, a middle-aged father and mother, a young adult son and daughter, John and Kate, apparently of German birth. In the spring of 1871 the family built a house, located some twelve miles from Thayer and five miles from Cherryvale, on the main road crossing Labette County, Missouri, which ran from Fort Scott and the Old Osage Mission to Independence. In the ensuing year they murdered six men and a five-year old girl in cold blood. When suspicion fell on them, they quickly fled. Their grisly crimes were then fully uncovered by the local citizenry. The Benders subsequent whereabouts and final end remains an unsolved mystery. Edith C. Ross, "The Bloody Benders," *Kansas State Historical Society Collections, 1926-28* (Topeka, 1928), XVII: 464-479.

Bernalillo. He had a full-rigged California saddle, was dressed in a handsome corduroy riding costume, and armed with a brace of Colt's forty-fives. The Messick Hotel, the only one in Bernalillo, was next to my store and office and my brother and I took our meals there. The stranger was seated at our table and opened a conversation by inquiring if I knew where he could get a guide to a small town about forty miles east of El Sandia Mountain. I replied by naming a stalwart young Mexican, Marino Lebya by name, a fine horseman and one who knew the country in every direction.

Marino was sent for, satisfactory arrangements made, and the next morning they started early. Several months elapsed and several men successively stopped over at Bernalillo, made inquiries about various matters, and went their way. Later, another appeared, and entering my store asked for the postmaster. I happened to be making up the mail for the next train, so I identified myself, whereupon he asked to see me privately.

Entering my office he showed me his credentials as a Government secret-service man, and swearing me to secrecy stated that a Government official on special business in that section had disappeared some months previously. He had been traced to Bernalillo, where his trail seemed to stop. I asked for his description and he handed me a photograph of a man whom I instantly recognized as the one I had turned over to Marino. A still hunt was on at once for Marino, the young Mexican, but it was learned that he had not been in Bernalillo for some time.

The detective went on to Albuquerque, where he found in a pawn shop a fine gold watch and chain that belonged to the man who had disappeared. Following this and other clues, a searching party was sent over the mountain trail the men were said to have taken and they found that Marino had led him into an ambush, where he was murdered. After taking his valuables, the murderers had covered the body with a pile of logs, set them afire, reducing to ashes everything except a half-dozen metal military buttons that were on his vest. These, and other clues, resulted in tracing the crime to an organized gang. And to the astonishment of all, Panteleon Miera was their leader!

This investigation was carried on with skill and secrecy and in such a way that not a suspicion was aroused in the minds of the guilty.

A short time before this secret-service man came to me, Panteleon entered my store one morning and presented me with a beautiful Navajo saddle blanket, which I have kept all these years and which adorns a couch by my side as I write. He knew I was very fond of fine horses, and when he gave me the blanket he said, 'This is only the *ante*. The first time I go to my ranch I bring you the best horse and saddle I own.'

In thanking him I remarked, 'I hope, Panteleon,

you won't fall dead before you fill the hand.' I have always regretted that the detective did not arrive a month later!

The discovery of the outrageous crime created intense excitement in Bernalillo. During the day Panteleon and one of his men, almost a dwarf in stature, had been seized and thrown into the calaboose back of the Alcalde's home just across the street from my office.[3] The word was passed around to assemble that night at a big warehouse near the railway depot, and nearly one hundred responded.

Details were quietly discussed. Then the meeting adjourned to the calaboose and the final act in Don Panteleon's career was brought to a close. In front of the Alcalde's house stood a stately cottonwood, the trunk of which divided into two branches about fifteen feet from the ground. A dry-goods box was placed on each side of the tree and a lariat was thrown between the two forks with each end suspended over a box. The two murderers were then brought out, one placed on each of the boxes, and the ends of the lariat properly fastened around their respective necks.

The dwarf was agonized with fear and begged hard for his life. Panteleon sneered at his pleadings, and in a strong, clear, and steady voice sang his death song as boastingly as the old-time American Indians we read about. He declared that he had

[3] An *alcalde* is equivalent to a justice of the peace or mayor of a town.

killed over two hundred Americans during his career and was proud of it.

The knots were tied, the boxes jerked away, and his song was silenced forever.

There were seven men in Panteleon's band, including himself. Four of them were captured by Don Perfecto Armijo, sheriff of Bernalillo County and stationed at Albuquerque. They were incarcerated in the jail at that place and later taken out and given the same punishment that their leader and comrade had received. The seventh was the Marino Lebya whom I had introduced to the murdered officer, and strange to say, he eluded all kinds of traps and efforts to apprehend him and for some years was not heard of. There was, of course, a big standing reward for his capture.[4]

I never knew his fate until a short time ago I ran across in a public library Mr. Charles F. Lummis's book 'A Tramp Across the Continent'—a very interesting narrative by the way—which tells of this murder and says that after Lebya escaped to the mountains he organized a band of outlaws which he handled for some years, but cupidity finally won and he was killed for the reward by two of his own band, as Bob Ford killed Jesse James.

[4]Hoyt's account of Miera and Lebya (often spelled Leiva or sometimes Leiba) is at variance with New Mexican newspapers. The more accurate story is found in Philip J. Rasch, "A Pat Garrett Item," *New Mexico Historical Review*, xxxvi (January 1961), 80–82. For more details, see Panteleon Miera entry in *Biographical Notes*.

XXI

I Testify in Court and Call on the Governor

IN MESSICK'S HOTEL in Bernalillo I met one day a stranger who told me of a man he, as a lawyer, was defending at Santa Fé. The man had been tried and convicted and was awaiting sentence. The attorney said he believed his client innocent and was on the way to Arizona for an important witness for the defense. In reply to my questions he said that the man's name was Webb and that he was accused of robbing passengers and mail from a stagecoach near Las Vegas, New Mexico, some time before.

This sounded familiar, so I at once identified myself and told him the story of Webb of Las Vegas, and of Parker's hunt with me, and learned that it was the testimony of this very man Parker that had convicted Webb. My story pleased the attorney beyond words. It was evidently a case of railroading an innocent man to prison for a reward. The penalty then for robbery of stage and U.S. Mail was imprisonment for life. Enjoining silence, the lawyer left for Santa Fé, made a motion for a new trial, which was granted, and in a few days I received a subpoena to appear at court in Santa Fé. Webb's attorney, whose name I cannot remember, had carefully camouflaged details of the new evidence and my identity, but it was rumored that a sensation was coming. As a result, the courtroom was crowded.

I did not enter until court had convened and took a back seat in the crowd where I could listen to the testimony. Parker was the star witness for the prosecution. He was a fine-looking man, and with his long beard, black broadcloth suit, and strong features, could easily be taken for a typical Mormon bishop. He positively identified poor Webb as the man who hired his team on the two occasions of the hold-up of the stage and described the condition of the horses when returned reeking with sweat. He was followed by the driver of the stage during the second robbery, who testified that the outlaws were masked, but that he saw the horses and wagon among the trees not far away and later identified them at Parker's livery stable.

While Parker was on the stand, a gentleman entered, and as he stepped toward the front, was saluted by the Judge and invited to a seat by his side. It proved to be the Governor, General Lew Wallace. This was the first time I had ever seen him.

The prosecution rested, and Dr. Henry F. Hoyt was called to the stand. A good many years have elapsed, but I can still visualize Mr. Parker. We were but a few feet apart, facing each other. His black eyes flashed fire; he glared at me like a wolf at bay, while his face slowly turned to an ashen gray. If a look could kill I should have perished right there.

After the preliminary questions were completed, I was asked to describe in my own way just what occurred in Las Vegas the night of the second robbery of the stage and mail. As the high spots of this story have already been described, I will not repeat them.

Webb's attorney, for reasons, had not even disclosed to his client my coming into the case, so I was as much a surprise to him as I was to Parker. Several times during the course of my testimony I had glanced at him and saw tears trickling down the poor fellow's face. I could imagine his feelings at seeing the life sentence to prison apparently fading away.

Upon completion of my direct testimony, I was naturally subjected to a vicious cross-examination, but I had told the truth and most of the prosecuting attorney's attacks were boomerangs. I was a tyro then as a witness—in fact, it was my first experience. Since that time I have appeared on the stand in court a great many times in all kinds of cases and I have never seen a cross-examination break down *true testimony*.

Before I left the stand the Judge himself took a hand. He had evidently observed the change in Parker's demeanor after I appeared on the scene.

The Judge: 'Dr. Hoyt, you have testified that you knew Mr. Parker in Las Vegas. What was his general reputation there for truth and veracity?'

Dr. Hoyt: 'Your Honor, my personal acquaintance with Mr. Parker in Las Vegas was limited to the night when we were together as I have testified. I do not recall ever discussing his character with anyone. But I listened to every word of his testimony here this morning and, judging him from what I heard, I would not believe him under oath. His testimony was absolutely false.'

More vicious looks shot from Parker and a deputy United States marshal who sat beside him and who, I afterward learned, was also interested in winning the big reward for the capture and conviction of any of the robbers. I do not think the prosecuting attorney was mixed up with it in any way.

The Judge then charged the jury, who brought in a verdict of '*Not guilty*.' From the unanimous demonstration of approval by the audience, it was very apparent that Webb had their sympathy.

As court adjourned I was introduced to General Wallace by the Judge and was heartily congratulated by him for my testimony. As I was pushing through the assemblage toward the front door which opened onto the plaza, some one caught me by the arm and pulling me in another direction, whispered, 'Come this way for God's sake, quick!'

I turned, and it was the Mr. Teats who had the 'star route' contract for carrying United States mail from Fort Bascome, New Mexico, to Las Vegas, and whose vouchers I had signed when I had charge of the post office at Las Vegas. He jerked me through the crowd to a side door into another room, thence through a back door into a sort of corral in the rear of the courthouse, eventually landing me in a back street, where he explained.

He said that Parker and the deputy marshal were so furious at me that they had arranged with a couple of Mexican 'knife men' to stab me from both sides as I emerged from the courtroom door. Fortunately Teats had one of his Mexican mail-riders with him, who overheard the plot and informed him at once. It was doubtless as narrow an escape as I ever had. Although I had a gun and knew how to use it, they would have struck me from behind and I should have had little chance to defend myself.

Modern readers may think this incident rather improbable, but if they will dig up some of the history of New Mexico at that period they will not wonder at the story. They will find records of many killings for less provocation than I gave.

I learned recently from some old-timer that my friend Teats was still living in New Mexico. If he should read this, I hope he will communicate with me. For a hark-back with him I would go a long way.

At first I was for going at once to the Judge to see if the villains could not be rounded up, but after discussing the pros and cons with Teats I decided to drop it. No real harm had been done and to give publicity to the affair would no doubt jeopardize his rider, so we left well enough alone.

When I arrived in Santa Fé I was surprised to

learn that Billy the Kid had been captured and was in the Santa Fé jail. News was not broadcast then as now. So I called on General Wallace at the Palace, told him of our former friendship, and asked for a pass to the jail that I might visit Billy. He sent for United States Marshal John Sherman, Jr., who went with me himself and left me with the Kid as long as I wished to stay.

Before leaving, the marshal called my attention to a pair of shackles he had made to order, not caring to take any chances with his resourceful prisoner. They were attached to Billy's ankles. They weighed fifteen pounds each and were made of the hardest steel known, and were connected to a short heavy chain and fastened with a Yale lock. He seemed quite proud of them, and boasted that there was no danger of losing his man with that brand of jewelry worn. Billy, with his usual smile, came back with 'There's many a slip 'twixt the cup and the lip, John!'

We had a long visit. Except for his irons he was much more comfortable than he had been for years. His life had been little more than hardship and danger since boyhood. His spirits were just as buoyant as if he were free. He was as well treated as possible under the circumstances and had no complaints.

We discussed at length what might have been had he kept his promised tryst with General Wallace, and also what might have happened if he had joined Jesse James. He did not doubt the Governor's good intentions anymore, but commented on the fact that the plan for the meeting placed him at the mercy of any one on the outside who was being tempted by the big reward. He was bitter against John Chisum, who, he claimed, was behind him until conditions in Lincoln County compelled the intervention of the Government and he was outlawed, after which Chisum faded away and left him to play a lone hand.

While in Santa Fé I was stopping at the Old Exchange Hotel on a corner of the plaza, often called the 'End of the Old Santa Fé Trail,' where, at the intersection of a side street and the plaza, stood a petrified tree-stump about two feet high and nearly the same in diameter. Being easy to see, it was one of the first objects to elicit questions from curiosity-seekers and there was always some old-timer near to unload the following:

'There used to be a big tree thar, stranger, all petrified, petrified branches, petrified leaves, petrified birds' nests, little petrified birds sitting on the petrified limbs with petrified songs stickin out from their mouths, ya'as. But during all these years it has been most all carried away by some curious fool strangers.'

I found at the hotel two invitations to receptions that evening. One was from Governor Wallace and his wife at the Palace, the other from Judge Bradford Prince and his wife at their residence. I first paid my respects to the Judge and lady and then to the Palace. At this time Billy the Kid was the principal topic of conversation and everything connected with him was discussed pro and con.

During the evening I strolled into the General's study, where I found him with a small group of friends discussing the Kid. I was made welcome and the occasion, to me, soon developed into a memorable event. The General said that he had heard and read many versions of the battle at McSween's home at Lincoln, and soon after the Kid was incarcerated in the Santa Fé jail, he decided to get a true account of it from one of the two survivors.[1] So, providing himself with a box of cigars and a bottle of whiskey, he went to the jail and, after announcing to Billy that he did not come as Governor but as man to man, asked him to narrate the exact facts of the McSween affair, and handed the Kid the box and bottle. Billy thanked him for the cigars, but said he had no use for the bottle; and in his own way he complied with the Governor's request.

This story the Governor now repeated to his guests in his inimitable manner and it proved to be one of the most thrilling I have ever listened to. The Governor himself was carried away with it and evidently full of admiration of the simple and modest manner in which the Kid told the story to him.

I took advantage of the occasion to refer to my

[1]The McSween battle, which lasted five days, July 15–19, 1878, is ably described in Fulton, *The Lincoln County War*, pp. 259–269.

meeting with Billy in Las Vegas in 1879—not mentioning Jesse James—and expressed my regrets that the Governor's plan in behalf of the Kid had miscarried, and hoped it might still be possible.

The General was thoughtful for a moment. Then he shook his head and replied, 'Too late.'

I have both read and heard all manner of stories about what happened, from first to last, between General Wallace and Billy the Kid. Some are correct and others are not. I knew both personally, have discussed each of them with the other, and with the copies of their correspondence before me, it is very difficult to understand what basis there ever was for the reports of serious trouble between them, threats from Billy, etc.[2] To be frank, I cannot believe them.

I had the pleasure of meeting General Wallace again, some time after Billy the Kid was removed from Santa Fé, and his opinion of the outlaw was exactly the same as it was when he paced back and forth before the fireplace in the 'Ben-Hur' room in the Palace and dramatically rehearsed his visit to Billy in the jail.[3] Returning to my hotel from the receptions about midnight, I found a small party of men discussing former days, and upon joining them learned that their subject was Kit Carson, famous

[2]The extant correspondence is in the Indiana Historical Library, Indianapolis.

[3]During his territorial governorship, Wallace wrote his famous novel, *Ben Hur*, in the study of the governor's palace.

hunter, scout, and Indian fighter. One of the party was an official of the First National Bank of Santa Fé, who, after a number of Carson stories had been told, asked if we would like to see a real souvenir of the old man. There were no negatives, so he led us to the bank, opened up the vault—there were no time locks then—and brought out the old muzzle-loading, octagon-barreled Hawkins rifle with his powder horn, buckskin bullet-pouch, and wiping-stick, the latter still in the bore of the gun, that altogether helped to make Kit Carson one of the outstanding characters of the old West.

Kit Carson was a member of the Montezuma Masonic Lodge of Santa Fé, which fell heir to this outfit when he died.[4] We all wished it might talk.

[4] Jack K. Boyer, director of the Kit Carson Foundation, Taos, New Mexico, states that "Carson did not will any of his personal effects to Montezuma Lodge. His Hawkins rifle later was given to Montezuma Lodge. The location of his powder horn, buckskin bullet-pouch, and whipping stick is not presently known by us." Personal letter, August 12, 1978.

XXII

Jesse Martin's Gold Mine

I was hardly seated in the train on my return trip to Bernalillo when I was joined by a former patient, Jesse Martin, a typical old 'desert rat,' who was in a state of partial intoxication. I tried hard to shake him, but he stuck to me like the business end of a cactus, telling me how much he thought of me and at last could repay me for all I had done for him, etc., etc.; and finally he pushed into my hands a big envelope full of papers which proved to be a lot of exceedingly rich assays of gold ore, the story of which he then imparted in a maudlin manner.

In some way he had succeeded in interesting General Wallace to the extent of 'grub-staking' him, and not wanting to absorb all the riches that might accrue from the deal, he generously (?) took in as a partner a Mr. Lucas, owner of the largest jewelry store on the plaza.

Jesse and his burro had faithfully prospected for some months over a wide range of country, and he had finally landed in a little hamlet, Las Placitas, I think it was called, only a few miles northeast of Bernalillo. He had arrived after dark and, as was customary with his class, slept on the floor of some Mexican adobe home.

There was but one street in the village, upon which the house fronted. As he stepped out next morning his trained professional eye at once detected a peculiar color and formation of the earth in the street. He at once decided it was mineralized and he promptly proceeded to declare and locate a mining claim, with one extension of same, the two covering the town and a good deal of land besides. The notices on these claims contained the names of his two backers and himself.

His activity naturally created intense excitement among the villagers and their first idea was to run him off, but old Jesse was game and, after showing them who was behind him and promising to make them all rich, he practically owned the town. Enjoining secrecy, he employed a number of the men at good wages and proceeded to sink a shaft right in the middle of the street, and when it was down about ten feet, he sacked up a lot of samples, took the train for Santa Fé, and obtained the assay reports he showed me. One can imagine the sensation he created when he reported all this to Messrs. Wallace and Lucas. He told me they were both wild. They gave him a fat roll of bills with instructions to keep his mouth shut, go back at once, sink the shaft as rapidly as possible, while they would prepare a camp outfit and be down in a few days.

On the way to the train Jesse had made several saloon stops and when he entrained and saw me, his gratitude for former favors I had done for him so overcame him that he forgot all about 'keeping his mouth shut'; and that was that.

I thought it all over carefully. Jesse was an old and experienced miner. Everything seemed to ring true. The two claims they had would produce millions. So I decided to take a hand myself. At Lamy Junction I wired my brother at Bernalillo to meet me at the depot with the best team in town prepared to take a trip into the country.

My brother was awaiting me with a very good friend of ours, Colonel Francisco Perea, and his spanking team of black mares hitched to a carriage. Perea was one of the prominent citizens of Bernalillo, formerly a delegate to Congress, and I decided to take him with us.

It was a beautiful moonlight night, the Colonel was a fine driver, and we rolled into the village between midnight and morning. Everything was dark, no one was stirring, so we quietly located an extension on the south end of the property, roused one of the families known to the Colonel, and turned in until morning.

Jesse was sober as a judge and seemed delighted to see us. I did not know whether or not he would remember meeting me on the train, but he did, and frankly told me he intended to stake a claim for me the first thing in the morning.

What seemed to be a well-defined vein of mineral matter, of a yellowish red color, and about twenty feet wide, ran almost directly north and south just about the middle of the street of the village. It was very easy to trace either way. We put two men at work sinking a shaft on the vein in our new mine, which we named 'The Christine' in honor of a daughter of the Colonel, and as Mexican homes of the class here are more or less 'buggy,' we pitched a camp right on our property.

In a couple of days General Wallace and Mr. Lucas arrived with a camp outfit and were surprised to find my outfit in the game, but were apparently glad to see us and pitched their camp near ours. With their sombreros, blue flannel shirts, overalls in the tops of their boots, and guns at their belts, they presented all the earmarks of true Western miners. In assembling their camp equipage, cups and saucers were by some mistake omitted and they substituted empty tin tomato cans for their coffee cups. About two years afterward—possibly longer— I picked up the morning paper at Columbus, Ohio, and read how General Wallace, who had in the meantime been sent as Ambassador to Turkey, had just been entertained at the Sultan's palace in Constantinople at a breakfast where the coffee was served in exquisite china cups rimmed with diamonds. I at once dropped him a few lines asking him if the coffee tasted any better than when he made it himself and drank it from an old tin can in Las Placitas, and enclosed the clipping. In due time I received a reply, written by Mrs. Wallace, to the effect that Turkish coffee did not begin to compare with our 'tin-can brand' even though it was served with diamonds.[1]

From now on the news of this wonderful strike spread like wildfire all over the country. People began to pour in from every direction. A number of newspaper correspondents arrived and kept the wires at the nearest telegraph station hot. Stories were sent out to the effect that all the houses in Las Placitas and the adobe walls around their yards were constructed from this mineral vein and were so rich in gold that people had all moved out and they were being torn down preparatory to being shipped to the smelters. A party came from New York City, sized up the situation, and before they had been there two hours made the Governor and Mr. Lucas a cash offer of three hundred thousand dollars for their holdings. This was in my presence, so I know it to have been a fact. They both laughed at it and would not consider it for a moment. They then had quite a deep shaft, the contents of which seemed to look better every foot they went down.

Remember that, so far as I know, up to this time all this excitement was absolutely due to that bunch of assays shown me on the train by old Jesse. These were conspicuously posted at the Wallace-Lucas camp and were a magnet that drew all who came to

[1]President James Garfield appointed Wallace ambassador to Turkey in 1881, an appointment which followed his governorship of the Territory of New Mexico. He served abroad in that post until 1885.

the new strike. Of course ore dumps around the shaft also helped.

The most picturesque object outside the mine, however, was old Jesse Martin himself. Well supplied with a pocketful of gold—I have always wondered just where it came from—he was dressed in the latest fashions, as he saw them, and was surrounded from morning to night by new arrivals to whom he told with thrilling variations the story of the wonderful strike.

The village beauty was a little Mexican señorita, fifteen years of age—and she *was* a beauty. Jesse began to buy her presents, and after a conference or two with her parents, the entire camp was invited to a wedding. Jesse did not spare expense and it was without doubt the most remarkable function Las Placitas had ever experienced before or since. A number of sheep and two beeves were barbecued, several barrels of native wine were on tap, while a good orchestra came from Santa Fé to supply the music for the *gran baile* that followed the wedding and *fiesta*.

But all good things must come to an end. I began to feel as if I might have come from Missouri after all, and after a private talk with my brother and Colonel Perea, I secured a few of the most promising looking specimens of ore from Jesse's mine and some from our own, took the train for Santa Fé, and spent twenty-five dollars in an assay office. Result, *not a trace of gold.*

Although not a word was said, I think about the same time others began to think they were from Missouri too. At any rate, the crowd—including the Wallace-Lucas outfit—began to fade away until old Jesse Martin was the only American left. The real inside facts of this famous fiasco, unprecedented in the history of mining in New Mexico, or elsewhere as far as I know, have been up to this time a complete mystery. Later I met both General Wallace and Mr. Lucas in Santa Fé and they were absolutely unable to explain it. They had investigated carefully. The assays were genuine. They had not given Jesse a cent after the day he brought in the reports and received one hundred dollars. But during the high tide of the bubble Jesse Martin spent many hundreds of dollars. Where did he get them? No one was ever able to find out.

This fact, however, is well known. Jesse Martin stayed right there, continued to work the mine, and always had plenty of money, at least he did, to my certain knowledge, until I left New Mexico about the first of September, 1881. Some years afterward I met some one just from that section and was told that old Jesse was still there.

His exothermic romance was of short life. He soon found his beautiful young bride trifling with a former suitor; although Jesse was liberal, this was over the limit and she and her entire family—whom he had supported since the wedding—were sent home. All were sad, but Jesse was adamant.

Page B. Otero offers a solution of the source of Jesse's mysterious income that is the most plausible of any I have heard. A few years ago Mr. Otero met a native of Las Placitas who told him that at certain places in this supposed rich and immense vein there occurred little pockets of almost pure gold. He believed that Jesse knew where to go after them, and would do so when he needed money, but that no one else had ever been able to find them.

XXIII

Silk Hats and a Last Meeting with Billy the Kid

ALONZO LIVINGSTONE had been appointed railway agent at Bernalillo and at a recent election we had wagered silk hats on the result. The railway was completed to Albuquerque, and on that date, April 22, 1880, a grand celebration was held in honor of the occasion.[1] Lon and I decided to attend and we donned our new hats for the first time. I suppose there were silk hats in Bernalillo, but I do not remember seeing one until ours arrived.

We arrived early and put up at a new hotel where I was delighted to find my old friends, Mr. and Mrs. Scott Moore, in charge. Everybody enjoyed the parade, and the banquet which was held at our hotel. I met a number of old acquaintances, among them being Mr. and Mrs. A. M. Conklin who had moved there from Las Vegas and who later settled at Socorro, as already told.

Lon and I soon discovered that we were quite conspicuous, as not another silk hat was to be seen,

[1] Although the Santa Fe reached Albuquerque on April 15, 1880, the official celebration was not held until April 22. It is graphically described in the contemporary press. Glenn D. Bradley, *The Story of the Santa Fe* (Boston, 1920), p. 205; *The Weekly New Mexican* (Santa Fe), April 19 and 26, 1880.

but we did not allow that fact to interfere with our pleasure. When we went out in the evening we had to run a gauntlet of wit and wise-cracks, but it was all good-natured. By and by we came to a typical Western dance and gambling hall which was going full blast. It was not long before we attracted the attention of some of the revelers who had been patronizing the bar and who were in the midst of a wild carousal.

We were greeted with wild yells of '*Shoot the hats!*' and the yells were quickly followed by several shots that went high. Since my arrival in New Mexico I had witnessed several similar incidents, but as a spectator only, never before as a victim. A tenderfoot—and we were evidently taken for such— was invariably hazed by oldtimers at these resorts by shooting off his hat, making him dance to the tune of bullets, and usually winding up by compelling him to 'set 'em up' for all hands at the bar. Although the hazing was usually just in sport and harmless, any stubborn resistance on the part of the victim meant trouble and not infrequently led to tragedy.

Naturally I felt that I did not belong to the tenderfoot class and glanced at Lon to see how he was standing the gaff. I knew this was his first experience at this game, as he had but recently arrived from the States. His poise was perfect and he appeared cool and self-possessed. I instantly decided to stand my ground.

We jerked our guns just as my hat was shot from my head. But before anything really serious happened, one of the men, yelling, 'Stop, he's my friend!' bounded toward and fairly hugged me. It was William Nickel, 'Slap Jack Bill, the Pride of the Panhandle,' whom I had met as the leader of a band of horse thieves, on the Staked Plains in the Panhandle in 1878, while in Jack Ryan's party rounding up stray cattle for the LX Ranch, as previously described.

The Lord alone knows, but I have always believed that but for the shooting off of the stovepipe hat from my red head, which Bill instantly recognized, my career would have ended right there. Maybe that bunch did not make up for their onslaught. We had a *bodyguard* from that moment. I wore the ventilated lid the rest of the evening with a good deal of pride and kept it many years as a souvenir; but it finally vanished.

A young man of Bernalillo, George Lewis by name, had owed me a bill of seventy-five dollars for service for some time. He boasted of his sprinting ability and declared he never had been beaten. From his talk I naturally concluded that he was a runner. One day I learned he had received a draft for seventy-five dollars and hoped he might call on me, but he did not. Meeting him with some friends I reminded him of his remittance and said that I had often heard of his prowess on the track, winding up with a challenge to run against him one hundred and fifty yards, the stakes to be a receipted bill from me for seventy-five dollars and his draft for a similar amount. He accepted with alacrity.

Although I had then been in Bernalillo for some time, I had never divulged to anyone that I had ever had any experience as a sprinter, and of course I was not in training. But as I had a feeling that my bill would never be paid in the regular way anyhow, I did not stand to lose very much.

The race was to be run right in the street. The distance was paced off and staked, judges were selected, the purse deposited in Landlord Messick's hands, we toed the mark, the pistol cracked, and away we went. I had always been quick on the start, and before we ran ten paces, I was perfectly confident I would win.

We ran even for one hundred yards, during which I was never pressed for a moment. With the idea that my opponent also might have some reserve power, I decided to *run* the rest of the way and as I passed him I yelled, for the benefit of the natives, '*Adios, Jorge*' (good-bye, George), and easily beat him by at least ten feet. I can't imagine where Lewis got the idea that he could run. I have rarely had an easier man to beat. Any sprinter will realize that when he reads that I did any *talking* along the way.

I was awaiting the arrival of the southbound train at Bernalillo one afternoon in company with two local merchants, Schuster and Bibo by name, and as the Pullman stopped, I recognized Billy the Kid through one of the windows near the rear of the car. I called the attention of my friends to my discovery and they both laughed at me. They had never seen Bonney. From the blood-thirsty accounts they had read of him, they had visualized a different-looking person from the handsome beardless youth in the window, and both declared I was mistaken.

Knowing the stop was brief, I hustled them into the front end of the car and down the aisle toward Billy, who was facing us. He instantly recognized me and attempted to give the cowboy high sign by throwing up his right hand. But his handcuffs compelled both hands to come up together, and this sight, with the rattle of the chain, so rattled the two doubters that they fled in a panic, amidst the laughter of the passengers.

Opposite the Kid sat Deputy United States Marshal Bob Ollinger and his companion Tony Neis, also a deputy. These men had been selected by Marshal John Sherman, Jr., as the best men on his force to convoy the outlaw from Santa Fé to Mesilla, New Mexico, where he was to be tried for the killing of William Brady when he was sheriff of Lincoln County in 1878.[2] It will be remembered

[2] According to Maurice G. Fulton, the Kid was taken from Santa Fe to Mesilla on March 28, 1881, by Tony Neis, deputy United States marshal, and Francisco Chávez, chief of police at Santa Fe. *The Lincoln County War*, p. 387. It should be noted that Olinger is the correct spelling for Robert Olinger, "whose hatred of Billy was well known."

that the race-horse, Dandy Dick, presented to me by the Kid at Tascosa, Texas, was owned and ridden by Sheriff Brady when killed.

After I identified myself to the escort, I asked Billy if there was anything I could do for his comfort. The marshal sat with a couple of forty-fives in his belt and a sawed-off double-barreled shotgun between his knees. The Kid was in high spirits and instantly replied: 'Sure, Doc, just grab and hand me Bob's gun for a moment.' Ollinger replied: 'My boy, you had better tell your friend good-bye. Your days are short.'

Said Billy: 'Oh, I don't know, there's many a slip 'twixt the cup and the lip,' the identical quotation he made to Marshal Sherman when we were together in the Santa Fé jail.

At that moment Ollinger little dreamed that within a month he would be killed by the Kid with that very weapon when Billy made his remarkable escape from the jail at Lincoln, April 28, 1881, by killing also J. W. Bell, a deputy sheriff of Lincoln County.

A farewell was spoken, the train rolled out, and I never saw Billy the Kid again. I have just learned,

---

Adams, *Burs Under the Saddle*, p. 273, states that Olinger was not a deputy U.S. marshal. However, William A. Keleher, *Violence in Lincoln County, 1869–1881* (Albuquerque, 1957), p. 347, *note* 2, states that U.S. Marshal Sherman appointed Olinger a deputy, a view concurred in by Larry D. Ball, *The United States Marshals of New Mexico and Arizona Territories, 1846–1916* (Albuquerque, 1978), pp. 99–100.

incidentally, that in January, 1928, a colorful drama
of 'Billy the Kid,' written and presented by Viola
Vivian, at the Temple of Music and Art in Tucson,
Arizona, was produced with success. In preparing
this play Miss Vivian collaborated with James H.
East, the only man now living of the posse that
captured the Kid.[3]

I experienced quite a thrill upon being told that
'Dr. Hoyt' was in the cast. Had I known of it, I
would have traveled quite a distance to have been
in the audience. Not often can one see one's self in
just that way. It seems that 'Dr. Hoyt' was played by
Mr. Sam R. Falvey. I shall be very much disappointed should I learn he was not 'red-headed,' and I
should like to know just what his rôle called for.

[3] This production was a benefit for the Temple of Music
and Art. It was presented on January 10–11, and was staged
in four acts. An account of what was truly a community
effort is found in *The Arizona Daily Star* (Tucson), January
11, p. 10, cl. 5, and January 15, 1928, p. 4 cl. 1.

XXIV

I Go Back to My Studies and Box with John L. Sullivan

THE RAILROAD had been completed to Albuquerque and construction was going on down the valley. The drug business was slowing up, and as I had accumulated money enough to take me through college, I decided to put the drug store in charge of my brother, ship it to Socorro, New Mexico, and to entrain for the East. I had decided to finish at the University of New York and estimated that it would cost me at least three thousand dollars, so with that amount I started, after turning the cash balance over to my brother to finance the new drug store.

There was no bank at Bernalillo, and as one half of my money was in gold, I packed it securely in my trunk, and with the rest in my pocket, I started about September 4, 1881, for Kansas City. At that time there were no through tickets and no through baggage-checking over several different railway lines. Somewhere between Bernalillo and Las Vegas, New Mexico, the train was stopped by a washout and passengers were obliged to walk about a half-mile to a train on the other side—a not very infrequent occurrence during the early days of the Atchison, Topeka and Santa Fé Railroad.

We arrived at Kansas City at 5 P.M. September

7, 1881, and I at once bought a ticket and secured a berth over the Chicago & Alton Railway for St. Louis, where I had a little business to attend to. Then I went to recheck my trunk, but learned that on account of the washout it had not arrived, and might not come for a day or two.

My first thought was simply to exchange my check and go on, but remembering the gold in the trunk, I finally decided to wait in Kansas City and canceled my berth reservation. At breakfast newsboys began yelling 'EXTRAS'! 'ALL ABOUT THE TRAIN ROBBERY!' and with astonishment and other emotions I read the story of the famous Blue Cut train robbery on the Chicago & Alton Railway by the Jesse James gang. This was the last the James gang ever pulled off, and strange to say the date of it was exactly five years from the day they attempted to rob the First National Bank at Northfield, Minnesota, and murdered Cashier Heywood because he refused to open the vault. At the Northfield affair the gang consisted of eight, as previously noted. At the Blue Cut there were six: Jesse and Frank James, Dick Liddil, Charles Ford, Wood and Clarence Hite.

I waited two days, but no trunk came. The agent assured me it would be all right to exchange checks and go on, and next morning I was in St. Louis. My business finished, I consulted a lawyer and learned I could not collect for my fifteen hundred dollars in gold if it was lost. I told my troubles to a doctor

Jesse James

Frank James
Photos Courtesy National Archives, Washington, D.C.

friend, who strongly advised me to matriculate at the medical school in Columbus, Ohio, where I would find a splendid faculty, receive more personal attention than at a big school in New York, and last but not least I could complete my college course of lectures and graduate at Columbus for less than one half what a similar tour in New York City would cost.

It began to look as if my trunk was gone for good, so I again exchanged baggage checks and in due course of time matriculated at the Columbus Medical College, now the University of Ohio. I found the faculty to be composed of the very best men in Ohio and the college facilities up to date in every respect.*

I lived at a very nice family hotel on Broad Street, just opposite the Capitol building. To keep in trim physically I took out a membership in the Y.M.C.A. Gymnasium and worked out faithfully from one to two hours daily, paying special attention to boxing and sprinting, my favorite exercises. The Sells Brothers' Circus wintered at their farm near Columbus and several of their performers were regular attendants also. Among them was an acrobatic clown, just three feet in height, who was a skilled boxer, and whenever the boys wanted a good laugh they would stage a burlesque bout between him and me. He could turn somersaults and

---

*Some time after I was settled in Columbus, Ohio, my trunk finally came along—gold and other contents intact.

while in the air land on me in fine shape, and after a little practice we could put over quite a show. The Athletic Superintendent was a young man from Boston who, when a boy, had been a schoolmate of that King of the Ring, John L. Sullivan.

Sullivan had climbed the pugilistic ladder until, at this time, he was matched to battle at New Orleans with Paddy Ryan, who then held the championship belt.[1] Sullivan and his staff were putting on exhibitions at principal cities and, while on their way to the battleground, stopped off at Columbus. The pugilist was welcomed by his former schoolmate, who in the afternoon brought him to the Gymnasium where he could carry out his daily training. It was a sheer coincidence that they should enter just as the Sells' clown and the Red Doctor— the name I received from the boys at the Gym— were in the midst of one of their performances. When we had finished and were introduced to the guest, we learned we had made a hit with him, as well as with ourselves.

During his workout, his manager-trainer, Billy Madden, gave the onlookers a cordial invitation to

[1]Sullivan (1858–1918) gained the title with a knockout in the 9th round and a purse of $5,000 from Ryan on February 7, 1882. The bare knuckles fight took place in a ring pitched in front of the Barnes Hotel in Mississippi City, Louisiana. Ten years later, in the first championship fight with padded gloves under Marquis of Queensberry rules, Sullivan lost to James L. (Gentleman Jim) Corbett. Bob Burrell, *Who's Who in Boxing* (Rochelle, N.Y., 1974), p. 181.

'put on the mitts' with the challenger, and several of us accepted, after stipulating it was to be 'sparring for points' only, no slugging. The Y.M.C.A. Superintendent telephoned me at 6 P.M. that Sullivan had sent word that his sparring partner was suddenly taken ill, and could not appear at the exhibition to be given at the Opera House that night, and urged him to 'get that red-headed doctor' to take his place.

Any man with red blood in his neck has more or less of a combative complex if he understands boxing. Taking everything into consideration, I confess I felt flattered by this invitation and my first impulse was to accept.

I had arrived in Columbus a stranger. I learned that the Reverend Frank Wakely Gunsaulus, a very popular minister, had erected a beautiful new church with a unique feature, the entrance being on each side of the pulpit so that one came in *facing* the congregation instead of from the rear. Mr. Gunsaulus explained that this naïve change was to permit ladies already seated to size up the new bonnets and styles without stretching and twisting their necks!

He also had a public reception at his home every Thursday evening, where strangers were specially invited, introduced, and treated generally with the utmost friendliness and hospitality. I had availed myself of this invitation, had become a regular attendant at both church and receptions, and through this medium, together with social favors extended by Professor Hamilton and his wife, I had become acquainted with many of the best people of Columbus, Ohio.

It was late in January of 1882 when I was invited to spar with John L. Sullivan at the same Opera House where I was to graduate in March. At that period pugilists were not classed as social lions. I quickly realized that to accept might mean a lot of very undesirable publicity, and as I was not looking for that, I declined. The Superintendent I think understood, and then invited me to join a box party he was giving for the exhibition.

The house was packed, and we had a fine close-up view of the performance. After our sport at the Gym that afternoon, Sullivan asked me to give his heart a once-over, which gave me an opportunity to look him over generally. He was in the pink of condition and the most perfect specimen of physical manhood I have ever seen, before or since. Since that time I have met James J. Corbett, Patsy Cardiff, Bob Fitzsimmons, and Jack Dempsey—the last-named having in my opinion the most symmetrical physique of them all.[2]

Sullivan was very dark-complexioned, with heavy hair, eyebrows, and mustache, all black. With his

[2]Corbett, Fitzsimmons, and Dempsey were all champion boxers and their ring careers are well documented. However, Burrell, *Who's Who in Boxing* and *The Ring Boxing Encyclopedia and Record Book* (New York, 1978), have no entry for a Patsy Cardiff.

massive form and supple movements he presented a formidable front to his antagonist that night of the exhibition. From his *entourage* he had selected Pete McCoy as his opponent to replace his regular sparring partner. McCoy was either a middle or light heavyweight, I have forgotten which, and was considered to be one of the best boxers of his time in America.[3]

In our set-to at the Gym, John L. was paying particular attention to his defense, and I was invited to hit him as often and as hard as I could, which I soon learned was not difficult to do.

They squared off on the stage, and it was not long before Pete McCoy landed on John L.'s face with a whack that resounded all over the house and was greeted with a roar of applause. In a very short time this was repeated with a harder blow than before. Sullivan's heavy eyebrows began to droop with a scowl, his eyes glittered, he crouched, and began to glide around with the speed and grace of a panther, his face plainly registering rage. An opening appeared and like a flash he landed a terrific blow on McCoy's jaw, knocking him into complete insensibility almost over the footlights. Exactly that would have happened to me had I accepted that invitation!

[3] It would appear that Hoyt is referring to Norman S. McCoy who was popularly called Kid McCoy or "The Corkscrew Kid," who "was a natural middleweight but fought men in the heavyweight and light heavy division." *The Ring Boxing Encyclopedia*, p. 64.

John L. Sullivan went on to New Orleans and, as all the world knows, became the heavyweight champion by defeating Paddy Ryan in nine rounds without gloves, under the London Prize Ring Rules.[4] Paddy confessed later that when struck by John L. it felt as if some one had hit him with a telegraph pole endways.

I saw Sullivan again at St. Paul, Minnesota, in the late eighties or early nineties. He was on a tour that was offering a purse of one thousand dollars to any man who would stand up before him for three rounds of three minutes each, under the Marquis of Queensberry rules.

An employee of the Northern Pacific Railway, Hafey by name, six feet six inches in height and roughly two hundred and twenty-five pounds in weight, was the acknowledged amateur champion among the railroad men in that section, and he decided to go after this purse.

I met him at the Merchants' Hotel during the afternoon and he was very confident. 'Doc,' said he, 'I don't expect to hurt John L., and I shan't try to— but say, there ain't a man on earth with a pillow on each hand that can knock me out. That I know!'

At this time Dr. Ames was Mayor of Minneapolis, Robert A. Smith Mayor of St. Paul, and I had be-

---

[4] Paddy Ryan (1853–1901), Irish by birth, had won the title in 1880 from Joe McAuliffe. He has the dubious distinction of having held the title for the shortest time for any champion. *Ibid.*, p. 181.

come Commissioner of Health of the latter city. Both mayors were friends of mine, and fond of sports, so I gave a party including them, our Chief of Police, Jack Clark, and a few others, and before the performance took them behind the scenes to the star's room and introduced them. John L. was then at the height of his popularity, and happened to be in an amiable mood, so we had a very pleasant call. Learning that we wished to get as close a view as possible, Sullivan had us conducted to the stage, where chairs were provided between the wings, giving us a fine opportunity to see without being seen by the spectators.

The champion stepped onto the stage from our side and Hafey from the other; they shook hands and the fun began. As they squared off, Sullivan actually looked small in comparison with Hafey.

In less than ten seconds an opening presented itself and Hafey was fairly lifted from his feet with a blow under the chin, and but for his staggering against a wing he would have been knocked flat. He was game, however, and came back with a rush, when Sullivan springing straight up in the air, shot his terrific right to Hafey's neck, crumpling him to the floor, where he took the count. The champion stalked to the front of the stage and delivered in a gruff voice one of his characteristic orations. Raising his hand to quell the applause, he said, 'This guy has been bragging around town that he'd win the purse. He lasted just thirty seconds.'

Hafey was dragged from the stage and a bucket of water dashed over his head before he knew where he was. 'Doc,' he said, 'after that first lick I never saw nothin' but stars.'

XXV

Getting On in My Profession

AFTER GRADUATING in March, 1882, in the same Opera House where John L. Sullivan lost his temper and knocked out Pete McCoy, I could not resist comparing the two occasions. As I stood on that stage and received my hard-earned diploma, I wondered what would have happened had I taken Pete's job.

Returning to my old house at St. Paul, Minnesota, in April, 1882, I soon became active in my profession.

During my tenure of office for nine years at the head of the Department of Health of St. Paul, Minnesota, I left a record of handling ten outbreaks of smallpox without the spread of a single case, after the discovery of the outbreak. While in that position I was responsible for the vaccination of over forty thousand persons without a death. There was no mystery or secret connected with my method of handling and checking an outbreak of smallpox. I had compiled a health law from legislation in force in the principal cities of our country and Europe, added sections adapted to local conditions, and had it passed by the State Legislature. That law granted me the necessary authority to act at once in an epidemic emergency, instead of having to call meetings, discuss, argue, and almost fight a lot of politicians before I could get authority to go to the expense of purchasing as much as a postage stamp for the department.

I had a right to be proud of this Public Health Act as well as the manner in which it became a law. I had been at the head of the Department of Health for two years, had made a good record, and expected to be reëlected. Just before the term expired I discharged an inspector for flagrant dishonesty. He was a typical 'ward-heeler,' and the City Council, considering politics only, served me with a private notice to reinstate him or lose my job. I was advised by a prominent political friend to *promise* this concession, and after my reëlection to *forget* it. This idea was quite different from certain principles taught me by my parents, so I promptly turned it down, and was just as promptly kicked out of office. It was understood that my successor had *promised*, but if he did he *forgot* it, and the 'ward-heeler' was loser after all.

I then compiled and drew up my Health Act, keeping it a secret from all but a lifelong friend, Eugene A. Hendrickson, then a member of the Minnesota Legislature. At the psychological moment Hendrickson introduced my bill and—by suspension of rules—passed it through the House before noon. Before 5 P.M. our Senators, Robert A. Smith and Albert Schaeffer, put it through the Senate, it was rapidly engrossed, and before midnight was signed by Governor William R. Merriam and became a law.[1]

This act reinstated me, and the howl that went up from that political Council was long and mournful. Their power and patronage were gone, in so far as all matters pertaining to the public health were concerned. I held the position of Commissioner of Health for the next seven years.

The moment a case of smallpox was discovered in St. Paul, I at once established an absolute quarantine—in one instance a shotgun quarantine—of the case or cases, including every man, woman, and child that had been exposed up to that time, and at once vaccinated the latter contingent. Smallpox cases were quarantined at a hospital for that purpose just outside the city limits, and those exposed were quarantined wherever they happened to be when

---

[1] Hoyt's handiwork is clearly seen in *General Statutes of the State of Minnesota in Force, January 1, 1889,* Volume 2, *Supplement, 1879–1888* (St. Paul, 1890), pp. 929–934.

However, Hoyt's account of the passage of the bill is a bit confused. Hendrickson served only one term in the state legislature in 1885. Although Smith was in the assembly at the same time as Hendrickson, he was a state senator from Ramsey County in 1887–1889. Albert Scheffer, not Schaeffer, served a single term as a state senator from Ramsey County which paralleled Smith's term, 1887–1889. It would appear that someone other than Hendrickson had to introduce the bill in the lower house since the measure in question was enacted in 1889 and signed by Merriam, who was governor from 1889–1893. *Minnesota Biographies*, pp. 319, 504, 675, 719.

discovered. The latter were held for two weeks and then turned loose after complete disinfection of clothing, bodies, followed by the fumigation of furniture and buildings.

Two of the outbreaks occurred in hotels, the first in the Merchants' Hotel, one of the most prominent in St. Paul at that time, owned by a member of the City Council and Chamber of Commerce. Two cases of smallpox were found there, a colored and a white man, both employees. The white man was in charge of the billiard room for years. The darky had never been vaccinated, and his case was the confluent form, while the other, having been vaccinated successfully about ten years before, had only a mild case of varioloid.[2] Both men were at once removed to the hospital, and the hotel, with all persons that had been exposed, was promptly quarantined. This did not set too well with the owner, who made a very strong speech at the Chamber of Commerce denying that there was any smallpox, declared that the Commissioner of Health did not know smallpox from the freckles on a turkey egg, etc., and announced that a suit against the city for a large sum for each day his hotel was shut up would be started at once.

I lost no time in getting a photograph of each of the two cases in the hospital and posted them in one of the windows of the Chamber of Commerce Building fronting on one of the principal streets of

[2]Varioloid is a medical condition resembling smallpox.

the city. In a short time I was visited by Chief of
Police Jack Clark, who said that there was an actual
blockade of the street in front of the photographs
by a curious crowd, and as fast as one group was
moved on another took its place. So I decided that
my object was accomplished and had them removed. No more was heard from the proprietor of
the hotel and the quarantine was kept on during the
usual time.

During that period everybody was not running
around with a Kodak, and those photographs were
considered to be the best photographs of genuine
smallpox in the United States. They became almost
invaluable to me in the matter of vaccination. As is
well known, there is a strong movement in certain
circles against vaccination. In St. Paul vaccination
was compulsory, and each year before the opening
of schools a large number of parents would come to
the Health Department with all kinds of excuses in
an effort to get their children admitted without vaccination. I would then ask these parents if they
had ever seen a case of smallpox. Invariably the
answer would be '*no*.' I would then hand out my
two pictures to them with the statement, 'The man
in this picture had been vaccinated, but the one in
the other had not.' In ninety-nine cases in a hundred one good look was sufficient and they were
glad to allow their children to be protected from
the disease as provided for by law.

A few last words regarding vaccination. It takes

all kinds of people to make a world, but it is absolutely incomprehensible to me how any human being, with any brains, intelligence, or education, can for a moment oppose it. The one fact disclosed by history is that before its discovery and introduction in the civilized world smallpox caused the death of *more people than all other diseases put together*, and that since the introduction of vaccination the mortality is less than that of *any other contagious disease*. This ought to settle the question at once and for all time.

After becoming chief surgeon of railways employing thousands of men, I learned that there was a great need of a complete physical examination of a man before putting him in charge of property of much value or the lives of thousands of human beings. All that was necessary then to be put on the payroll of a railway company was to pass a rather simple examination for color-blindness, and to have the ears tested.

A few of the older lines had what they called a physical examination, but it was far from thorough. After considerable experience and observation I prepared, in May, 1897, and read before the tenth annual meeting of the International Association of Railway Surgeons at Chicago, a paper entitled, 'Observations upon and Reasons for a More Complete Physical Examination of Railway Employees.' It aroused a good deal of interest, was strongly endorsed by a long editorial in 'The Railway Age,' and eventually many railway companies adopted the method suggested.[3]

A political position is anything but a bed of roses, as I learned many, many times during my official term of nine years. The 'in' party of course controlled the appointment and during my entire tenure of office there was scarcely a month passed in which the 'outs' did not make an effort to wipe me off the political map. A voyage in a political ship is a stormy one, from start to finish. I had to meet not only political tricks of every description, but personal attacks of all sorts, even attempted blackmail.

When I first took charge of public health affairs there was no inspection of foods. It was not long before I had a tip that led to an investigation of our meat supply. I had one of my best inspectors—am sorry I cannot remember his name—disguise himself as a laborer and go from one to another of the slaughter houses adjacent and obtain work, staying long enough at each to make a complete report to me of their methods employed.

It was not long before he caught a burly German selling meat from 'lumpy-jaw' cattle. Judge W. T.

[3]The Association's meeting was held in the Medinah Temple and extended over three days. Hoyt presented his paper on Wednesday morning, May 5. The discussion which followed was lead by Dr. W. D. Middleton. The paper was labeled "especially interesting," although no editorial has been found endorsing it. *The Railway Age*, 23 (1897), 385; *The Railroad Gazette*, 29 (May 14, 1897), 344. However, the text was published in *The Railway Surgeon*, IV (June 29, 1897), 51–54.

Burr, of the Municipal Court, fined the culprit the limit, one hundred dollars, and ordered him to the workhouse for ninety days, at the same time saying he only regretted he could not give a more severe sentence.

When this affair was made public, there was a wave of indignation over the city. The result was the establishment of a careful inspection of all meat sold in St. Paul.

Another sequel of this adventure was that there was scarcely a piece of beef consumed as food in St. Paul for a month. Not long afterward a milk inspection also was established.

During the first eight years of my incumbency there were numerous cases of diphtheria every winter, but few during the summer. In 1894, not long after the discovery of the antitoxin, Dr. Kinyoun, of the Marine Hospital staff at Washington, D.C., was sent by Surgeon-General Wyman to Paris and Berlin to investigate and report its efficacy. He returned a very enthusiastic convert.

I at once went to Washington and spent several days with him in his laboratory there. I knew him well, as we were both members of the American Public Health Association, and I was shown the entire technic of the propagation and exhibition of this great boon to humanity. Returning home I reported my findings to the City Council and urged the establishing of a bacteriological laboratory, which was later provided.

In the early days of my service sanitary science was virtually in its swaddling clothes. Its progress and advancement during the past fifty years have been marvelous. Wherever its provisions and methods are utilized, one will find smallpox, diphtheria, typhoid fever, yellow fever, cholera, bubonic plague, scarlet fever, and other infectious and contagious diseases almost extinct.

The human viewpoint is a strange thing. People accept the experience and advice of their shoemaker, plumber, etc., implicitly, with rare exceptions, while in matters concerning the most important asset they have in this world—their health—they will accept suggestions and advice—often a matter of life and death—from any Tom, Dick or Harry they may happen to meet; totally forgetting or ignoring the expert, educated physician who spends the greater part of his life in accumulating knowledge for the benefit of the human race.

XXVI

Chief Surgeon of Volunteers
in the War with Spain

IN THE SPRING of 1898 we were at war with Spain. The world was electrified with the victory of the American fleet at Manila.

My family has been represented in every war of our country beginning with the Revolution. With the promise of being sent to the Philippines, I accepted a commission as Major and Chief Surgeon of Volunteers and was much disappointed at being ordered for duty at Chickamauga Park, Georgia. I served on the staff of General Frederick D. Grant, commanding the First Division, Third Army Corps, during June, July, and August. I was then assigned as Chief Surgeon of the Third Army Corps, commanded by General Frank, which had been transferred to Anniston, Alabama, as the general sanitary conditions were better there.

At that post we were visited by the General Grenville B. Dodge Commission, 'inspecting the conduct of the War' by order of President McKinley. They made a favorable report of conditions there. When I first assumed charge of the First Division Hospital at Chickamauga, it was in bad shape. After sizing up the medical officers of the division, I selected Charles M. Drake, Brigade Surgeon with the rank of Major, who proved to be a good one. He was from Georgia and I picked him for two reasons: he had red hair and he had been chief surgeon of a Southern railway.

Much fault was found with the Medical Department at Chickamauga during the summer of 1898, and General H. V. Boynton was sent by the Secretary of War to inspect it and report. This report he submitted August 31, and about every hospital in the camp was criticized adversely, except Major Drake's which was commended.

When ordered to duty at Anniston, Alabama, I took pains to see that Drake came also. I had gone down in advance of the troops and selected a site for the General Hospital, Third Army Corps, on a beautiful elevation near the city. The water supply at Anniston was an immense spring, which was tapped and piped to the camp of each unit including the hospital. The hospital was laid out in the form of a Maltese cross, surrounded with a wide walk of white sand edged with cobblestones, and in front of the main entrance a fountain played constantly. There were board floors everywhere and drainage was perfect. The ingenuity and resourcefulness of Major Drake was apparent at every turn. I was in the service nearly five years, and saw many field hospitals, but in comfort for the patients, picturesque surroundings, and completeness of equipment, this was the outstanding one of them all.

Secretary Alger arrived early one morning in a

General Frederick D. Grant and Staff
Chickamauga Park, Georgia, June 1898
(Hoyt is seated at far left)

special train, sent for me, and asked to be shown the hospitals of the Corps. There was a switch and side track that enabled his train to pull up very close to the General Hospital. This the Secretary and staff, including Surgeon-General Sternberg, inspected very thoroughly. I instructed Major Drake to keep his staff busy and away from the visitors that the patients might be free to enter complaints if any cared to. Mr. Alger noted this and commended us for it later. No complaints were made that we ever heard of.

On the way to the train I was informed by the Secretary that from what he had seen at the General Hospital he did not consider it necessary to inspect the different regimental hospitals and we returned to the headquarters in the city. He was evidently pleased with what he had seen, and while we were on our way to the city I made bold to tell him of my disappointment in being sent South and requested that I be ordered to the Philippines should any more troops be sent there. He looked at me a moment and answered: 'Major, I will remember you.'

At that time he was doubtless the most harassed and worried man in the country. He was being blamed by many of the leading newspapers for bad canned beef, for typhoid fever among the troops, as well as for about every other mishap since the war began.

Arriving at headquarters he instructed the commander, General Royal T. Frank, to order a review of the Corps and after it to assemble all the officers at headquarters that he might meet and say good-bye to them. This was done, and after a very interesting talk, he shook hands with and said good-bye to each officer as he passed out. When my turn came, he grasped my hand, slapped me on the back with his left, and smiling, again said, 'Major, I will remember you.'

I now decided that he was a diplomat and a good politician, but gave up all hope of ever getting to the Philippines. October 24, 1898, I received one of the surprises of my entire military career. A special order from Secretary Alger sending me to the Philippines arrived with the following clause: 'Upon completion of his attendance before the Commission to investigate the conduct of the war.'

It appears that this was an unusual order. It at once attracted the attention of the newspaper men at Washington who arrived at different conclusions concerning it.

Next morning the 'Cincinnati Enquirer' headlined me on the front page with:

'WARNING TO ARMY OFFICERS. Major Henry F. Hoyt banished to the Philippine Islands for his very radical testimony against the administration when before the Commission, etc., etc.' Wise Washington correspondent!

I sailed from San Francisco in November, 1898, on the Pacific Mail Liner, Rio Janeiro, commanded by Captain William Ward. Some years afterward,

General Royal T. Frank and Staff, Anniston, Alabama,
September–October, 1878 (Hoyt is seated at far left)

this steamer entered Golden Gate in a fog, struck a reef near the shore, and went down, drowning almost all the passengers and officers, including Captain Ward. There was a large shipment of gold from the Orient aboard, but, although searched for by divers from all over, no trace of the missing ship has ever been found.[1]

From the fact that I had friends in Shanghai, my two-day layover there was most pleasant. When the famous Chinaman, Li Hung-Chang, toured the world, he met, and signed up a ten-year contract as Imperial Director of Railways in China, with Captain W. W. Rich, then Chief Engineer of the Soo Railway lines, at Minneapolis, Minnesota, who had been a friend of mine for some years. A former classmate at the University of Minnesota, John Goodnow, was

[1]On the morning of February 21, 1901, the *City of Rio de Janeiro*, owned by the Pacific Mail Steamship Company, was anchored in the fog at the Golden Gate, some three and a half miles from where she foundered. When the fog lifted, Captain William Ward ordered the anchor weighed at 4:00 a.m. and the vessel proceeded on a northeast course at a speed of about eight to nine miles an hour. Shortly thereafter thick fog rolled in engulfing the ship. As soundings were not taken, her exact position was not known to the officers on the bridge. She struck a rock and sank in fifty fathoms of water, taking 131 passengers with her to the bottom. The sinking was near Fort Point. Eighty-two passengers and crew survived. Although her mail bags included valuables, those that floated to the surface were fished out of the water and looted. There is no evidence that supports the assertion that she carried a valuable cargo of gold. This legend has been dispelled in Harold Gilliam, *San Francisco Bay* (Garden City, N.Y., 1957), pp. 185–192.

then the United States Consul-General at Shanghai, and as his charming and accomplished wife had been a patient of mine when a young girl, I was quite sure of a hearty welcome.

I found my friend Captain Rich in a fine building, its furnishings and equipment palatial. His staff were high-caste Chinese who spoke better English than the average American. The state reception- and dining-rooms of Consul-General Goodnow's palace were the most elaborate, richly furnished, and altogether ornate apartments I had ever visited.

After two delightful days, farewells were spoken and our good ship steamed away for Hongkong, where I took the United States Transport Zafiro, commanded by Captain Whitton. I arrived at Manila December 13, 1898.

XXVII

To the Philippines and Service under Fire

UPON REPORTING at headquarters I was assigned as Chief Surgeon, Second Division, Eighth Army Corps, commanded by Major-General Arthur Mac-Arthur, one of the finest men I have ever known, and served with him for nine months. That period included the Malolos and San Fernando campaigns of 1899, in which I personally participated in over twenty battles against Emilio Aguinaldo and his insurgent army.

General MacArthur's headquarters was the Palace, formerly the home of Admiral Montojo, commander of the Spanish fleet destroyed by Admiral Dewey. It was a beautiful building fronting on Calle Gran Solano, its rear flush with the Pasig River, where, by descending a few stone steps, the Admiral could step into his launch and be carried to the fleet. The building was lighted by over a thousand electric lights. The front lawn was guarded by a five-foot stone wall surmounted by an open iron fence of exquisite design, behind which grew a profusion of beautiful tropical flowers and foliage. The building was elaborately furnished in solid mahogany, with silk or satin upholstering, and the floors were polished until they could almost be used as mirrors.

The lower story we used as offices and our commissary; the upper as sleeping apartments. The Filipino bed is unique, much larger than ours, usually of solid mahogany, the posts supporting a canopy in addition to the inevitable mosquito bar, and instead of our springs and mattresses there is a cane bottom, over which is spread a very thin bamboo mat. Two sheets and three pillows complete the affair. One of the pillows, round and larger than the others, is used, when sleeping on one side, between the knees for ventilation. It is known as the 'Dutch wife.'

In the Philippines metallic articles, if not kept oiled, will quickly rust. One of the duties of my 'boy' was to look after my emergency instrument case, always ready in my room, weapons, etc., and for this I had furnished him with a pound can of vaseline. Evidently he was watched by a colony of monkeys on the premises, for on returning from a few days' absence I found an empty can and absolutely everything get-at-able in the room smeared with vaseline by the little rascals.

During December, 1898, amicable relations between the Malay and the American had ceased. Our trenches, occupied by our troops, ran from sea to sea like a horseshoe, just outside the city, while about a mile away Aguinaldo's army and trenches paralleled ours. Manila was under martial law and a ten o'clock curfew obtained. Returning home one night about eleven o'clock in a victoria alongside the big moat surrounding the old walled city, we

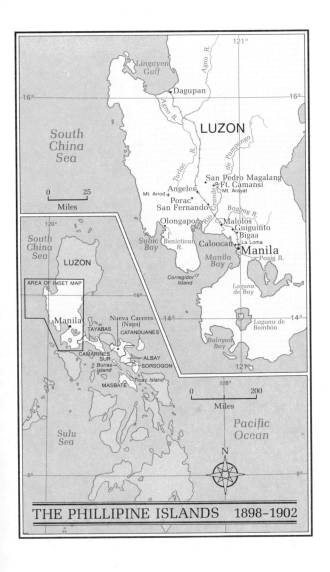

THE PHILLIPINE ISLANDS   1898–1902

heard an unearthly din caused by the croaking of millions of frogs that infested the moat. A boiler factory would be music compared to them. There was a fog. Approaching a street intersection it seems we were halted in the regular way by a sentry who was neither seen nor heard by my *cochero*, and the next instant there was a flash in the fog in front and a Springfield bullet grazing his right side missed me in the rear seat by an inch and passed on through the back of the carriage top, mute evidence of our narrow escape. The *cochero's* seat was in the middle and a little above the back seat, on the right of which I sat.

At the crack of the rifle—that could just be heard above the frolic of the frogs—the horses were pulled up quickly, and I hailed the sentry, who then approached and was worse frightened than the *cochero* when he sized up the situation. A sentry had recently been bolo-ed and very strict orders had been issued that he no doubt complied with. I assumed the role of attorney, judge, and jury and convicted and sentenced the frogs—and we went on our way rejoicing. My *cochero* was different from the average native. He was taller, very dignified, wore a 'Valentino' set of sideburns, and was in fact rather a distinguished-looking chap. He was very faithful and took fine care of my team and victoria.

A few days before the insurrection he came to tell me that his father was very ill in Malolos, and while *mucho* sorry, he would have to go to him at once.

He brought a substitute with him and went his way.

On April 25, 1899, the battle at Bagbag River was fought. General Hale's brigade crossed the river, and flanking a trench on its north side, left it literally full of dead insurgents. I stood watching our soldiers pulling the bodies out of the trench to have the wounded cared for, should any be found, when one of our boys called out, 'Look, here's a Comandante' (Major).

I stepped up and there lay my poor *cochero* shot through the brain. I had him buried and the grave marked, but never knew whether his people found it or not.

Starting about December, feeling between the Americans and Aguinaldo's men became more tense each day. Although the latter were permitted to enter Manila at will, Americans were taboo inside of the insurgent lines.

About 10 P.M., February 4, 1899, Private William Grayson of Company 'D,' First Nebraska Volunteer Infantry, on sentry duty at San Juan Bridge, shot and killed an insurgent lieutenant who paid no attention to repeated orders to '*Halt!*' and the war was on.

In a few moments a roar from thousands of rifles resounded through and around the city, the sound accentuated by the smashing of bullets against the corrugated iron roofs and buildings in all parts of Manila.

General MacArthur established temporary headquarters in front of the famous Bilibid Prison and I parked the ambulances nearby. It was a battle in the trenches on both sides all night long and until about noon February 5, when a general advance of our army was ordered. The boys had been awaiting this a long time.

In due time General MacArthur and staff rode the lines beginning at the extreme left. It was my first experience under fire in battle. We paused for a while when we reached a section of the Utah Volunteer Light Artillery which was in action on an eminence to the left of La Loma Cathedral (Chinese Catholic) just north of Manila. The Utah Artillery was commanded by Major Richard W. Young (grandson of Brigham Young), Chief of Artillery on the staff of General MacArthur. He was a West-Pointer and made a splendid record in the Islands.

While we were watching the effects of Young's shell, Sergeant Bernard Sharpe of the Third Artillery—an organization supporting the Utahs as infantry—was seen to fall a short distance away. As no surgeon was near, I rode over and found he had sustained a severe gunshot wound through one of his knees; so I gave him first aid and sent him back, the first soldier I had treated in battle. Later he was commissioned and is now retired as Major. To illustrate the wonderful progress in my profession I will say that if Sharpe's wound through a knee joint had occurred in the Civil War, his leg would have been amputated at once. In 1899, however, it was saved by aseptic surgery. He returned to duty within two months and later was wounded again, but is still enjoying life thirty years after.

As I rode into the corral at headquarters that night at nine o'clock, my faithful little mount, of Arabian descent, fell dead. We were galloping down a steep decline after leaving La Loma, I near the center of the cavalcade, when my horse tripped over a stone and fell headlong. As I also went down head first, I should doubtless have been severely injured but for the fact that by special permission I was wearing a white cork East Indian helmet, being fearful of sunstroke in the tropics under a campaign hat. I was the only man in the army wearing a white helmet in this campaign.

The battle of Caloocan, February 10, 1899, was fought by our First Brigade, commanded by General Harrison Gray Otis. The center of the battle-line was too broken for horses, so I accompanied General Otis on foot. It was over a mile to Caloocan, and when about halfway, Lieutenant Colonel Bruce Wallace not far away, leading the First Montana Volunteer Infantry, was shot by a Mauser, the bullet entering just to the right of his heart, coming out close to the spine. He tried to tell me something which I quickly stopped, as the blood was gushing from his mouth at each gasp, and as he was carried away on a litter I never expected to see him alive again. He lived, however, and returned to duty much sooner than he should. He was young, ambitious, and as this seemed his chance, he could not resist the urge. As a result, he did not last very long in the service, was sent home, and soon after passed away.

After the battle, Caloocan became General Mac-Arthur's headquarters. In my department the regulations called for two men of the Hospital Corps to be assigned to each litter. My experience in the first two battles demonstrated that even *six* white men could carry a man but a short distance in that hot, humid, tropical climate. I anticipated trouble, as poor or no roads in that rough country, with other reasons, often made it imperative that the dead or wounded be carried on litters for long distances. In Hongkong I had often seen two Chinese coolies with a rope and bamboo pole pick up a piano, or other article as heavy, and trot along with it all over town if necessary with little apparent exertion or fatigue.

I decided to experiment, and made an official recommendation that Chinese coolies be substituted as litter-bearers, giving reasons. My recommendation was at once approved and one hundred and fifty were sent to me by the Chief Quartermaster for that purpose. Except twelve held in reserve, they were distributed *pro rata* among the different units. I detailed Major F. J. Adams of the First Montana Regiment to drill and train them, to be assigned to a litter in charge of a Hospital Corps private.

One night a call came from the trenches for three

litters, and six of our coolies had their first tryout. It was dark, the trenches some distance off, they were exposed to desultory firing all the way, and only one was in at the finish, in spite of the fact that the Americans did their best to pull them along.

Next morning Major Adams got a little leather rosette that decorated some saddle or bridle, lined up the column of Chinese, had the sole remnant of the rout step to the front, and after a spread-eagle eulogy on his bravery, passed on by the interpreter, pinned the badge of honor to his blouse, gave him a hearty handshake—in fact handed him everything that usually goes with a function of this kind, except kissing him on both cheeks—and it is an historical fact that never again did a coolie litter-bearer flunk under fire.

We were at Caloocan for some time, awaiting reënforcements, and had many visitors. The British cruiser Powerful was at anchor in the bay, and one day General MacArthur was visited by Captain the Honorable Hedworth Lambton, Commander Ethelston, and a party of junior officers from that vessel. Lambton and Ethelston were middle-aged men who had seen real service, while the others were youngsters who as yet had never smelled gunpowder. They wanted to look at the trenches, and as everything was quiet, General MacArthur was willing and we started. A broad street led from the church door straight to the trenches. There were at least twenty in the party, and as we neared the trench, a hot

General Arthur MacArthur and Staff at Malolos
Left to right: Capt. Edgar Russell, Maj. Putnam Bradlee
Strong, Capt. James Lockett, Maj. John S. Mallory,
Gen. MacArthur, Maj. Hoyt, Maj. J. Franklin Bell,
Professor Becker (U.S. Geological Survey)

fusillade came from the insurgent lines just across from the Tuliajan River at a range of about a mile, provoked of course by the sight of our party. The music of the Mauser bullets as they 'pinged' over and about us no doubt produced acute attacks of tachycardia in many of us, especially the young Englishmen, as demonstrated by sudden involuntary twitching of their heads. This being observed by one of their veteran commanders, they were further stimulated by an angry scowl and a sharp command from him, 'Gentlemen, gentlemen, no ducking, no ducking,' and the way those sickly spines stiffened up from then on was amusing.

That there were no casualties was due to the poor marksmanship of the Filipino. If they made a hit it was by accident. They were brave and very expert with the weapons they were familiar with, but as the Spaniards never allowed a native to possess firearms, the rifle game was new. Before the advent of the American in the Islands most of the fighting between the Spaniard and native was what might be termed a trench duel. Fighting in the open, or a charge, was unknown.

A young Spanish officer, a prisoner in the insurgent army, escaped and entered our lines. He was a bright chap and entertained us by comparing the fighting methods as he saw them: 'The Filipino, entirely concealed in the trench, simply elevates his gun over the top and pulls the trigger. The Spaniard peeps over the trench top, takes aim, shoots, and instantly ducks out of sight. The American looks over, takes aim, and, as his gun cracks, springs to his feet and looks to see if he has made a hit.' The Spaniard's physical demonstration of this was a scream. He was a good actor.

XXVIII

I Get a Wound in Action

WHILE THE TROOPS were at the front, the Division headquarters in Manila were in charge of a sergeant with twenty-five men, and usually one of the staff would spend the night there. The Thirteenth Minnesota Volunteer Infantry was serving in Manila as the provost guard. The committee on rumors had reported a number of conspiracies and all kinds of plots and uprisings, the usual objective being a massacre of all Americans, but so far all were either dreams or a flash in the pan. But finally the cry of 'wolf' was a real one.

February 22, 1899, it was my turn to come to town and on this occasion I was joined by Captain Charles McClure, Acting Judge Advocate of our staff. We came in about 11 P.M. from a downtown show and were about to retire when, with the suddenness of a thunderbolt from above, the ball opened. In an instant the roar of rifles in action spread over the city, the din being almost as great as in the first battle, that of February 4.

Admiral Montojo had constructed an observation tower on the roof. We quickly repaired to this and were thunderstruck by the scenes all about us. It seemed as if most of the city was on fire. Flames were shooting skyward in every direction and with the shooting and shouting, created a condition that would terrify almost anyone. We did not have to be told that the long-prophesied uprising was on. Several bullets had already entered the building, and after a short conference we divided the guard, McClure taking the Pasig River side while I stationed my men behind the stone wall fronting the street. The headquarters was so well known we felt confident it would be attacked, either by *cascos* (native boats) on the river, or on the street side, possibly on both sides at once.

The headquarters guard were picked men and as both McClure and I were good shots, we felt we could put up a fight. After arriving in the Islands and learning the character of the native, I recommended another departure in the Medical Department, 'that the personnel be armed,' which was approved. I was carrying a Mauser pistol, a ten-shot automatic, the most deadly weapon of its size and weight I have ever run across.

Opposite our headquarters was the palatial home of Don Eduardo Eugester y de la Deheza, a remarkable character. His father was Swiss and his mother a Spanish *mestiza*. He could speak and write fluently five different languages, was an artist, musician, and a successful businessman. With his remarkable baritone voice he had toured Europe several times with Adelina Patti during his earlier career.

He was a strong pro-American and we became

close friends. He had a very beautiful lawn adorned with typical tropical shrubbery, and glancing in that direction I could see a shadowy form of a man skulking through it. I called to him both in English and Spanish to 'throw up his hands,' but he paid no heed, and turning to my detachment I prepared to give the order to fire, but for some unaccountable reason my voice simply refused to work.

During the few seconds that I was dumb, the skulker vanished, and I had one of my men make a détour to investigate and warn Don Eduardo. Returning he reported it was the Don himself whom we had seen. He had heard a suspicious noise and was investigating on his own account. He almost collapsed when told of his narrow escape.

The Minnesota regiment did splendid work that eventful night. Several times bodies of insurgents working toward our building were beaten back by them and by daybreak the enemy had disappeared. They made no attempt to attack by way of the Pasig. Reënforcements having arrived, the army began the northern advance at daybreak, March 25. The battle-line was several miles long, the General and staff near the center. Fighting began from the start and continued all day.

At noon we rested under a gigantic mango, and coffee was being prepared in a nearby ravine sheltered from bullets. An officer from the Japanese army had joined us to observe our military methods in war. Italy was also represented. I started to see if the coffee was coming along all right, and passing a large tree found our Japanese friend squatting on its safe side, his watch in this left hand, the fingers of his right on his pulse. Thinking he was ill, I questioned him.

'No,' he replied, 'I am not sick. Before ze bullets my pulse he seventy-two, after ze bullets he one hundred and twenty. I no like ze bullets.'

He actually made an official report of this to his Government. Japanese efficiency!

The next day we arrived at a bamboo hut in a rice field where a large *olla* full of cool fresh water was found from which everybody was quenching the thirst that Kipling tells us about—only I think he sidesteps water. We were all oblivious of the fact that bullets from a long trench a half-mile away were coming along thick and fast. By this time it was a case of familiarity breeding contempt. An orderly was passing out the water in a tin cup, and just as the Japanese grasped the handle, a large Remington (the insurgents were armed with Mausers and Remingtons) bullet smashed through its center. He evidently knew when he had enough, as he disappeared next morning *sans* any farewell and we saw him no more.

A few minutes after the crushing of the cup, Private Donavan from Minnesota, chief clerk for General MacArthur, had his horse shot dead from under him, and almost before he was on his feet a spent Remington bullet buried itself in his left elbow joint. I at once cut out the bullet and Donavan retained it as a souvenir. This was another wound that in the Civil War would have cost an arm and possibly a life. Donavan made a very rapid recovery and returned to duty.

Even General MacArthur, with all his *sang-froid* under fire, looked homesick, so we moved. When I wrote up my diary that night I find as a finis: 'And I am still alive.'

March 29, 1899, was for me a red-letter day. We advanced early and fighting soon became hot all along the line. The rough country and impenetrable jungle compelled a long détour of our horses by the right flank of the army while the General and staff advanced on foot along the railroad. About 9 A.M., from a thick bamboo hedge, several bands of men could be seen coming, and with the idea they might be bringing in some wounded, we all stopped to train our field glasses on them.

There had been a lull in the fighting for a short time as the insurgents were retreating, but the moment we stopped a brisk sniping began right in front of us at a range of four hundred yards—from a concealed trench, we learned later—and I had the bad luck to be the one man hit in our party. A Remington bullet tore off the iron brace supporting the outside of a heavy leather legging on my left leg, causing a slight flesh wound, and at the same time a spent Mauser bullet buried itself in the muscles of my left thigh just above the knee.

My first impression was that some one had given me a violent kick, but as I staggered back, I glanced down, and the little hole through my riding trousers, together with the dilapidated legging, told the story. Assisted by my hospital steward and orderly, I quickly cut out the bullet and gave both my wounds first aid, and as we were within a day or two of our objective, Malolos, I decided to go on, although General MacArthur urged me to go into Manila and not take any chances. I confided in him that I would rather lose a leg than miss the capture of Malolos, and he said no more.

We entered Bigaa about noon, halted, and I was soon resting on a big Filipino bed upstairs at the railway station, my mind full of the problem of how to transport all our casualties from our advancing front. The retreating army had destroyed all bridges over the numerous streams, except those iron railway bridges over which ambulances and bull-carts could not pass. This resulted in all our transportation facilities being far in the rear.

Before the outbreak Aguinaldo outgeneraled us by getting behind his lines all the engines and most of the rolling stock on the railway in the Islands which ran north from Manila. An old broken-down engine and a few damaged box- and flat-cars were found, repaired by our men, and were now used as fast as the railway track, which the insurgents also destroyed as much as they could, was repaired. But our advance was extremely rapid and our crippled

Manila Limited was always some distance behind us.

The bugle call of 'Forward' broke my rest, and as I limped downstairs I saw in the yard the remnants of a hand-car. Calling my men, I quickly improvised, with these remnants and the big body of the bed from upstairs, the first Philippine palace-car ever turned out in Luzon. With a silken canopy for shade, a bunch of Igorote prisoners as motive power,[1] my train *de luxe* would comfortably carry six to eight wounded men south to the dressing-station, rapidly change from palace to freight-car, and return with a much-needed cargo of rations and other supplies.

Although I was never given credit for this device in pictures, I have seen mention of it in historical publications. The following quotation from the official report of General MacArthur placing its origin may be interesting: 'The excellent service of the Medical Department, as previously reported, has been continued throughout the campaign. The Chief Surgeon, Major Henry F. Hoyt, displayed skill and ingenuity in providing for the wounded under the exceptional conditions which arose in consequence of the ambulances being unable to cross streams over which all the bridges had been destroyed, and the substitution therefore of hand-cars improvised into practical vehicles for the conveyance of the wounded.'

[1] The Igorots, a proto-Malasian people, inhabit central Luzon Island.

The insurgents were so badly whipped at Bigaa that not a shot had been fired before we arrived at the next station, Guiguinto, into which I limped sore, weary, and hungry. In the morning I had pocketed a couple of biscuits for lunch, but I had come across an insurgent hid in a clump of bamboo with his leg broken by a bullet. He had almost bled to death and was crying for water and food. After giving him first aid, I supplemented it with one of my biscuits, which he gratefully devoured.

Guiguinto is on the south side of a wide, deep river with a swift current. The General and staff were on the railway track near the entrance to the iron bridge watching our troops debouch from both sides and slowly pick their way across the river on the iron ties, and incidentally munching chucks of fresh cocoanut passed around by Major J. Franklin Bell (who later became Major-General and Chief of Staff of the United States Army), who had picked up a bag of them as he came through the town.

That scene, with a marvelous Oriental sunset as a background, would have furnished an inspiration to an artist.

In an instant that panorama changed and Mausers poured in a rain of bullets from a concealed trench several hundred yards straight away up the railway track. In much less time than it can be told, five of our men were killed and thirty-nine wounded, many of them in our vicinity.

At my left stood our debonair Division Adjutant-

General, Major Putnam Bradlee Strong, who was shot in his right arm. Between us, a few paces back, Lieutenant F. L. Perry, First Colorado Infantry, was struck over the heart with a flattened bullet, which had ricocheted from the bridge, and was knocked senseless. Private Albert Shaughnessy, Company E of the Twentieth Kansas Infantry, on my right, was shot through his left leg below the knee.

While I was attending these casualties, Lieutenant Davis of the Navy dashed up with his squad and one of the few machine guns in our army, a Colt's rapid fire, had it jerked across the river on the iron ties, followed almost instantly by a gun from the Utah Battery, and between them they soon silenced the volleys from the insurgents.

The welcome rattle of the little hand-car was now heard, as it conveyed the wounded toward Manila and rations for a hungry army on its return. We dined on hardtack and canned salmon and bivouacked on rice straw spread over the railway station platform.

This affair of March 29, 1899, was doubtless the occasion named in the belated distinction with which I was honored in February, 1925, by order of President Calvin Coolidge, as illustrated in this book.[2]

[2]Unfortunately, the original citation certificate has been lost. Therefore, it cannot be reproduced here but may be seen opposite p. 204 in the original edition.

XXIX

'With General Funston's Compliments'

THE ARMY advanced from Malolos on April 25, 1899, and in the forenoon fought the battle of the Bagbag River, a wide, swift stream where the north span of the iron railway bridge had been cut, a spot made historic by Colonel Frederick Funston's swimming from there to the shore, the only *swim* he ever indulged in during a battle in the Islands, various newspapers to the contrary notwithstanding. The battle was fierce while it lasted, and when it was over there were thirty wounded, four dead, and eleven heat exhaustions of our men, and quite a number of wounded Filipinos, all to be transferred from the north to the south side of the river.

The cut span in the bridge made it impossible to use my hand-car. The insurgents had done away with every craft in sight and my men hunted for some miles up and down the stream before they finally found a small canoe with which, paddled by a Kanaka boy and a Filipino prisoner, I had the casualties brought over one at a time. I directed this movement from the south bank. It was hot. The river swarmed with soldiers enjoying a refreshing swim. One in the middle of the stream in front of me threw up his hands and went down. His comrades, thinking he had been pulled down by a crocodile, swam straight for shore, excepting two who dived after but could not find him. Two days later the body was recovered, when it was learned that cramps caused the tragedy.

I had given strict orders that the canoe was for casualties only, and when a soldier with his rifle came over with a dead body and climbed the bank, I was cross all the way through and reprimanded him sharply. He looked up at me, tears trickled down his face, and pointing to the dead soldier he said in a trembling voice, 'Major, he is my brother.'

Registering a canoe-load of mental chagrin, I am not ashamed to record that I apologized and sent him on his way. Military men will understand, as he was a private.

In 1903 I told the story of this incident to a group in an office at Muskogee, Oklahoma. As I concluded one of them shook hands with me and identified himself as the man I had 'bawled out' on the banks of the Bagbag.

A short distance north of the Bagbag is the Rio Grande de Pampanga, by far the largest stream in that part of Luzon. On its north bank, opposite the town of Calumpit, the insurgent army was strongly entrenched and now commanded by General Antonio Luna. He was the only real military man the insurgents had, and in my three years of active field service in the Islands was the only Filipino general

U.S. Army entering Malolos, Philippine Islands
Courtesy National Archives, Washington, D.C.

officer I ever saw on a battlefield. He was equipped
with artillery and we were facing a real problem.
General MacArthur called a council of war, and after discussing the situation stated that there was a
Medal of Honor for the man who presented a practical plan for crossing the river. Many times in later
years I have heard the late General Frederick Funston's exploits belittled, even by military men.
These men always get 'a rise' from me. There were
many officers in that army with much longer military experience and training than Funston. Every
officer there had the very same opportunity to distin-
guish himself. April 27, 1899, he won the star of a
Brigadier-General by his famous crossing of the Rio
Grande on a raft, putting the entire army under
General Luna to flight, as all the world knows. He
was a big little man.

May 31 the army crossed the Rio Grande, the
objective being San Fernando, which was captured
and entered May 5 after a hotly contested battle at
Santa Tomas the day before. Colonel Funston was
wounded there, and while the injury was being
dressed, he was handed a cablegram by the signal
officer, Captain Edgar Russell (who later became
a Major-General and Chief of the Signal Corps
of all the American forces during the World War),
from Washington, promoting him to be a Brigadier-
General.

San Fernando was quite a city, built on the north
side of a river of that name. It had many beautiful

homes, richly furnished. But all of them were abandoned. A proclamation was issued, however, that soon brought many of the inhabitants back. I utilized most of my spare time in going among them with the strongest American propaganda and did all I could to gain their confidence. My knowledge of conversational Spanish, picked up in the Panhandle, was of immense advantage to me.

I learned that they firmly believed that few Filipinos were killed in battle, but that the American losses were enormous. Aguinaldo had a portable printing press on a bull-cart and issued a daily edition of war statistics, every word of which the natives believed. We found these bulletins scattered along the entire route—or should I say rout? According to Aguinaldo's figures the United States was almost depopulated, killed in battle by his brave Filipinos.

This information I imparted to General MacArthur one day in the presence of General Funston, now commanding our First Brigade, and suggested that after the next scrap—they were attacking us every few days—we bury their dead in the cemetery right in San Fernando as an object lesson, instead of on the battlefield as was customary.

In my copy of my official reports I find that we were attacked in considerable force June 16, 1899, most heavily in front of the First Brigade. We had one man killed and fifteen wounded. The Filipinos had thirty wounded and fifty-nine dead. This very unusual proportion between wounded and dead was due to the fact that they always had about four men to a gun and made the most strenuous efforts to remove all casualties as fast as they occurred.

This affair was on our left, some distance away, and I did not get out to it. A soldier entered, saluted and announced, 'I have something for the Major downstairs with General Funston's compliments.' I stepped to the window and saw a strange sight. At the curb in front of our headquarters, the beautiful home of a wealthy planter, stood two Government wagons with sideboards, each filled with dead Filipinos. It was a gruesome spectacle. General Funston had evidently remembered my suggestion and had done his part. Most of the San Fernando refugees had returned and the street was filled with very surprised and excited natives. Never again did they accept the report of no Filipino losses in battle.

I sent for a large squad of prisoners, who dug a long deep grave in the cemetery, but when ordered to transfer their dead comrades from the wagons, they absolutely refused. I learned that for some superstitious reason they never touched with their hands a body killed in battle. With ropes, however, they did the work readily enough.

While at San Fernando we had a number of guests. Senator Albert J. Beveridge visited us for nearly a week. I had just established the first Field Hospital in the Islands by selecting five commodious houses adjoining and connecting them in the rear by a sheltered bamboo porch. Mr. Beveridge several times visited my new hospital. He visited the firing lines also with all the nonchalance of a veteran, and all in all he proved to be a very welcome visitor. He delivered a notable speech in the United States Senate, July 9, 1900, on the 'Policy of the Philippines' and, in referring to the climate, mentioned me as his authority.[1]

An ambulance brought four young physicians from Johns Hopkins University, Simon Flexnor, Llewelyn F. Barker, Joseph Flint, and W. F. Jay, to study tropical diseases. Like most young Americans, they were wild to get a taste of real war at the front, and I made it my business to see that they did. As I remember, they acted also as vets and I was quite proud of my company.

Conditions at San Fernando were ideal if one wished to show a visitor just how it looked and felt to be on a real 'firing line.' The enemy were strongly entrenched but a short distance away on three sides of us. All that was necessary to start something was to walk or ride a short distance beyond our outposts. The Filipinos did the rest. I should also add that it was not always necessary to throw out bait.

They were fighters, and if they had been trained

[1] Beveridge in his speech commented: "Major Hoyt, chief medical officer with MacArthur, told me San Fernando is as healthy as the average town." *Congressional Record*, 36th Cong., 1st Sess., p. 705.

Town Square, Malolos, Philippine Islands
after its capture by U.S. Army
Courtesy National Archives, Washington, D.C.

as marksmen as is the average American, we should be fighting them yet, if there were any of us left. That little bantam-lightweight champion boxer—Pancho Villa I think was his name—is a good representative of the race.

Aguinaldo, suffering a continuous performance of defeat, forced the population of each city, town, or village to evacuate as his army retreated, after setting fire to their homes and buildings. He had read of the historic victory due to the burning of Moscow and aspired to the title of Alexander I of Russia, as well as to that of the 'George Washington of the Philippines,' as he was already called by his people, but he had overlooked the difference in climatic conditions and no one suffered from *his* bonfires but the poor natives.

Where they disappeared to or how they subsisted for a time would be difficult to say. The Filipinos were so cocksure of victory that no thought of defeat was even dreamed of. It all happened so suddenly that they could carry but little of their belongings in their precipitous flights and consequently millions of dollars' worth of their personal property had to be abandoned.

Fortunately for them our advance was so rapid that this incendiary plan was necessarily incomplete. It was certainly pathetic to enter these abandoned communities and find the utmost confusion there. Every imaginable kind of household goods, clothing, silverware, beautiful paintings, and musical instruments, including pianos and harps, were all scattered about in almost every direction.

Under Spanish rule, if the native prospered, some charge would be trumped up against him, he would be thrown into the famous Bilibid Prison, his wealth confiscated and he himself forgotten. Therefore they concealed their funds as best they could, avoiding banks as they would rattlesnakes.

The Mexican peso was the most common medium of exchange, and as this is both heavy and bulky, many thousands of them were left during this exodus. When Malolos was captured, several large safes were found in the Treasury building of the Philippine Republic, containing a considerable sum in silver and a lot of valuable bonds, etc., showing how confident they were of victory.

After the return of many of the inhabitants, an old Chinese merchant came one day asking that he be allowed to take some money to Manila in a box-car I had fitted up as a hospital car, fearing robbery if he took it in the usual way. I consented, and down he came in a vehicle with five good-sized baskets of pesos, amounting to thousands of dollars.

General Lloyd Wheaton, commanding a brigade in our division at San Fernando, selected for his headquarters a very beautiful residence adjoining General MacArthur's. On the ground floor was a fine billiard table on a most handsome tile floor. After confidence was restored and people were returning, the owner of this property appeared with a retinue of peons one day and requested authority to 'remove some of his property,' which was granted.

Under the eyes of our soldiers, the peons dug up a section of the floor under the billiard table and took out some twenty thousand pesos!

XXX

Home and Back Again

DURING THE advance from Malolos I was seized with a severe attack of amœbic dysentery. I gradually grew weaker until we reached San Fernando, where, on July 25, 1899, after fainting away, I had a conference with General MacArthur and decided to go to a hospital on Corregidor Island at the entrance of Manila Bay. Major G. F. Shiels, Brigade Surgeon, was announced as my successor.

I had, however, delayed too long, and in spite of the best of care and treatment, grew slowly worse. A consultation was held and I was ordered home on sick leave and sailed, August 23, on the good ship Valencia commanded by Captain Lane.

The change and sea air did wonders and I began to gain strength at once. The day we arrived at Nagasaki we encountered a terrific typhoon in which several thousand Japanese fishermen were caught out and drowned.

After a stop-over of two days, the anchor was weighed, steam on, and the ship just beginning to swing around, when we were signaled to stop by an official launch that dashed alongside. Two Japanese officers, in full dress, brass buttons, gilt trimmings, and armed with guns and swords, climbed up the rope-ladder and over the rail like nimble acrobats.

'What's the matter, gentlemen?' says Captain Lane.

'You no pay ze laundry bill,' was the reply.

'!!!!!!!!!!?' says the captain, turning to his first officer, who replied, 'Wait a moment,' and went below. Returning with a large bundle, he spread out on the deck five white uniforms which were absolutely ruined. They were full of holes and discolored in spots, evidently the result of a strong acid or chemical.

With a disgusted look and a wave of his hand toward the exhibit, Captain Lane indicated that the incident was closed. But not much! With a most elaborate Oriental salaam, accompanied with a shrug of the shoulders and a gesture of his hands— such as may be seen occasionally on the East Side, New York City—the little official said, 'You pay ze bill o' you no go. If you like you sue ze laundry man'—just like that. 'Ze bill' was paid.

As the departing officers slid over the rail I asked Captain Lane what would have happened if he had refused to pay up. Pointing to a battery of big guns on the side of a mountain overlooking the harbor, he replied, 'They'd have blown the ship out of the water with one volley.'

The United States Transport Valencia had on board a regiment of American soldiers, the First Montana Volunteer Infantry. I wonder if an incident like this could have happened with people of any other nation in the world? I thought of the little Japanese officer making a governmental report of the effect of a battle on his pulse.

The Valencia, some years later, was shipwrecked and lost on the west coast between San Francisco and Alaska. I landed at San Francisco September 24, and rejoined my family in Chicago four days later.

Near the end of my leave of absence I learned that the United States Transport Thomas was to sail in a few days from New York to Manila via the Suez Canal, and wired the Secretary of War for permission to return to duty on that ship. My request was promptly granted and I climbed up the gangway of that fine vessel the morning of November 3. On board was the Forty-Seventh Regiment, Volunteer Infantry, which was commanded by Colonel Walter Howe. Being fresh from the Philippine campaign I was a welcome guest, as but few of that command had ever experienced real war.

The Transport Thomas—just remodeled at the Cramp Shipyard—was very much in the news and was visited that morning by a party of New York ladies whom I assisted in escorting on a route of inspection over the vessel. Among them were Mrs. Russell Sage and Miss Helen Gould.

During the day I renewed my friendship with Major Putnam Bradlee Strong and Captain Francis Burton Harrison, and in the evening, still having some sporting blood left, I watched Jim Jeffries knock out Sailor Sharkey in twenty-five rounds in a fighting match held at Coney Island.

After a most delightful voyage the Thomas arrived at Manila the last week in December, 1899. I found many changes had occurred during my absence. Aguinaldo's army, after sustaining numerous defeats without a single victory, disbanded, hid their rifles, and for the next two years a guerrilla war was on. During the war many letters from American soldiers describing the Filipino people were published in their home newspapers. These sometimes came back to the Islands and were seen by the natives. At first they were amused, but eventually became indignant at continually being described as savages, head-hunters, and even cannibals.

Before the war began I had met and known many of the better class of the people of Manila. A few days after my return to Manila I was waited upon by many of my former acquaintances and presented with a photograph of a group of typical Filipino ladies of the *gente fino* class of Manila, dressed in their national costume. I was requested to have this circulated among my friends in America, that they might see for themselves that all Filipinos were not savages. A copy of this photograph is shown in this volume and speaks for itself. Thirty years have passed since it was taken and it might provoke a smile from the Manila flappers of today, but I doubt if they could produce a better picture.

General MacArthur had become Military Governor of the Islands. General Frederick Dent Grant had arrived and at his request I was assigned as Chief Surgeon on his staff and at once reported for duty at his headquarters at Angeles, a station on the Manila-Dagupan Railway, some distance north of San Fernando.

The guerrilla war was a succession of ambushes and night attacks by the enemy and retaliatory raids by the Americans. To obtain reliable knowledge of the situation General Grant called a meeting at Malolos of the heads of the municipalities in his district—which encompassed the most populous and wealthy section of Luzon. At this conference the Filipinos informed the General 'that they had all signed a document *with their own blood*, never to submit to any government but their own.' Thanking them for their frankness and stating in substance that he was glad to know just where they stood, General Grant adjourned the meeting and began active preparations for war. Wearying of having his troops chasing bushwhackers through tropical jungles on foot, he made request for and was supplied with about four hundred broncos from Oregon, and after he organized what was known as 'Grant's Mounted Scouts,' the war became another story. In all official and War Department records this remarkable organization appears as the 'Fifth District Scouts.'

One of their 'hikes' was during the rainy season, lasting over twenty days, during which there was a

daily downpour, with one exception. On this hike
we discovered, captured, and destroyed over a million pounds of rice, concealed in almost inaccessible strongholds high in the mountains, along
with a considerable quantity of various military
supplies. During these hikes both officers and men
shared alike in food, shelter, and hardships.

One day we were on a jungle hike following a
sinuous trail, single file, that brought us to a boggy
spot, and after plunging through it, the General and
staff halted to see that all crossed in good shape.
After about a hundred had passed, the bog, especially in one spot, became almost bottomless and
warning was passed back the line. Finally a troop-
er's horse in crossing became unmanageable, and
while floundering, both horse and rider went down
out of sight in the mud. Struggling out, the soldier
paused a moment to wipe the mud from his eyes,
and taking one look at himself and the horse, he
remarked, 'Damned if I seed any pictur like this in
the office whar I 'listed!' Even General Grant, stern-
faced in war, got a good laugh.

On one of our night raids we were on a jungle
trail more or less muddy most of the way. With
foliage and vines meeting above us, intensifying the
darkness, our progress was slow. The General preceded me on an iron-gray horse which I could see
but dimly and I was closely followed by my orderly. A drooping vine jerked off my cork helmet, and
as it struck the mud just behind my horse I called to

Filipino Maidens, about 1899
Courtesy Library of Congress, Washington, D.C.

the orderly to pick it up. He didn't see it or hear me and the helmet sank deep in the mud under his horse's hoof. My temper was usually under control, but this was just too much and I warmed up the atmosphere with some real old Panhandle profanity. Next day after dinner the adventure was being discussed when, turning to me with a droll expression, General Grant remarked, 'Doctor, I have known you some time and was under the impression that you were a very pious man, but last night I *changed my mind.*'

Some distance from Angeles stands, in the center of a fertile plain, an extinct volcano, Mount Arayat, a beautiful majestic peak, almost a perfect cone, and covered with a dense tropical forest. In an almost inaccessible part the insurgents established a supply dépôt defended by a large garrison in a position they thought impregnable, part of the approach to it being the bed of a winding mountain stream where they could ambush an attacking enemy in a hundred places.

Through the medium of *their* signal corps, the pounding of a club against a tree-trunk, producing a booming sound that carried a long distance, the Filipinos were kept advised of our movements, and often sallied out, ambushing our supply trains, and other small bands of troops. In one of these attacks they had captured five Americans.

Their stronghold, long a secret, was finally found, stormed, and captured by our troops—one of the most remarkable achievements accomplished during the guerrilla war. The stronghold was built on the edge of a sixty-foot precipice. Just before they abandoned it, the insurrectos dragged out the five starved, emaciated, and manacled Americans, placed them on their knees along its edge, shot them, and boloed them.

Three were dead, but two managed to roll off the edge and, their fall being arrested by shrubs along the wall, they reached the bottom still alive and were tenderly taken to the hospital at Angeles.

They hovered between life and death for weeks, but finally recovered. The surgeon who had brought them back was First Lieutenant P. C. Fauntleroy.

They were kept in a private room and their recovery kept secret. In all the publicity given this affair at the time, the five were reported killed. Commissary Sergeant Christian Peterson and Private Edward H. Norvell of Company B, Twelfth United States Infantry, Privates Joseph E. Cook, C. C. Cook, and Brown of Company B, Ninth United States Infantry, were these unfortunate heroes. The two first named were the survivors.

Later General Aquina, who commanded this stronghold, was captured and tried before a military commission for murder. He positively testified that he ordered the Americans released and then fled (excepting Antonio Luna, all Filipino generals *led* retreats), but a major commanding the rear guard had committed this atrocious crime, with a squad, all of whom he later court-martialed and shot. At the completion of his testimony a dramatic scene was presented. The two supposedly dead victims were carried in and gave *their* testimony. They had been dragged to the edge of the precipice, shot down with one volley, followed by a second, by the order and in the presence of this perjured man, who, to make sure his work was complete, personally attended to the *golpe de gracia* (stroke of mercy) by having them carved up with bolos. General Aquina received the punishment he deserved.

The gallant assault and capture of Fort Camansi was by Companies B, K, and L, Twenty-Fifth United States Infantry (colored), commanded by Captain Leonhaeuser. It was a remarkable performance and deserves unstinted praise.[1]

As a rule, General Grant and his staff accompanied these punitive expeditions, but missed that one, fought January 6, 1900, on account of being on an inspecting tour in another part of the district.

[1] The action referred to began on the night of November 17, 1899, when 400 black soldiers of the Twenty-fifth Infantry, headquartered at Bamban, learned that a large number of insurgents were some fifteen miles distant at O'Donnell. Taking a roundabout way through the foothills of the Zambales Mountains, Captain Leonhaeuser and his command caught the insurgents by complete surprise at sunrise. The white officers in charge of the attack force praised the black troops in the highest terms for their gallantry in action, as did an Associated Press story. One sergeant was recommended for the Medal of Honor. Willard B. Gatewood, Jr., *Black Americans and the White Man's Burden, 1898–1903* (Urbana, Ill., 1975), pp. 266–267.

XXXI

Raids, Hunts, and House-Parties

BUT WE did not play the game of war all the time. We lived in a beautiful house where many visitors were attracted by the hospitality and social qualities of General Grant, who was also fond of week-end and house-parties selected from his numerous friends at Manila.

A most delightful house-party was held at the Angeles headquarters, the guests including the reigning belles at Manila, the two beautiful daughters of Judge Henry Clay Ide, member of the Taft Civil Commission, who later became Governor-General when Mr. Taft was appointed Secretary of War.[1] Other members of the party were two charming New York girls, Miss Margaret Astor Chandler and a Miss Livingstone, on a trip around the world, and

[1]President McKinley appointed a Second Philippine Commission, headed by Federal Circuit Judge William Howard Taft, on April 7, 1900. The commission's charge was to establish a civil government in the islands. Its success was steady: on June 21, 1901, all military government in the islands was terminated except in those areas still in a state of rebellion. Congress confirmed the Taft Commission and provided for its retention as an element in the governance of the islands in the Philippine Government Act, July 1, 1902. Richard B. Morris, ed., *Encyclopedia of American History* (Rev. ed.; New York, 1965), pp. 292, 294.

Judge George R. Harvey, wife and son, and others whose names are forgotten. Mrs. Harvey is my sister. General Grant, never having seen Fort Camansi, arranged for the party a picnic in the vicinity of this wild picturesque scene of tragedy and battle. The party was escorted by a strong body of his mounted scouts, and the ladies were transported in ambulances. Miss Anna Ide (who later married W. Bourke Cockran) decided she preferred to go on horseback. A Filipino racing pony was brought with a Whitman saddle which she mounted *sidewise*, having no riding habit, and we were off. On account of the dust I suggested to Miss Ide that we take the point. After passing the ambulances and the long column of troopers at a lively gait until we led, I called to her to slow down. But she kept right on. Thinking she did not hear me, I spurred up to overtake her. My mount, a good American horse, but not fast, was unable to lessen the distance between us and it dawned on me that her pony was running away.

Turning in my saddle I saw that the first man behind was a handsome young surgeon I had detailed with the scouts. Knowing he had by far the speediest horse in our District, I yelled to him to overtake Miss Ide, as her horse was running away, and he passed me almost as if I were standing still. I kept on at top speed, and to my wonder the young surgeon—whom I had already visualized as a life-saver riding to a romantic dénouement—instead of catching or stopping Miss Ide's pony, flew on past, and my romance faded. He had hardly passed her when I saw her sway in her saddle, and the same instant a swerve of her mount threw her to the left, headlong into the jungle skirting the trail. I reached her first. She was unconscious and had sustained a fracture and dislocation of an arm and wrist. Giving her first-aid treatment, I carried her back to Angeles and sent her home. It appeared that as the surgeon came up behind the pony, his own horse began to swerve, so he kept on with the idea of getting ahead, blocking the trail with his horse, and stopping the runaway, a plan that would have failed even if Miss Ide had not been thrown, as her pony would have dashed into the jungle. If my surgeon had ever been a cowboy with his fast horse he would have made a wonderful rescue.

So that the reader may realize that these house-party mounted escorts were not for show only, I will tell of a jaunt to Porac, a small town some distance from Angeles. It had been captured and re-captured several times and now was said to be pro-American. It was a picturesque spot, the town built on both sides of a beautiful mountain stream, and had never been visited by a white woman.

Sending word to the Presidente that on a certain day a party of Americans would call and pay their respects, General Grant, with the usual escort, took a house-party, and after a ride through all kinds of tropical scenery landed at Porac, where we were received with the utmost cordiality and hospitality. Natives had flocked from everywhere to see the *mujeres blancas* (white women). A splendid collation was served, each guest receiving a unique menu, made by a barefoot native with his pen, coached in his English and spelling, not entirely successfully, by a soldier in the small garrison there, his artistic sketch on each a bit different. Barring his natural artistic talent and dexterity with a pen, he was totally uneducated.

A very excellent native band discoursed sweet music and after the feast provided the music for a *gran baile* (grand ball) in our honor. They had even shipped ice from Manila, nearly a hundred miles away, for the champagne.

After all this peaceful and delightful affair, when just about halfway home, the advance guard, under Lieutenant Chauncey B. Humphrey, was vigorously attacked by a strong force, which were quickly put to flight with considerable loss, but with no casualties on our side. In looking over the war reports I found no mention of ladies being behind this affair.

Three young American bachelors of prominent families, Stephen B. Elkins, Jr., of West Virginia, W. S. Wheeler, of Philadelphia, and Earle Alexander, of Elizabeth, New Jersey, supplementing a visit to the Paris Exposition by a trip around the world, landed one day at Angeles.

Among other entertainments they were given a grand hunt on Mount Arayat after deer and wild boar, of which there were plenty in the great canyons and almost impassable jungle forests of that mountain. I describe this, as it was about the most interesting sport I had ever enjoyed, although I had been after game during the seasons every year since I was big enough to handle a gun. In addition to the game mentioned, there were monkeys, parrots, and the jungle fowl, the latter a beautiful bird from whence evolved the domestic fowl.

Don Luciano, the *Alcalde* (mayor or justice of the peace) of San Pedro Magalang, a small *barrio* (village) at the west foot of Mount Arayat, was notified by General Grant to prepare for a hunt. We arrived at the *barrio* the evening before the day set for the hunt, and found Don Luciano had provided quite an entertainment in our honor. An orchestra of fifteen pieces gave us a concert during a dinner of six or eight courses and kept it up till bedtime.

The preliminaries had all been arranged and we had nothing to do but enjoy ourselves. At four o'clock in the morning our slumbers were broken by musical blasts from a hunting horn, made from the horn of the *carabao* (water buffalo). While waiting for horses to be saddled, after a breakfast of eggs, fried potatoes, bread, butter, bananas, oranges, and coffee, we found a small army ready, seventy-five natives, thirty *carabao* packing hunting nets, and over one hundred dogs. As we appeared, the natives, each carrying a bolo, at once fell into line and saluted, showing conclusively that they were

ex-insurgent soldiers. In addition to our orderlies
and my hospital steward, we had come with an escort
of only ten troopers.

A big bolo hitched to a native in the jungle is bad
medicine, and as I knew we should later be strung
out some distance apart and as I had been 'close up'
with the Oriental character for two years, I began to
feel just a little dubious, commonly called *scared*.
Glancing around I saw several upright hardwood
posts, each about the size of a man, portions of the
ruins of a sugar mill. They were in line to the right
of the natives and about fifty yards distant.

An observer would naturally think I was unarmed, as I usually carried my Mauser pistol concealed, and not wishing the natives to think I might
be an easy mark, I decided to give them an object
lesson. There was a light spot about the size of a
man's hand on the flat side of one of the posts facing me, and jerking my gun from under my left arm
I put ten bullets into that spot as fast as I could pull
the trigger, shooting as accurately as when I used to
knock down the beer bottles behind Howard &
McMasters' store with Billy the Kid.

As I anticipated, this diversion astonished them,
and, although the Malay is more or less stoical, they
quickly broke ranks and crowded around my target
chattering away like magpies, evidently impressed
as much as I could wish.

My 'object lesson' was doubtless unnecessary, but
it did no harm, and one can never tell.

The 'hunting nets' were constructed of hempen cordage a half-inch in diameter, four-inch mesh, six feet high, and fifty feet long. The mountain we found intersected with trails of loggers where the logs were dragged down by *carabao* tandem teams, and one of these was selected by the *cazador* (head hunter) who directed the pitching of the nets as the *carabao* passed along. One after another the nets were securely fastened in an upright position to the foliage edging the trail, and when all were up, they formed a six-foot fence of at least a half-mile in length, with a native stationed at each section.

All this was accomplished with military precision, the *cazador* giving his orders partly with his horn and partly by strange shrill cries that could be heard for a long distance through the forest.

All our party had noticed the military manner of the natives and their unexpected numbers, and on our way to the mountain we quietly decided on a plan of distributing ourselves along the line to our best advantage in case of treachery and arranged what action to take. We were placed along the line at regular intervals a short distance inside the net by the *cazador*, I between my orderly and hospital steward. While not so very far apart, we could not see each other for the dense jungle growth. Our men carried Krag carbines in addition to revolvers.

During these preparations the remaining natives with the dogs made a détour around the mountain several miles, and after forming a line paralleling the nets, slowly advanced toward us, both men and canines making all the noise they could, which drove the game in our direction. It was understood that all shooting at game must be directed toward the beaters, never toward each other. The natives behind the nets carried the bolo, in addition to a savage-looking spear eight feet long. Their function was to spear or cut up any game that became tangled in the net after being wounded or missed by the hunters.

It was not long after the unearthly din from the beaters and dogs reached us before we began to hear noises in every direction, putting us on the alert and tense with anticipation. As no one could see through the undergrowth more than ten to fifteen paces, there were thrills aplenty when a wild boar would tear through everything before him with a noise like a threshing machine. They are very dangerous animals, and with five-inch tusks in the lower jaw and three-inch in the upper, they can quickly tear a hunter to pieces unless he kills them first or is an agile tree-climber.

Like the rattlesnake, a boar definitely advertises his advent, and if the hunter is doubtful as to his skill, there is always a handy tree in a jungle. Deer are just the opposite, gracefully gliding through the forest with scarcely a sound. I was very ambitious to bag a boar, but was disappointed. I could very easily fake a fine adventure here, but am under contract to write a true story; so that's that.

After quite a wait I was gladdened by sounds indicating that a boar, pursued by a pack of dogs, was crashing through in my direction. I took up a position under a tree, with a *very convenient overhanging limb*, and with my Mauser pistol full of dumdum bullets—which we used when hunting—was quite prepared for developments.

But, to my great disappointment, just before entering my area of vision, the animal turned at an angle, dashed straight away to my orderly, who, after missing two good shots at point-blank range, took to a tree, while the big brute, landing in the net, was quickly assassinated by the native standing guard. The trophies of this drive were three boars and four deer.

A certain blast from the horn indicating the hunt was over, we assembled in a beautiful spot on a mountain stream, with water cool and clear as crystal, where we made camp and with ravenous appetites enjoyed a toothsome tiffin provided by our host while the beaters were packing the nets and other impedimenta on the *carabao*. Then with the game added to their burdens, the small army of ex-insurgents—whose anticipated treachery we had forgotten—the numerous canines, together with our cavalcade, made a motley procession.

We arrived at Don Luciano's at 6 P.M., tired and hungry as wolves. Game was quickly dressed, and in a very short time we were enjoying a feast of wild pig chops, venison, sweet potatoes, fresh tomatoes, radishes, lettuce, fried bananas, guava jelly, and coffee, in a way that was no trouble to us.

A young wild pig is simply delicious, but not the old ones. All the game, excepting two saddles each of venison and wild hog, was turned over to the natives, who soon had a grand *fiesta* going, winding up with a *baile*. To offset our suspicions of their loyalty, General Grant gave them a talk, our host interpreting, after which we distributed one hundred pesetas (ten dollars gold) among them, thus furnishing a climax to a wonderful day, on both sides, no doubt handed down by their traditions to the present time.

The late famous writer and traveler, Frank G. Carpenter, arrived at Angeles just as we were starting on an important hike, and, by invitation of General Grant, gladly joined us. The objective was a secret cache of rice and war munitions, supposed to be located somewhere up a very remarkable and hard-to-get-at canyon called 'Ypo,' away up Mount Ariod, quite a distance from Angeles. At one time our trail was the bed of a tortuous mountain stream, the luxuriant foliage on the sides forming a veritable tunnel over us, for a distance of about five miles. This proved to be a very successful adventure, as the cache was finally discovered and nearly a half-million pounds of rice, many guns, and considerable ammunition were destroyed.

We were shot up a number of times, once while at the bottom of a very deep canyon, the enemy on both sides at the top blazing away at an almost vertical range. It was here one of the mounted scouts received a very unique wound, the first of its kind in history and the source of one of my best surgical stories.

The bullet, from a Mauser, entering his face, between the cheekbone and nose, passed through the hard palate, thence through his entire body, finally coming out just in front of the lower end of the spine. Remarkable as it may seem, this man fully recovered and was again on the firing line within a month.

In narrating this extraordinary incident, at any indication of incredulity or doubt from my listeners, I would at once explain, but, if my story was *swallowed*, as the soldier did the bullet, I always let it go at that.

This hike occurred in November, 1900, and Mr. Carpenter pronounced it the outstanding adventure of his entire life. The day after our return I gave him another. Don Florentino Paumintuan—musical name, don't you think?—whose home was our headquarters, like most wealthy natives had a secret cache for his silver and other valuables. He also had a billiard table on the ground floor, under which was an invisible trapdoor that opened by a spring nearby. I had dubbed it the 'crawl cache,' as we entered this door on hands and knees, and after descending two or three steps crawled along the ground, under the floor three feet above, some little distance to an opening, where a pair of stairs took us into a subterranean apartment about fifteen feet below the surface, where on the floor were a number of large *ollas*, now empty. Some of our soldiers could have spun a yarn about this cache when the town was captured.

We had each lighted a candle as we started downstairs, but our visit was very, very short, as a young boa constrictor was trying to tag something among the vessels. No traffic cop was present, so the going was 'on high.' At our first, and last, glance the snake seemed to be about fifty feet long, but friend Frank and the 'Red Doctor' were both too busy trying to get through that door at the same time, to measure him.

If Frank had been my size, we might both have been stuck in that door yet, but he was very slender and wiry, and the way we eeled it up those stairs and out was a caution. It was my first and last subterranean sprint and brought to my memory my adventure with a snake in the Panhandle of Texas in the long ago, as previously told. I never did have much real affection for a snake—except as an emergency ration. Later our boa was captured and turned loose in the attic as a rat-catcher. He was a youngster and only about six feet long.

XXXII

A Typical Hike after Guns

THE EDUCATED Tagalo, the leaders of the country, are haughty, dignified, proud, deceitful, and cruel, yet withal they are the acme of polished politeness, hospitable, and brave in their way, with a strong complex of mystery and intrigue of all kinds.[1]

Their guerrilla tactics, while simple, were effective. To Americans at this time all natives looked alike. When their army disbanded in 1899, the insurgents repaired to their respective homes, concealing weapons and uniforms, and appearing in the white habiliments of peace were *apparently* from that time a harmless peaceful *paisanaje* (peasantry), but under the surface and behind the scenes conditions were reversed.

They divided the country into districts, each under the command of the ranking insurgent officer who resided within its boundaries. Each district had its secret rendezvous, where the patriots, armed and in uniform, assembled at regular intervals, usually at night. When attending these meetings each attached a small package to his belt containing a

[1] *Tagalo* is the name given to the aboriginal Malay people of the Philippine Islands.

white coat and trousers, and if a force of Americans were encountered, our 'brown barefoot brethren of the beach' would quickly vanish in the jungle and 'presto change,' would emerge innocent *amigos* clad in white.

As they were past-masters in double-dealing and deception, this was easy for a while. They had learned they were safe in meeting Americans unless armed and in uniform. One of their bag o' tricks was to apply a certain bruised herb to a man's back that would raise a crop of harmless swellings resembling welts. He would appear at our headquarters with a pitiful tale of being badly whipped by his people for befriending us, show up his back as proof, and offer to guide us to a secret location where many guns were kept, all in revenge for his punishment.

Out we would go and after we had silently stolen after him for miles through the wildest, roughest country in the world, he would suddenly vanish in the jungle and leave us to get home the best we could. It was an Oriental imitation of our old 'snipe game' in the Panhandle, as described previously.

We were not always beaten at the game, however. It was known that in the heart of one of the richest sugar districts was a favorite rendezvous of the guerrillas, but all plans to surprise them in action or break it up had failed.

It was sugar-harvest time and long trains of the two-wheeled squeaking carts with bamboo mat awnings and drawn by *carabao* were transporting sugar to market, often at night on account of the cooler temperature. Getting reliable information about a meeting night at this rendezvous, a detachment of scouts secretly and silently stole away in the darkness and were fortunate enough to overtake a sugar train *en route* for the same *barrio*. Holding it up, the drivers were compelled to shift their cargoes from sugar to scouts, and comfortably reclining under the awnings, the latter proceeded on their way. The frightened drivers, well knowing that treachery or disobedience of orders meant instant death, slowly conducted the train within a short distance of the meet, when, at the signal from their leader, the scouts sprang from cover, and instantly surrounding the building, opened a fusillade through doors and windows. The surprise was complete and the fight soon over. The insurgents surrendered after quite a loss, and the bull-carts were again utilized to convey the scouts and their booty, some twenty guns and other plunder, to Angeles. The survivors were listed and turned loose with a warning that if caught again they would be shot.

One evening word was quietly passed for the staff to be prepared to take the field at 9 P.M., with emergency rations for one day, destination unknown. We learned that with a detail of one hundred mounted scouts we were booked for one of the night raids after guns for which 'Grant's Mounted Scouts' had become famous, a diversion welcome to all.

It is 9 P.M., and the column is off. Angeles was a large *pueblo*, and in order not to excite the suspicions of the native populace, not a move was made out of the ordinary before 8:45, when horses were saddled, carbines and revolvers inspected, all with scarcely a sound until the column dashed away at a gallop, toward a mountain gorge twelve miles away, in a defile of which we hoped to surprise a rendezvous. The rapid start was to prevent any advance warning by natives. We galloped for a few miles, then slowed down to a steady trot of about six miles an hour.

It was a beautiful tropical night with a brilliant moon just rising as we pulled out, almost bright enough to read by. Would it were possible to describe the beauty of moonlight in Luzon, but it must be seen and its softness actually felt to be appreciated. The first ten miles led through an undulating country broken at intervals by clear rapid streams from the mountain, easily forded and very refreshing to our horses. The trail, a very good one, was fringed with the feathery bamboo, many varieties of stately palms, different kinds of fruit trees, which, with the many varieties of the famous hard woods of the Islands, presented an ever-changing panorama of nature beautiful to behold. At interval breaks in the forest were a vigorous growth of the *cogon* grass, often rearing its silvery plumes full fifteen feet from the ground, which, gracefully fanned to and fro by the cool night breeze, produced an effect under the shimmering moonlight that was simply indescribable.

Several small *barrios* were rapidly passed, but all was dark and silent except the angry barking of the dogs, in the number of which, as in number of children, the Filipino excels. Many of the *barrios* were supplied with tame geese which as alarmists often discount the dog. They detected strangers at night before the dogs did and the alarm they raised left nothing to be desired. That these alarms might not defeat our objective, the men at the point were instructed to lead at a gallop through these *barrios* and for some distance beyond at the first bark or cackle. Between ten and eleven o'clock the column halted at a *barrio* in the foothills to commandeer a guide, our men not being acquainted with the trails.

When it was necessary to surprise and round up a *barrio* in night raids, the scouts were trained to dash in at full speed, the first four falling out to surround the first house, the next four the next house, and so on. These villages are usually built on each side of a main street.

This plan was generally a success in a surprise, but occasionally conditions were reversed, and instead of silence, or surrender, our troops would be met with volleys from the Mauser, after which the insurgents would vanish like phantoms in the forest, the *barrio* would be burned, and, with casualties, if any, the column would face homeward.

This time the surprise raid was a success, with a

completeness and rapidity truly remarkable. Native houses, built of bamboo and elevated on posts several feet from the ground, were entered by a small bamboo ladder. From one of the first information was gained as to the whereabouts of the *cabeza* (head man) and he was soon brought into the presence of the General. When told what was wanted, he produced a stockily built native who was well posted in all the trails in the vicinity. This chap, after being told that the first sign of treachery or disobedience of orders meant for him instant death, was tied on a pony connected with a rope to a man on the point; and away we went.

We were still advancing in column of twos, but in a short time the trail narrowed and we moved in single file. The First Sergeant, Morris by name, a Westerner, a splendid horseman, a dead shot, in fact, an all-around first-class soldier, was given the post of honor at the front, and right well did he do his duty. Progressing rapidly for a mile after this delay brought the column to a trail so rough and broken that speed was considerably reduced. Progressing thus for a short distance, we came to a sharp angle in the trail which was hardly entered before two shots rang out into the night a few rods from the point, quickly followed by shouts of the men and desultory firing along the advance guard.

The instant the first shots were fired, all put spurs to their horses and the troop dashed forward, but in a few moments firing ceased and at the sight of a dead horse in the trail with prostrate forms beyond, the command halted, and the cause of the fusillade was explained. As the sergeant turned the angle, two mounted men were seen rapidly approaching less than fifty yards away. They both instantly fired at him with revolvers, but missed, and whirling their horses endeavored to escape, shooting over their shoulders as they rode. Unslinging his carbine the instant they fired, Sergeant Morris was after them on one of the best mounts in the troop, his first idea being to capture them, but they, being also splendidly mounted, paid no attention to his challenge to halt, but fled all the faster. Morris then fired and one of the fleeing horses dropped, dashing his rider to the ground. Recovering himself, he sprang to his feet, bravely firing his last shot at the same instant that his brain was pierced by a bullet from the unerring weapon of the sergeant. Without pausing a moment the intrepid soldier leaped his steed over the fallen horse and rider, as they lay in the trail, and had scarcely touched the ground when his deadly carbine crashed for the third time bringing the remaining fugitive to the earth with a mortal wound.

The wounded man survived long enough to reveal that they were insurgent officers with important papers concealed under the peaceful white garb they wore and that they would have surrendered but for them. Their white garments also made better targets under the moonlight than if clad otherwise. The poor fellow must have been turning to fire when shot, as the bullet, in addition to piercing the upper spine, had severed an artery in his neck, and being beyond all aid, he soon passed away.

From a military standpoint, this exploit of Sergeant Morris in taking the initiative, his instant action, his remarkable skill with the rifle as exhibited by its deadly work while on horseback at full speed under the shadows of night and the fire of his adversaries, was altogether a most brilliant performance and he well earned the hearty commendation bestowed by General Grant. Sergeant Morris is mentioned in War Department records.

Examination of the clothing of these unfortunate men disclosed their commissions as captain and lieutenant in the insurgent army, a map of the very location we were seeking, but, most important of all, a complete roster of their command.

This find was doubly valuable, for, during the rush and excitement incident to the above, the guide either loosened a hand or removed the halter from his pony with his teeth, and they both suddenly disappeared in the jungle, leaving an empty halter and nothing more. A hot fire was poured after him, but it was never known whether it was effective or not.

Leaving the bodies of the officers covered with plantain leaves under a bunch of beautiful palms, with a note in Tagalo directing passing natives to bury them (which later we learned was done), we pressed on with the new-found map as guide.

Silence was enjoined and all communication between the men prohibited except in whispers. Progress became much slower, as the trail abounded in soft spots, pitfalls, slippery roots of trees and vines over which horses frequently fell, impossible to avoid with the impenetrable thorny wall of jungle growth at each side of the narrow trail. This part of the journey was weird and ghostly, for while the moon was shining brightly in the heavens above, its rays were so obstructed by the interlacing of the massive growth crowning the crests of the lofty giants of the forest that along the trail all was either fitful deceptive shadows or deep darkness. By the few silvery rays that filtered through, dim outlines of the tree-trunks could be seen, many gigantic in size and height, a perfect maze of vines and creepers surrounding and festooning their bodies or intermingling with their boughs. These, with shadowy ferns rearing their graceful fronds, oftentimes to a height of fifty feet, produce effects that are easily heightened by the imagination into many varieties of fantastic fancies.

But this did not get guns.

The column halts. We wonder why. I can just see General Grant on his iron gray in my front. I press forward and hear a whispered report of a light or campfire some distance in front and on our left. The General directs that 'the first twenty-five men dismount, every fifth man hold horses while the remainder make a reconnaissance, surround and capture, without bloodshed if possible, all at or in the vicinity of the fire, not a shot to be fired unless absolutely necessary.'

The orders go forward by *wireless whisper*, while we, filled with suppressed excitement, wait, note the possibility of a near ambush by insurgents concealed in the shadows and dark recesses on every side—happy thoughts which, augmented by the death-rattle voice of the tree lizard and the angry chatter of monkeys disturbed in their lofty nests by the night raiders, all help to keep us awake.

We move forward for some distance when the General receives the report. The light came from a shack in the forest which we silently surrounded and entrance demanded. Excited voices were heard, lights put out, and a man sprang from a window in the rear in a frantic effort to escape, only to fall into the hands of two husky scouts. He surrendered and called to three comrades inside to do the same.

He was a first lieutenant in uniform and all were armed, the place being a sort of outpost. The lieutenant's name was found on the captured roster, and securing him with a lariat fastened to the saddle of the man on the point, he was given the choice of being shot or guiding us to the rendezvous. The latter was his choice, and acting as an infantryman— there being no extra horses—we were soon moving forward again.

It was now past midnight and for two hours or more the trail was one of the most difficult imaginable. Forests, swamps, stretches of *cogon* grass thick and high, rice paddies in which some horses mired down completely, a wide stream deep enough to necessitate swimming that we crossed twice, mountain spurs and sub-spurs—once for a half-mile the trail being the rocky, broken tortuous bed of a mountain stream—were all obstacles encountered in weary succession. The activity, endurance, and jungle craft displayed by the new guide excited the wonder and admiration of us all.

Entering an imposing-looking canyon about three in the morning, he stopped and announced the goal was nearby. Placing him with a guard to join his comrades when they came up with the rear, the signal to charge was sent down the line.

A night attack upon an unknown, unseen foe in a strange country requires courage. Would they fight or run was the question in the minds of all the men charging up the valley of the canyon. All were hoping for the former and were eager for the fray, all toil and hardship incident to the long march forgotten as they thundered into the clearing under the excitement of anticipated battle. But they were doomed to disappointment, as everything in the vicinity was silent as the grave and apparently deserted.

There was one large building, probably a barracks, and a number of smaller ones, each of which was instantly surrounded in the usual way. The large one was entered first by a detail, and to their surprise was filled with occupants and the same was found to obtain in the smaller. They were brought out in squads to a level place, evidently a drill ground, and proved to be over one hundred men and fifty women and children.

Men were in white, and not a weapon of any kind was found. We learned that we had been followed by runners and during the delay at the forest outpost one, worming his way through the jungle near enough to overhear the orders to the guide, took a short cut to the rendezvous and sounded the alarm. Deciding our column was too strong to attack, guns were concealed, and but for the women and children, the men would have also vanished.

The men were lined up and all denied ever having been soldiers. Guns? Never had seen one until we came.

During the campaign of 1899 prisoners reported great dissatisfaction in Aguinaldo's ranks, and our Government at the suggestion of General MacArthur tried an experiment, offering thirty pesos (fifteen dollars gold) for every gun brought in, but the response was disappointing. The majority that *did* arrive were damaged and practically worthless; consequently the large bulk of their guns were finally captured during the more than two years of guerrilla war by just such raids as I am describing.

Very noticeable in the motley line was a young lad of about fifteen—handsome, his appearance and bearing much different from the rest. Hearing him reply to the interpreter's questions in Spanish, I interviewed him myself, and learning he was the son of the cabeza, who was away, became convinced he knew all about the gun question. I urged him strongly to tell me the truth, but he was still positive in his denials of any knowledge of guns or other military munitions.

In the meantime our lieutenant guide—who apparently had suddenly become pro-American—had segregated about thirty of his countrymen, declaring them to be soldiers. Dismayed, they tremblingly fell to their knees, praying and begging for their lives, evidently expecting to be executed on the spot.

The guide then urged the young lad to tell the truth, but the youngster was game. He stood facing us without a tremor, his remarkable nerve exciting the secret admiration of all, denying emphatically any knowledge of concealed weapons.

At a signal from Lieutenant Burr, scout commander, the brave little fellow was taken to one side, bound hand and foot and lashed to a tree. A squad of scouts were drawn up a few paces in front of him where they were ordered to 'make ready, take aim,' but before the order to 'fire!' Burr, watch in hand, said in Spanish, 'My boy, if your memory does not come back in two minutes you will be shot dead!'

It was a sight and scene not easily forgotten. To me, twenty-nine years later, it is still as vivid as if it were yesterday. Burr counted the minutes by halves with a voice vibrating with the solemnity of the occasion, and at the beginning of the last half the boy's nerve broke and, begging for his life, he promised to tell the truth.

He was quickly released and this incident resulted in over twenty-five rifles, in good condition, together with a considerable quantity of ammunition and war bolos, being dragged from concealment. They were mostly hidden in the hollow of the bamboo, where they are easily concealed and kept dry.

Even had he remained silent, the boy, of course, would *not* have been shot, but in that event the raid would have been very close to a failure, and while the measures taken looked cruel, the end justified the means.

Knowing that to remain meant certain death, this boy and the lieutenant guide were taken with us as we returned to Angeles, and they took the oath of allegiance, the boy later being the means of our capturing over one hundred guns. Mario was his name. We learned early in 1899 that any native favoring us in *any way* was doomed to die if he fell into the hands of his people.

Both by heredity and training they are cruel to the limit, as shown by their methods of punishment. Leaving a victim bound hand and foot across a giant anthill, burying them alive, casting them into a pit to be impaled on the points of upright sharpened bamboo were a few of their modes.

A good deal has been published in this good old country of ours about the cruelties inflicted upon the Filipino during the war by the American soldier. I have strong opinions in favor of humane measures. My profession, followed for over fifty years, demonstrates that; but there are exceptions to all rules, and after four years of active field service in the Philippines I know that if it had not been for our stern measures and for an occasional 'bluff,' as above described, the insurrectos would still have guns and *we should be fighting them yet.*

The 'soldiers' taken in this raid were marched back as prisoners of war and placed in a military prison. Under ordinary conditions escorting thirty prisoners was a comparatively simple proposition, but marching them single file through a tropical jungle is another story.

Our captives were divided into squads of ten, each man fastened by his neck to a rope, which was then secured to the saddles of two scouts, and the long tramp to Angeles was made without further incident.

I have entered into greater detail than usual in describing this affair, that my readers may realize something of the nature of the experiences and duties of the American soldier serving in a war with a strange people, on the other side of the world and under conditions unique in our military history. This affair was selected, as it was a typical hike.

XXXIII

An Attempted Tobacco Cure

I WAS associated with General Frederick Dent Grant for over two years, under conditions of all kinds, and I had always found him the same kind-hearted, courteous gentleman. While I was with him at Chickamauga Park in June, 1898, he was taken very ill and was joined by Mrs. Grant, who assisted in nursing him. She, a very charming woman, was naturally very solicitous as to his health, and during our consultations his habit of smoking was discussed. After giving her my opinion, she entreated me to use my influence to induce the General to stop, which I gladly promised to do.

In a short time I was promoted and sent to Anniston, Alabama, and did not see General Grant again until I joined him in Angeles, Philippine Islands. I do not remember ever seeing him without a cigar in his mouth except when he was eating or asleep. I took every opportunity that offered to drop a suggestion that seemed timely, hoping to open his eyes to the truth about tobacco as I saw it. One would think this unnecessary after observing the fate of his illustrious father, whose life—as all the world knows—was shortened by this filthy, poisonous weed.

I began to see light ahead when one day he informed me that he had been seriously considering this matter of tobacco, and had decided to make an effort to stop using it. He had for years averaged not less than twenty cigars a day, and as a starter was going to begin the reformation by cutting that number right in two, and was now smoking but *ten*.

This pleased me very much, and I hoped for another cut soon. I was away for a few days, and when I saw him again I asked if he was holding out all right. He replied in the affirmative and, with a twinkle in his eye, held up his tenth cigar for the day, that he had just lighted. It was just *twice* the size of any cigar I had ever seen.

A large cigar factory in Manila had introduced a new brand, naming it after General Grant and sending him several complimentary boxes. His reformation stopped, and like his father, he passed away, long before his time.

I realized early in my career the danger from tobacco, and for more than forty years have advocated the idea that it is more harmful to the health and longevity of the human race than alcohol.

Later the remarkable activity and success of the mounted scouts began to bear fruit. That band of leaders that defied General Grant at Malolos, with their dramatic tale of signing papers with their blood never to submit to any government but their own, were weary of war and now came in again, this time under a white flag and, figuratively speaking, on their hands and knees, pleading for peace.

This was granted, and the courteous and kind treatment they received from General Grant apparently won their hearts. If my memory is correct, the insurgents in General Grant's District (the Fifth) were the first to sue for peace, and as it was the most populous portion of Luzon, their example was soon followed by the rest.

The people returned to their homes, resuming their former conditions, activities, and vocations as best they could. The machinery of the new government under the new flag was put in motion and affairs in general began to assume a rapid return to normalcy.

The *cabezas* of the cities, towns, and villages in the Fifth District held a meeting, and as a result, an invitation was extended to General Grant and staff, including friends, to be their guests at *Un Gran Fiesta de Paz* (a grand feast of peace) to be held at Malolos. This affair lasted a week and *was* grand in every way. It would take a much abler pen than mine to do it justice. Malolos was decorated as never before. A number of bands provided music. Processions of various kinds, serious and comic, were held daily. There was a grand ball in Aguinaldo's former Congress Hall. And last but not least, a six to eight course tiffin and dinner were served every noon and night during our entire visit.

Over the years I have been entertained in many

countries, but have never seen anything that excelled—and but few that equaled—the lavish hospitality of the Filipinos.

With their primitive method of cooking, it was a mystery to us, especially to our ladies, how they ever prepared and served the most dainty and delicious dishes in such abundance, without delays or confusion.

Their stove was a simple platform of brick three feet high, six to eight feet square, covered with a shallow layer of sand, all under a large open chimney. Their cooking utensils were nothing but shallow clay bowls, very similar to our old-fashioned 'wash-bowls,' and their fuel was charcoal. Their barefoot servants seemed to be trained with almost military precision and their service was faultless.

One evening, while we were at dinner, a charming young Spanish *mestiza*, seated opposite General Grant, arose, and with modest mien yet flashing eyes, threw her very soul into a most thrilling and pathetic song. Her voice was most remarkable—a deep, rich, melodious contralto, one of the best I had ever heard. It seems the fiancé of the young beauty was a general in the insurrection, had been captured and was then an inmate of a military prison in the General's district. At the conclusion of her song she stepped around to General Grant, seized his hand, kissed it, and, falling to her knees, pathetically besought him to liberate her lover.

The General, visibly embarrassed, arose, and lifting her to her feet, very gently and courteously explained how it was impossible to grant her petition.

This method of invoking clemency from high authority had its origin during the centuries of Spanish rule, the unselfish maid ready to sacrifice all to save a loved one from punishment or death. But Uncle Sam's generals are different, she learned.

Her wonderful voice did so impress one wealthy American in our party that he made an effort to have her come to the United States with a chaperon and have her voice trained, all at his expense, but, although grateful for the offer, she refused to leave the vicinity of her beloved.

The educated Filipino women have many splendid traits and I saw many happy families in that country.

Another diplomatic and appropriate tribute to General Grant was an elaborate testimonial of their regard, respect, and admiration in the form of an exquisitely engrossed, rosetted and beribboned manuscript, from each community in his District, the total filling a good-sized trunk. A marvelous contrast, the above, with the day these same people denounced the Stars and Stripes. Even now, there are people who do not know when they are well off.

After peace came the disbanding of General Grant's famous Mounted Scouts commanded by First Lieutenant Frank S. Burr, Fifteenth United States Infantry, than which no more efficient organization served in the Philippines. A history of their activities during the two years of guerrilla warfare would be very interesting reading.

When the Scouts were assembled at headquarters for their farewell review, General Grant gave them a heart-to-heart talk, telling how much he appreciated their splendid work, and that he would be delighted to see them should fate ever throw them together after they returned home, a discourse that brought tears to the eyes of many a stalwart seasoned veteran. After shaking hands with each man as he passed by, the General presented him with one of those *full-grown cigars*, a souvenir from the new brand, some of which may still be unconsumed. There was no necessity of warranting that brand to last.

XXXIV

The Battle of the Eggs

Augoust 30, 1900, I was ordered on temporary
duty to Dagupan as Chief Surgeon of the
Third District, commanded by General Jacob H.
Smith. Dagupan is a seaport on the west coast of
Luzon and was then the terminus of the railway
from Manila, and some distance north of Angeles.

The railroad was still torn up north of us and I
traveled overland with an escort. The trip was uneventful except for a comical incident as I was
crossing a large river in a canoe. In addition to the
two native boatmen and myself, there was in the
craft a half-drunken soldier with a pretty little par-
akeet attached to one of his thumbs by a cord. The
soldier, returning home from a furlough, had made
strenuous efforts to conceal his condition from me,
and of course the more he tried, the more evident it
became. When part way across the river, he lost his
balance and went overboard head first, nearly upsetting the craft.

The water was deep, the current swift, and the
man could not swim, but the natives were very
skillful and in a moment had swung around and we
were beside him and I pulled him in. The bath had
sobered him, but the poor little bird, his brilliant

plumage drenched and bedraggled, after giving himself a good shake, turned loose with a string of Spanish profanity that was perfectly astounding. He must have been raised with a bull-whacker.

While at Dagupan I had another experience that was somewhat extraordinary as well as amusing. A part of my duties was the inspection of the garrisons, and as quite a number in General Smith's District lay along the west coast of Luzon, I had at my disposal the gunboat Samar, a small vessel belonging to the 'Mosquito Fleet,' a branch of the navy for coast service among the Islands. We had a crew of twenty-five or thirty men under the command of a young Ensign.

The Ensign regretted that, although he had been on duty in the Islands for about a year, he had never heard the whistle of a hostile bullet. I jokingly told him that I was very lucky in that way and as I was to be with him, he would soon smell gunpowder.

The weather was perfect and we had a very pleasant voyage all along the coast. There was no wharf or dock at any of the landing-places above Subig Bay, so after anchoring the steamer out some distance I would be taken in a small boat to shallow water and carried to shore on the back of a native. As my weight was about two hundred and twenty-five pounds, how those little chaps lugged me in without giving me a ducking was a surprise to me.

We arrived at Subig Bay about September 21 and tied up at the dock, which is unique in that it was made by Nature, the water right up to the shore being deep enough for large ships. The small town there was called Olongapo.

In addition to weapons carried by the crew, the Samar was armed by a machine gun at each end of the bridge and a six-pounder mounted on the deck at the stern. There was an awning over the deck, and as it was hot in the stateroom below, I had been sleeping on deck on a cot but a few feet from the cannon.

The starboard side of the vessel paralleled the dock. Over the port side a dense forest could be seen skirting the edge of the bay just six hundred yards distant. With the foot of my cot toward the port side, I had retired and was almost asleep when, like a thunderbolt from a clear sky, a large force of insurgents in the edge of the forest across the bay opened up with volley after volley from their Mausers. The bullets sang through the air all about us and many struck the ship. In fact they seemed to have our range exactly. Raising myself on my elbow, I had a perfect view of the scene. My first thought was, 'How this will gladden the heart of the Ensign!' That officer was already on the bridge, his voice vibrating with excitement as he shouted his orders.

Now came the gunner from below, and in bounding across the deck to his gun, he failed to see me there in the shadow of the awning. He tripped as he struck my cot amidships, falling headlong over it and partially upsetting me. I heard a loud groan and some emphatic, inarticulate muttering as he scrambled to his feet and jumped to his gun.

As my cot began to tip, I involuntarily put out my hand as a brace and it landed on a very moist deck, my brain instantly registering *blood*.

In an instant—as it was already loaded—the cannon, paralleling my cot a few feet away, roared and shortly was fired again. In the meantime the machine gun on the bridge began its *pur-rrrrr*, which was quickly echoed by the rifles of the crew, but all this, including the Ensign, was forgotten in my intense admiration for my hero at the six-pounder, evidently badly wounded and yet doing his duty nobly, as he was serving the cannon alone.

I even formulated in my mind a perfectly splendid report that I would make of his bravery and courage as exhibited in this exploit.

Unless some one was hit, there was nothing for me to do, so I lay still through it all. But for the bullets, I could easily imagine I was at some Fourth-of-July celebration, with the fireworks along the edge of the forest, the exhibition of activity on the Samar, the silvery waves of the bay between reflecting the brilliancy of the moon and stars above, all together presented a most beautiful and exciting panorama that I shall never forget. It would be difficult to imagine a more luxurious manner in which to participate in a war scene.

But the show was soon over. Our boys evidently

had the range, for before a half-dozen shells—accompanied by a shower of bullets from the rifles of the Marines—had flown across the bay, the fireworks in the forest ceased almost as suddenly as they had begun.

Later it was learned the enemy had ten killed and about thirty wounded. Although hundreds of bullets came our way, not a man was hit.

The Ensign, happy and jubilant, came back to shake hands and put me on record as the mascot of the Samar. As we shook, I—for a joke—mournfully put out my left hand to show him my *blood*, but much to my amazement it was *gone*.

An official investigation was held on the spot and the mystery was solved. To keep them cool, the cook had put a big basket of eggs on the deck, between my cot and the gun, and my hero(?) had landed head first in it, a curious climax to his acrobatic performance. The sequel—no more eggs for breakfast.

Who says I didn't have a *hand* in the first authentic case of 'shell-shock' in this world's history?

With the exception of the date, taken from my inspection records at Subig Post, the entire story of that 'shoot-up' of the Samar, I wrote from memory. Desiring the name of the officer in command, which I had forgotten, I had written a short time before to the Secretary of the Navy requesting it if possible, and also his status if still living. Not hearing from him, I proceeded to write the above as stated.

A short time afterward, the Pension Board at Long Beach, California, Drs. Charles S. Evans, George O. Gordon, and myself, examined a man named Harry Harvey, an ex-sergeant of the United States Marines, for pension.

He was decorated with a Congressional Medal of Honor, the greatest and most highly prized of the three decorations authorized by our Government for valor, bestowed only for some deed voluntarily performed outside the line of duty, without reference to rank. It took persistent questioning of this modest hero to bring out the explanation of the medal.

In February, 1900, he was on duty at Olongapa, Luzon, Philippine Islands, as sergeant in a company of Marines. During a raid General Grant captured a small insurgent gunboat, the Don Francisco, up the Benictican River, a tributary of Subig Bay. Being cunningly camouflaged with palm leaves and other foliage, a short distance away it was easily mistaken for an island. This boat was brought down near the river mouth, where it was guarded by twelve Marines in charge of Sergeant Harvey. 'They were all from Georgia and the greatest fighters I have ever seen,' said Harvey.

February 16, 1900, a scouting detachment of Marines from Olongapo proceeded up this river in a launch. When some distance above the Don Francisco, they came to a sharp bend in the river and had hardly entered it when they were shot up by a large force of insurgents concealed in the jungle on the left bank.

At this time Harvey and his crew were all in the river enjoying a swim. From the crashing of the rifles they instantly decided that the little party of Marines were outnumbered, so quickly clambered on board their little vessel, all eager to go to their assistance. The response to Harvey's call for volunteers was unanimous and, selecting seven, away they paddled in a small boat, armed to the teeth, but stark naked. Landing just before they reached the bend in the river, they tore through the jungle— a remarkable feat itself for a white man clad in his birthday uniform—and as they reached the bank of the river, an exciting scene was before them.

The little boat of the Marines was beached on the opposite shore, Private Welch was dead, his body lying partly on shore and in the water, and just as Harvey's band hove in sight, Corporal Wallace Sullivan, while fighting for his life in the boat, was shot through the brain and fell overboard, sinking to the bottom of the stream.

Instantly ordering his men to open up a barrage on the insurgents to keep down their fire as much as possible, and throwing down his gun and ammunition, Harvey leaped into the river, swam across, and, after diving the second time, found the body of Sullivan, returned with it and, after passing it up to two of his men, swam over the second time and brought back the body of Welch, all under a most galling fire. Although the bank on the insurgent side was only a foot or two above the water level, on Harvey's side it was about ten feet straight up and down.

Hurrah for the Marines!

We learned while examining Harvey for pension that he still carried some of the thorns he picked up in that wild dash through the jungle. Incidentally I asked Harvey if he had ever seen the gunboat Samar while he was at Olongapo and to my surprise he told me the following: 'I remember the Samar very well. She arrived one afternoon in September, 1900, and finding an old friend aboard, I was visiting with him until the wee small hours of the morning. Right in the midst of our yarns the ship was shot up in good shape, but strange to say not a man was hit. The only loss was a basket of eggs that the cook had put on deck to keep cool. They were sure scrambled raw by a gunner who, rushing from below to his gun, fell over a surgeon asleep on the deck, falling head first in the basket. The doctor got a liberal squirt of the juice, and thinking the man mortally wounded, did his best to have him go below and be attended to.'

Harvey's surprise at learning I was the surgeon on deck at the 'great little battle of the basket of eggs'—as he expressed it—was no less than mine at hearing him tell of it. He even remembered that the name of the officer in command was Day.

After examining Harvey, I returned to my office

and found the following letter which had arrived during my absence:

Navy Department,
Bureau of Navigation
Washington, D.C., 28 April, 1928

Dear Doctor Hoyt:

By a strange coincidence your letter addressed to the Secretary of the Navy was referred to me for preparation of the data desired therein.

Since I was one of the two officers attached to the gunboat Samar during the time referred to, I am taking the liberty to reply direct.

I remember very well the incident of the shooting up of the Samar by the insurgents, while lying alongside dock at the old Spanish Navy Yard at Olongapo, at about 3:00 A.M. of September 22, 1900. A battalion of Marines was stationed at Olongapo, and the gunboat Samar and the smaller gunboat Gardoqui were lying alongside dock. Lieutenant George C. Day, U.S.N., and you were sleeping on deck aft on army cots when the fire opened. Some of the crew rushed aft to man the six-pounder gun, and one of them stumbled over your cot and fell to the deck and into a basket of eggs. You awakened just as the man was falling and thought he had been hurt, and reaching out your hand to the deck and feeling the eggs running over the deck made sure that the man was seriously injured, and undertook to assist him below: in the language that followed I fear the man somewhat forgot the respect due an officer.

As stated, the Samar was commanded by Lieutenant George C. Day, who is now a Rear Admiral commanding the Light Cruiser Division 2 of the Scouting Fleet (U.S.S. Trenton Flagship), and I was a Naval Cadet and the only other officer attached to the ship. The total crew numbered thirty, and the armament consisted of one six-pounder, three three-pounders, and two one-pounders.

At present I am a Commander in the Naval Reserve on duty in the Bureau of Navigation of the Navy Department. If you should ever wander this way, I trust you will give me the pleasure of again recalling with you these interesting events.

Yours sincerely
J. A. Schofield
Comdr. U.S.N.R.

This belated memory test of three individuals, from different sections, after a lapse of twenty-eight years, is remarkable, so I have reproduced it here *egg'zactly* as it occurred.

XXXV

Back to the States and Private Life

SEPTEMBER 1, 1901, I sailed from San Francisco, California, on the U.S. Transport Sheridan for Manila, accompanied by my wife and twelve-year-old son, intending to make the islands my permanent home.

General Frederick D. Grant, also a passenger, had been visiting his daughter, Julia, the Princess Cantacuzene, at her home in Russia. As the General and I were the ranking officers on board, we occupied the two best staterooms on the ship, side by side on the upper deck facing the bow.

Among the passengers were a Mr. A. W. Hastings and his daughter, Miss Charlotte, very agreeable, charming people from Minneapolis, both on their way to Manila, Miss Charlotte to meet and marry her fiancé, Judge Charles A. Willard, of the Supreme Court of the Philippine Islands.

During my two years at Angeles, among the occasional recreations of the headquarters mess was a modest game of draw poker in which both General Grant and I often joined.

Meeting me on deck one evening, he said that he

and one of the officers were going to have a game in his cabin, and after giving me a cordial invitation to join them, suggested that I bring Mr. Hastings, to whom he had taken quite a fancy.

I found Mr. Hastings quite willing, so we left our respective ladies, our itinerary unknown, and quietly slipped into the General's cabin.

We were in the midst of the game when a sudden exclamation caused us to look up, and in the two bull's-eyes overlooking the deck and open for ventilation were two faces, each registering expressions of astonishment verging on horror; one was Mrs. Hoyt and the other Miss Charlotte, who, while taking their evening promenade and passing casually, glanced through the openings! Caught *flagrante delicto*.

During this voyage to Manila, a remarkable coincidence occurred. With a favorable breeze blowing, a large sail would be hoisted to increase speed. One night, just at sundown, the ropes supporting this big sail became loosened and it had fallen part way down, its folds wrinkled and lying in such a way that, when standing at a certain place on the deck, a large and perfect profile of President William McKinley could be seen silhouetted against the sky. Many of the passengers saw this and some even noted it in their diaries.

Before we anchored in Manila Bay our ship was circled by a launch and we were megaphoned the news of the assassination of the President, and its date was the *same as that of the incident* of the sail.[1]

In due time General Grant was ordered to Nueva Caceres, Camarines Sur, P.I., to take command of the Fourth Separate Brigade, I accompanying him as Chief Surgeon.

General Grant established his headquarters in a fine commodious residence, formerly the home of a native planter. He had secured the services of two Japanese boys while in Manila, one an expert cook and the other his valet, who, with a retinue of native servants to assist, soon transformed the headquarters mess into a very delightful place. Peace was now established, and as many of the officers had been joined by their families, these, with a number of schoolteachers, formed a pleasant social circle.

At this post my duties extended over the following areas: The provinces of Tayabas, Camarines Sur, Albay, and Sorsogon, and the adjacent islands of Catanduanes, Burias, Masbate, and Tiaco, with a total population of 654,186, and covering an area of 8229 square miles.

The roads were very poor and we relied chiefly upon water transportation, so we had no ambulances. There were several launches and one small vessel at our disposal.

As elsewhere mentioned, I have always been very

[1] While on a visit to the Pan-American Exposition in Buffalo, New York, McKinley was fatally wounded by an anarchist, Leon Czolgosz, September 6, 1901. The President died eight days later.

fond of field sports, especially shooting. For a number of years before the Spanish-American War, I was a neighbor and also family physician of Mr. Frank B. Kellogg, recently our distinguished Secretary of State, and as he too was a devotee of the rod and gun, many of my pleasantest recollections are of our hunting and fishing excursions together. He gave me a Greener shotgun, made to order in London to fit my shoulder. It was a twelve-gauge, double-barreled, and with an automatic ejector, a beautiful and most accurate weapon—and I may add, is still shooting strong, although with close to thirty-five years of service in the field. This gun was with me in the Philippines.

There was fine shooting in the vicinity of Nueva Caceres, all kinds of water fowl, as well as plenty of snipe, pigeon, quail—the latter a very diminutive bird compared with our 'bob white'—parrots, fruit bats, and jungle fowl. There were also monkeys if one cared to kill them, something I never could do.

There were numerous rice paddies still containing some water near Nueva Caceres where one could get a good bag of snipe or ducks at almost any time. General Grant was also fond of bird shooting, and as he had no shotgun I would loan him my Greener. He went out one day, forgetting his rubber boots, so instead of wading, he walked about on the narrow tops of the dykes that surround the paddies. A fine flock of mallards came sailing over. The General fired and missed, and as he turned quickly to fire the second barrel, forgot where he was standing, and went headlong into the mud.

I wasn't there, but I heard several versions of his *soothing* remarks as he crawled out. I am not certain the mud is all out of that Greener yet, as he used its muzzle first to break his fall.

I had now been in the Philippines some years, was beginning to understand the people, enjoyed Oriental life, the climate suited me, and foreseeing the future possibilities in the Islands, I had brought my family from the other side of the world with the idea of making a new home.

But that *something* which controls our destinies brought complete change to these plans. My wife, my son, and I were all injured in varying degrees in an accidental fire in our quarters. But for the prompt help of General Grant himself and his aide, Lieutenant Miller, we should all have perished. My own hurts included burns of the first degree on my hands and forearms, my wife sustained a severe injury, and my son was terribly burned. Realizing, before my own injuries were healed, that my boy would never recover in that climate, I wired my resignation to General Chaffee in Manila and requested passage home on the next transport.

Arriving in Manila, I reported to General Chaffee, who for some time had absolutely turned down every request by an officer for a leave of absence.

After greetings, 'Why this resignation?' asked the stern-visaged old soldier.

'To save my son's life,' I replied.

'Why didn't you ask for leave?'

'Because I didn't think you'd grant it,' I said.

'Umph,' he grunted, and tearing up my resignation, he dictated an order for two months' leave, which I still have among my treasured souvenirs.

When several days out from Japan, the good transport Meade ran into a typhoon that raged for more than a week, and it was then learned that a very inferior quality of coal had been palmed off on us by that noted group of native beauties at Nagasaki. Their method of coaling ship is by passing it up in an endless chain of baskets, the maidens standing on a series of gradually elevated platforms from the bottom of the coal barge to the opening in the side of the ship far above. This is one of the sights one looks forward to on a tour of the world. There is nothing just like it elsewhere.

The ship's officers evidently had their weather eye on beauties instead of baskets. The price and quantity of the coal was all right, but the quality dropped off about fifty per cent as it was converted into steam.

This discovery compelled a change in our course and the ship was re-coaled at Honolulu, a side-step that no one objected to. Two days were very pleasantly spent there, the outstanding diversions being a swim at Waikiki Beach and a visit to the Museum where numerous curious relics of early Hawaiian history are seen.

Henry F. Hoyt
Major and Chief Surgeon, U.S.V., 1902

In the evening we were entertained at a ball in the Hawaiian Hotel, the music for which being furnished by the famous Royal Hawaiian Band. They were the first band I had ever heard sing as they played for the dance, and it was certainly thrilling. I might also add, and not very difficult to dance to.

On arriving at San Francisco, I found that although my boy was much better, he was far from well, so again I wired my resignation, this time to the Secretary of War direct. This was in March, 1902, and my reply was an order to report for temporary duty at Fort Douglas, Salt Lake City, Utah, where I was honorably discharged on October 10, 1902, and returned to private life. I learned after my long tour in hot countries that I could not live in a cold climate, and after visiting our Eastern cities and making a tour through Old Mexico, I again took up the practice of my profession at El Paso, Texas, later settling in Long Beach, California, the queen of the beach cities in this State, which has now been my home for nearly twenty years, and where any of the old-timers I have ever known are welcome. There are only a few of us left.

Biographical Notes

BIOGRAPHICAL NOTES

F.J. ADAMS is not listed in Francis B. Heitman, comp., *Historical Register and Dictionary of the United States Army*, 2 vols. (Washington, D.C., 1903), hereafter cited *Army Register*, nor is he listed in the official reports relating to officers who served in the Philippine theatre of war.

EMILIO AGUINALDO took command of an insurrection against Spain in 1896. When peace was restored, he went into exile with fifty followers, supported by a Spanish subvention of $300,000, to live in Hong Kong. With the Spanish-American War he returned to the Philippines and again led the insurrectionary forces in concert with American military forces. At the conclusion of the war, which brushed aside Philippine independence, he established a republic at Malolos, June 12, 1898, with himself as president, the following year. From 1899 until his capture by General Funston, March 23, 1901, he led the rebellion against U.S. occupying forces. In 1935 he was defeated for the presidency of the Philippine Republic by Manuel Quezon. He died in Manila, February 6, 1964, age ninety-four, a much revered and respected patriot. *New York Times*, February 6, 1964, p. 1, cl. 6; p. 29, cl. 3–4; February 7, 1964, p. 32, cl. 6.

RUSSELL A. ALGER (1836–1907), born and raised in Ohio, on admission to the bar settled in Michigan. He enlisted in the army, in August 1861, as a private, but advanced through the ranks to colonel in the Michigan Volunteer Cavalry and was brevetted brigadier general and major general in the volunteers for wartime meritorious service and bravery. He was elected governor of Michigan and served one term, 1885–1886. President

McKinley appointed him secretary of war on March 5, 1897, and he resigned under fire on August 1, 1899. Appointed to the vacancy in the U.S. Senate in 1902, he subsequently was elected in his own right and died in office January 24, 1907. *Biographical Directory of the American Congress, 1774–1961* (Washington, D.C., 1961), p. 468 (hereafter cited *Biographical Directory of U.S. Congress*).

ALBERT A. AMES was born in Garden Prairie, Boone County, Illinois, on January 18, 1842. When he was ten his parents relocated in Minneapolis, where he graduated from high school. He commenced his medical education with his physician father and graduated from Rush Medical College on February 3, 1862, in time to serve the Union with distinction. After a term in the legislature, he served four terms as mayor of his city, 1876, 1881–1882, 1886–1887, 1900–1902, and ran unsuccessfully for the Minnesota governorship in 1886. He died November 16, 1911. Horace B. Hudson, *A Half Century of Minneapolis* (Minneapolis, 1908), pp. 515, 517; *St. Paul Dispatch*, September 14, 1886; Warren Upham and Rose B. Dunlap, comps., "Minnesota Biographies, 1655–1912," *Collections of the Minnesota Historical Society* (St. Paul, 1912), XIV: 11.

GEORGE T. ANTHONY (1824–1896), New York born, made his reputation in Kansas as a newspaperman and editor. After a number of political appointments, he was elected governor of the state in 1876. He was appointed general superintendent of the Mexican Railroad in 1881. *Who Was Who in America, Historical Volume, 1607–1896* (Chicago, 1963), p. 26.

BILLY ANTRIM. See the entry for Henry McCarty.

SERVILLANO AQUINO was brought to trial in Manila,

December 6, 1900, charged with murder and assault with the intent to murder. Brigadier General Grant served as president of the military commission. Specifically Aquino was accused of having five American soldiers in his custody, Privates Alonzo Brown, Charles C. Cook, and Joseph C. Cook, all of Company B, 9th U.S. Infantry, and Regimental Commissary Sergeant Christian Pederson, 12th U.S. Infantry, and Cook Edward E. Norval, Company B, 12th U.S. Infantry, ordered shot. The first three were killed; the latter two survived, though wounded and left for dead. This tragic incident took place in the barrio of Camansi, Pueblo of Magalang, in the province of Pampanga, Luzon. Declared guilty, Aquino was sentenced "To be confined at hard labor for the remainder of his natural life at such place as the reviewing authority may direct." *Affairs in the Philippine Islands* . . ., 57th Cong., 1st Sess., Document 33, 3 vols. (Washington, D.C., 1902), 2: 1205-1206. His sentence was commuted when general amnesty was declared.

LEWELLYS F. BARKER (1867-1943), Canadian by birth, after preliminary education in Ontario, took his M.B. from the University of Toronto in 1890. After a year's internship locally, he became an assistant resident physician at Johns Hopkins, becoming an associate professor of anatomy in 1887. On his return from the Philippines, in 1900 he accepted appointment as professor at the University of Chicago, but returned in 1905 to Johns Hopkins as chief physician to the university hospital. A prolific author, he retired in 1921. *National Cyclopedia of American Biography*, 32: 308-309 (hereafter cited *National Cyclopedia*).

SAM BASS, orphaned early in life, was born on a farm near Mitchell, Indiana, in 1851. Leaving home at eighteen, he commenced his wanderings, finally ending up in Denton, Texas. By 1874 he fell into bad company in the person of Joel Collins. As partners in 1876, they drove a herd of 500 to 700 beef steers to Dodge City. Changing their minds about selling there, they headed for the Black Hills and disposed of the cattle there. In short order robbing stage coaches became their obsession. After a year of lean pickings, in August 1877, they turned their faces south toward the Union Pacific; their number now included Bill Hefferidge, Jim Berry, Tom Nixon, and Jack Davis. At Big Springs, Nebraska, the gang copped $60,000 in $20 gold pieces from a UP train. The gang then drifted back to Texas where it met up with the Texas Rangers; numbers reduced, it soon began to disintegrate. Through an informant Bass was mortally wounded in a bank robbery attempt in Round Rock. He died on July 12, 1878, his twenty-seventh birthday. Helena H. Smith, "Sam Bass and the Myth Machine," *American West*, VII (January, 1970), 31–35.

W. H. "DEACON" BATES, in partnership with David T. Beals, both Boston shoe manufacturers, established their first ranch in Colorado on the Arkansas River. Drawn to the Panhandle, they moved the LX Ranch to Ranch Creek on the Canadian River, some twenty miles north of the later site of Amarillo. William C. Moore was their second foreman. In 1884 the partners sold out their holdings to the London-based American Pastoral Company—210,597 acres, 45,000 head of cattle, 1,000 horses—and returned to Boston. *Handbook of Texas*, II: 1.

JAMES FRANKLIN BELL (1858–1919), Kentucky born, graduated from West Point in 1878. He began his active military career as a 2nd lieutenant in the 9th Cavalry, June 14, 1878. He served in the 7th Cavalry on the Plains from 1878–1894. At the outbreak of the war with Spain, Bell was appointed major in the engineer volunteers, May

17, 1898; colonel by April and a brigadier general in the volunteers by December 5, 1899. On November 27, 1899, he was awarded the Medal of Honor for his gallantry in action, September 9, 1899, near Porac, Luzon, Philippine Islands. In February 1901, he was promoted to brigadier general in the regular army and became a major general, January 3, 1907. After his service in the Philippines, which ended in 1903, he served as army chief of staff, 1906–1910. He died January 8, 1919. *Army Register*, I: 207; *Who Was Who in America* (Chicago, 1942), I: 80.

ALBERT J. BEVERIDGE (1862–1929), Indiana born, raised, and educated; when admitted to the bar, commenced his legal practice in Indianapolis. Elected to the U.S. Senate on January 17, 1899; he was reelected in 1905, but was defeated for a third term. Returning to Indianapolis, he pursued a literary career and published several distinguished historical works, including a life of Lincoln. He died in Indianapolis, April 27, 1927. *Biographical Directory of the U.S. Congress*, p. 550.

BILLY THE KID. See entry for Henry McCarty.

WILLIAM H. BONNEY. See entry for Henry McCarty.

HENRY VAN NESS BOYNTON joined the 35th Ohio infantry at the start of the Civil War, July 29, 1861, with the rank of major. Discharged September 8, 1864, with the rank of lieutenant colonel, he was brevetted brigadier general the following year for his wartime gallantry. The Medal of Honor for his courage at the battle of Missionary Ridge, Tennessee, November 25, 1863, in which he was severely wounded, was bestowed November 15, 1893. On June 17, 1898, he was appointed brigadier general in the volunteers and was discharged on April 12, 1899. *Army Register*, I: 236.

JOHN BALL BRISBIN was born in Schuylerville, New York, January 10, 1827, and died in St. Paul, March 22, 1898. He graduated from Yale in 1846 and was admitted to the bar in 1847. He moved to Minnesota in 1853 and opened his practice in St. Paul. He served as the city's mayor in 1857 and was a representative in the state legislature in 1858 and 1863. "Minnesota Biographies," p. 77.

THOMAS S. BUGBEE (not Bugby) was born in Washington County, Maine, January 18, 1852. During the Civil War he served the Union's cause. In 1869 he started business in Kansas. On moving to the Panhandle, he founded the Quarter Circle T Ranch, headquartered at Adobe Wells on the Canadian River. Selling out in 1882 to the Hansford Cattle Company, he reentered the cattle business the next year. He had a long career as a stockman, being a partner in a succession of ranching ventures. He died at Clarendon, Texas, his home, October 18, 1925. He married Mary C. Dunn, August 13, 1872. They had eight children. *Handbook of Texas*, I: 243; L. F. Sheffy, "Thomas Sherman Bugbee," *Panhandle-Plains Historical Review*, II (1929), 128–134.

FRANK SMITH BURR joined the 2nd Nebraska Volunteer Infantry as a private at the start of the war in 1898, but swiftly was made a 2nd lieutenant. By 1899 he was a 1st lieutenant, serving with the 21st Infantry, followed by assignment with the 11th Infantry, and by August 17, 1900, with the 15th Infantry. *Army Register*, I: 266.

JAMES CAMPBELL, a Scotchman, ran both sheep and cattle. During his ranching days he sold out twice and had two different partners, both Englishmen, Ledger and E. Godwin-Austen. Campbell's first headquarters was on the Rita Blanca Creek northwest of Tascosa. McCarty, *Maverick Town*, pp. 36–37.

MARTHA CANARY, better known as Calamity Jane, was born near Princeton, Missouri. Her life is immersed in a sea of legends, much of it manufactured by her overly active imagination. She came to the Black Hills in 1875, accompanying the scientific expedition led by Dr. Walter Jenney, most likely as a camp follower. She remained in the area throughout the heyday of the gold rush until 1880, living with a succession of men and turning to prostitution whenever necessity demanded. Her reputed relationship with Hickok remains unsubstantiated. In 1895 she returned to spend her twilight years in Deadwood, most of them in an alcoholic haze. On her death, August 1, 1903, in Terry, South Dakota, she was buried in Mount Moriah Cemetery, Deadwood. J. Leonard Jennewein, *Calamity Jane of the Western Trails* (Huron, So. Dak., 1953), for full details.

FRANK G. CARPENTER, six years after his graduation from the University of Wooster in 1877, became a legislative correspondent at Columbus for the Cleveland *Leader*, later performing the same job in Washington, D.C. Subsequently, he became a free lance writer and spent the remainder of his life traveling, lecturing and writing. Born in Mansfield, Ohio, May 5, 1855, he died in Nanking, China, June 18, 1924. *New York Times*, June 18, 1924, p. 19, cl. 5.

ADNA R. CHAFFEE enlisted in the army as a sergeant in the 6th Cavalry at the beginning of the Civil War and ended that war with the rank of captain. He was made lieutenant colonel by 1897 and colonel two years later. With the 1898 war he was appointed a brigadier general in the volunteers, May 4, 1898, and was promoted to major general, volunteers, July 19, 1901, a rank that was conferred in the regular army on February 4, 1901. He was promoted to lieutenant general in 1904 and served as army chief of staff. He retired on February 1, 1906, and settled in Los Angeles where he became active in local affairs. He died there, November 1, 1914. *Army Register*, I: 292; *New York Times*, November 4, 1914, p. 7, cl. 7; Allen Johnson and Dumas Malone, eds., *Dictionary of American Biography*, 20 vols. (New York, 1928–1936), III: 589–590.

JOHN SIMPSON CHISUM, born in western Tennessee, Madison County, August 15, 1824, spent his early childhood years on his grandfather's extensive plantation. In 1837 his family moved to Paris, Texas. Aided by a partnership with an Easterner interested in Texas ranching opportunities, in 1854 Chisum launched what was to become a notable career as a cattleman.

Highly successful in various livestock ventures, famed for his Jinglebob brand and unique ear marking, by the early 1870s Chisum pushed his stock operations into the sparsely settled Pecos River region of territorial New Mexico. By 1873 he had occupied an immense range in and around Bosque Grande; within two years his herd numbered 80,000 head. New headquarters were acquired on the South Spring River, situated five miles south of Roswell. There he built "Square House" from which he would manage his ranching activities.

In that same year, 1875, at the height of his prosperity, he transferred the majority of his Pecos stock holdings to the prominent St. Louis beef commission concern, Hunter, Evans and Company, with the understanding that he would remain in titular charge and that the herds would be removed piecemeal. Between 1875–1880 over 50,000 beefs were supplied to the Kansas City cattle market on demand of the new Pecos owners. This was a prudent decision: Chisum was aware that the days of running cattle on the open range were drawing to an end; herds had to be reduced as former pasturage was occupied by smaller ranchers and farmers. In the bargain, the market began to demand graded and quality beef, which in turn required a more restricted and controlled approach to stock raising.

However, the magnitude of Chisum's short-lived Pecos operations won him the sobriquet, "The Cattle King of New Mexico." The origin of the appellation appeared first in *The Grant County Herald*, published at Silver City, April 11, 1875: "We hear of cotton being king, of railroad kings. But J. S. Chisum of Bosque Grande is our stock king of New Mexico." In popular usage, cattle or cow quickly replaced stock.

Restricted range operations after 1880, coupled with increased competition, Chisum's affairs declined perceptibly. He took a lively role in the various stockmen's associations commensurate with his pioneering ranching role in New Mexico.

His last years were plagued with a tumor which stubbornly resisted surgery. A major operation in Kansas City in the summer of 1884 was followed by post-operative complications. He was advised by his local physician to spend the winter in Eureka Springs, Arkansas, famed for its mineral baths. But fate would have it otherwise: on December 22, 1884, Chisum died at the spa. His brother James escorted the body to Paris; there, on Christmas Day, it was interred in the family plot. Harwood P. Hinton, "John Simpson Chisum, 1877-84," *New Mexico Historical Quarterly*, XXXI (July 1956), 177-205; (October 1956), 310-337; XXXII (January 1957), 53-65; C[laude] L. Douglas, *Cattle Kings of Texas* (Dallas, 1938), pp. 107-126.

SAMUEL L. CLEMENS (1835-1910), partly to avoid Civil War service, went to Nevada in 1861 with his brother, who had been appointed to a territorial government post. Failure as a miner forced him to take a job as a feature writer on the *Virginia City Territorial Enterprise*.

During his tenure on the newspaper, he adopted "Mark Twain" as his pen name. Moving to San Francisco in 1864, he continued in journalism while beginning to develop a reputation as a popular writer. Charles Van Doren, ed., *Webster's American Biographies* (Springfield, Mass., 1974), p. 207.

W[ILLIAM] BOURKE COCKRAN (1854–1923), Irish born, immigrated to the U.S. in 1871 and entered education, first as a teacher, later as a principal in Westchester County, New York. After admission to the bar in 1876, he moved to New York City two years later to practice law. Subsequently he became involved in Democratic party politics which resulted in his election to Congress in 1887. He was elected again in 1891 for two terms in the House, followed by two more terms, 1904–1909, and was elected again for a final term in 1921. He died in office. He married Anne Ide on November 5, 1906. *Who Was Who in America*, I: 236; *Biographical Directory of U.S. Congress*, p. 715.

A.M. CONKLIN, according to one source, was born in Ohio in 1841, but was raised and educated in Westfield, Indiana. After service for the Union cause in the Civil War, he married and raised a family. A newspaper man by trade, he apparently worked for a short time with the *Las Vegas Gazette* before going to Albuquerque. When the *Socorro Sun* was acquired by Conklin, he and his wife took their children back to Westfield and placed them in a boarding school. On reaching Socorro, along with a few fellow Presbyterians, a small congregation was formed, with the Rev. S. D. Fulton as pastor, in October 1880. F. Stanley [*pseud.*], *Desperadoes of New Mexico* (Denver, 1953), p. 221.

Hoyt's facts, in respect to Conklin's death, are confused. The Christmas festival took place in the Methodist

Mission Chapel. Rev. Thomas W. Harwood, superintendent of missions for the Methodist Church, North, arranged the affair with the cooperation of Socorro's other
Protestant clergy and churchgoers.

Conklin, acting as an usher, did try to stay a disturbance caused by three young Mexicans, kin of the town's
leading merchant, Juan José Baca, scion of a longtime
and influential New Mexico family. Antonio, Enofre and
Abram Baca were involved. The Baca family was "one of
the largest and most influential in the territory." During
the church service the three young Bacas "persisted in
placing their feet on the shoulders of some American ladies who occupied the pew in front of them. Several times
they were asked by Mr. Conklin to desist, and the last
time they cursed him vigorously and left the church." As
a result of this confrontation with Conklin, the three
waited outside the church and there took their revenge.
As to precisely who shot Conklin, that remains unre-
solved. In the confusion that followed the shooting, however, the Bacas fled.

Harwood describes the church scene in his book, *History of New Mexico Spanish and English Missions of the
Methodist Episcopal Church from 1850 to 1910*, 2 vols. (Albuquerque, 1908–1910), I: 333–336. As to the Bacas, Stanley in *Desperadoes of New Mexico*, p. 226, presents one
version which has Antonio a son of Juan José Baca, while
Chester D. Potter in his "Reminiscences of the Socorro
Vigilantes," p. 27, states that the three Bacas were brothers and nephews.

Hoyt's account of the death of Conklin closely parallels that given by Gillett, with two exceptions. Gillett
merely notes that there was "a church festival during
Christmas week of 1881," and spells Enofrio, Enofre,
which is correct.

In 1881 Gillett was stationed at Ysleta where Judge
Baca also had a store and home. Receiving the territorial

governor's reward proclamation, which contained good descriptions of the two brother killers, Gillett had the judge's property closely watched to no avail. In March, however, a fellow ranger, Jim Finch, spotted "two well-dressed Mexicans, strangers to him, sitting on the porch of Judge Baca's home." Quickly, Gillett and a band of rangers arrested the two suspects and started with them to New Mexico. Near El Paso the judge overtook Gillett, and through an interpreter, tried to bribe him. Rebuffed, Gillett delivered the two prisoners to Socorro, only to find that he had Abram, but not Enofre. The second captive turned out to be an innocent cousin, Massias Baca, who was promptly released. Gillett received half the reward, $500.00.

A month later Gillett received intelligence that Enofre was clerking in a big store at Saragosa, Mexico, about four miles from El Paso. To make sure, he sent his informant back to double check. It proved true. With the aid of George Lloyd, Gillett was able to capture Enofre and bring him back to El Paso, which cost him a severe dressing-down by his superior, Captain George W. Baylor, Company A.

Reprimand aside, Gillett transported his prisoner to New Mexico. On the last leg of the trip, taken by train, a telegram from the governor ordered Baca brought to Santa Fe. Showing the message to a band of men led by the Socorro deputy sheriff, who abruptly ignored it, Gillett had his hands full in trying to prevent a lynching while transporting his prisoner to the jail. He dissuaded the vigilantes by calling to their attention the fact that he would receive no reward since part of the terms was to deliver the prisoner safely to the jail. When this was done, and again in spite of Gillett's remonstration, the luckless Baca was taken to a nearby corral and hung from "a big beam of the gate." *Six Years with the Texas Rangers, 1875 to 1881*, ed. by Milo M. Quaife (Chicago, 1943), pp. 299–314. Gillett's book was initially published by Yale University Press in 1925.

The *Albuquerque Daily Journal*, March 31, 1881, provides graphic details of Enofre's death, though spelling the name Onofrio. The execution took place about 3:00 A.M. that morning.

As for Abram, still languishing in jail, he survived. Brought to trial in the fall, he was defended by Colonel Thomas B. Catron, while the prosecution was handled by Colonel J. Francisco Chavez. He was acquitted.

ROSCOE CONKLING (1829–1888) served in the House of Representatives 1859–1863, 1865–1867, and in the U.S. Senate from 1867–1881. *Webster's American Biographies*, p. 218.

CUSHMAN K. DAVIS (1838–1900), after graduating from the University of Michigan in 1857, studied law and was admitted to the bar two years later. After military service in the Civil War, he moved to St. Paul and became active in politics. He was governor of Minnesota in 1875 and 1876; elected to the U.S. Senate in 1886, he was reelected in 1892 and 1898. *Biographical Directory of the U.S. Congress*, p. 782.

GEORGE CALVIN DAY was born in Bradford, Vermont, November 8, 1871, and made the navy his career. He graduated from Annapolis in 1892 and received his ensign's commission in 1894. During the Spanish-American War, he was stationed on the *Topeka* on duty in the Philippines. His service record included extensive sea and land duty and important ship and shore commands. He became rear admiral, July 18, 1924. On retirement in 1935, he resided in Washington, D.C., where he died on November 3, 1940. *New York Times*, November 4, 1940, p. 19, cl. 5; *Who Was Who in America*, I: 306.

GRENVILLE M. DODGE (1831–1916) won fame during the Civil War, rising in rank from colonel in the volunteers to major general. At the end of the war he became chief engineer of the Union Pacific Railroad, interrupted by one term in the House of Representatives, 1867–1869. He subsequently was associated with numerous other railroad projects. In 1898 he was appointed by President McKinley to head a commission to investigate the army's conduct during the Spanish-American War. That eight-volume report, published in 1900, led to many significant changes in army organization. *Webster's American Biographies*, pp. 281–282.

CHARLES M. DRAKE served as a major and surgeon in the volunteers from June 4, 1898, until his discharge on February 22, 1899. On July 5, 1899, he joined the volunteers in the Philippine Insurrection, serving until December 31, 1902. *Army Register*, I: 382.

JAMES H. EAST was born in Kaskaskia, Illinois, August 30, 1853. When he turned sixteen, he headed for Texas, inspired by having read of Davy Crockett and the fall of the Alamo. He got a job near Seguin, herding cattle on the range in the employ of John F. Tom. In 1870 he participated in his first "long drive" to the New Orleans market, followed by many more. In 1880 he moved to the Panhandle, taking a job with the LX Ranch. His life there proved exciting as detailed in J. Evetts Haley, "Jim East—Trail Hand and Cowboy," *Panhandle-Plains Historical Review*, IV (1931), 39–61. He died at Douglas, Arizona, age seventy-seven, on May 14, 1930. "Biography of Orrie Clark," p. 1, Information File, Panhandle-Plains Historical Museum.

WINFIELD S. EDGERLY made the military service his lifelong career. Born in New Hampshire, he became a cadet at West Point on July 1, 1866, and graduated in June 1870 as a 2nd lieutenant, posted to the 7th Cavalry. By 1893 he held the rank of captain. On the eve of the Spanish-American War he was promoted to major and during that war served as a lieutenant colonel. He returned to regular service in 1901. *Army Register*, I: 397.

JESSE EVANS, alias Davis, alias Graham, was born in Missouri in about 1853 and came to New Mexico in 1872. He became a drifter and entered Lincoln County with his small gang of cattle and horse thieves in 1876–1877. He was named and indicted as one of the men who killed John H. Tunstall. Billy the Kid was with the pro-Tunstall side in the ensuing conflict. In February 1879, long bitter enemies, the two agreed to make peace, but "on the heels of the parley came a startling renewal of the old lawlessness," beginning with the murder of Houston I. Chapman, the lawyer for Mrs. Alexander A. McSween, whose husband had been the second important figure to die in the Lincoln County bloodshed. McSween had been a partner in business with Tunstall. Again, Evans was involved with Chapman's murder and was arrested. Escaping, he was captured with the remnant of his gang by Texas Rangers on Alamito Creek near Fort Davis on July 3, 1880. Brought to trial in October, Evans was convicted for manslaughter in a robbery at Fort Davis. Sentenced to twenty years, he entered Rusk Prison, December 1, 1880. He escaped from there "about a year and half" later "and became lost to history." Fulton, *The Lincoln County War*, pp. 67, 125, 201, 324–327, 331, 333, 372–378.

POWELL C. FAUNTLEROY began his service as an assistant surgeon in the volunteers, November 15, 1898. He held the rank of major surgeon from November 30, 1900, until the time of his discharge, June 30, 1901. *Army Register*, I: 415.

SIMON FLEXNER (1863–1946) took his M.D. at the University of Louisville in 1889, having previously graduated from the Louisville College of Pharmacy. He went to Johns Hopkins Medical School when it opened in 1892 as assistant in the Department of Pathology. This marked the beginning of a brilliant career. After a year's work in Europe, by 1899 he was a full professor. In that year, accompanied by two medical students, Joseph Flint and W. F. Jay, and assisted by Dr. Lewellys F. Barker, he spent several months in Manila as head of the Johns Hopkins Commission on Tropical Diseases, especially created to investigate such diseases in the Philippine Islands. During his stay there, he isolated the *Bacillus* (now *Shegilla) dysenteriae*, which causes a prevalent form of dysentery. He continued to rise in eminence thereafter as a pathologist and bacteriologist. Charles C. Gillispie, ed., *Dictionary of Scientific Biography*, 11 vols. (New York, 1972), v: 39–41.

JOSEPH M. FLINT (1872–1944), after study at Princeton and graduation with a B.S. from the University of Chicago, entered Johns Hopkins Medical School in 1897, graduating in 1900. From 1901–1907, he was on the University of California medical faculty and taught at Yale, 1907–1921. *National Cyclopedia*, 33: 458–459.

ROYAL T. FRANK graduated from West Point in 1858. From a 2nd lieutenant, he rose in rank: captain, 1862; major, 1881; lieutenant colonel, 1889; colonel, 1894; brigadier general, May 4, 1898. He retired October 18, 1899. *Army Register*, I: 434.

FREDERICK FUNSTON, born November 9, 1865, in New Carlisle, Ohio, entered the service of the U.S. Department of Agriculture as an agent in 1890. Six years later, in 1896, he joined the Cuban insurgent army, which

launched his military career. With the outbreak of the
Spanish-American War, he was commissioned a colonel
in the 21st Kansas Volunteer Infantry, May 13, 1898, and
was posted to the Philippines. He was promoted to brigadier general in the volunteers May 1, 1899. For his gallantry in action at his Grande de la Pampanga, Luzon,
April 27, 1899, an engagement in which he was wounded,
he received the Medal of Honor, February 14, 1900. In
January of that same year he was assigned the command
of the 4th District in the Philippines and organized the
expedition which captured the insurgent leader Aguinaldo on March 20, 1901. He was promoted to brigadier
general in the regular army, April 1, 1901. On his return
to the states he saw duty as commander of various departments. He is particularly remembered for his efforts to
save San Francisco in the wake of the disastrous 1906
earthquake and fire and for his efforts in trying to capture
Pancho Villa while in command of the Texas-New Mexico
Department. Promoted to major general on November 17,
1914, he died in San Antonio, February 19, 1917, and was
buried in the Presidio in San Francisco. Bailey Millard,
History of the San Francisco Bay Region, 3 vols. (Chicago,
1924), II: 28–32; George D. Bogert, "The Man Who Saved
San Francisco," *Sunset Magazine* (May 1928), 38–39, 62;
New York Times, February 24, 1917, p. 9, cl. 5; *Army
Register*, I: 441.

PATRICK FLOYD GARRETT (1850–1908) has one
claim on history, indeed, it made his place in history, his
slaying of Billy the Kid. Born in Alabama, reared in Lou-
isiana, he became a Texas cowboy in 1869; in 1877 he
drifted into Tascosa, and in 1879 he moved to Lincoln
County, becoming sheriff the next year. He subsequently
turned to ranching, but he reentered law enforcement
with a brief stint as a Texas Ranger, and as sheriff of
Doña Ana County. From 1901–1905 Garrett served

as U.S. customs collector at El Paso, Texas. Returning to New Mexico to resume an unprofitable career in ranching, he was slain, shot on February 29, 1908; his confessed killer was acquitted in a verdict that satisfied few. Leon C. Metz, *Pat Garrett* (Norman, Okla., 1974), affords the best biography.

GERONIMO (1829?–1909) was the famed medicine man and leader of the Chiricahua Apache. His name, Spanish for Jerome, stands squarely in the history of Apache-U.S. relations in the turbulent years following the Civil War in Arizona and New Mexico. Angie Debo has authored an excellent biography, published in 1977.

CHARLES A. GOODNIGHT, born in Macoupin County, Illinois, March 5, 1836, was brought to Texas at age ten by his mother and stepfather. When he was twenty-one, he became a ranger, an Indian scout and guide. During the Civil War he served as a scout and guide with the Frontier Regiment of Texas Rangers. By 1857 he was a budding cattleman, running a herd in Palo Pinto County, Texas. In 1866 he moved to the Pecos River in southern New Mexico. Two years later he established a ranch on the Apishapa in Colorado, and in 1870 settled on the Arkansas, four miles from Pueblo. He married Mary Ann Dyer in Hickman, Kentucky, July 26, 1870. She was born in Madison County, Tennessee in 1839 and died in 1926.

In an effort to find a more lucrative market for his cattle, in association with Oliver Loving, a trail was blazed in 1866 from Fort Belknap, Texas, to Fort Sumner, New Mexico, famed as the Goodnight-Loving Trail and destined to become one of the most heavily trafficked cattle routes in the Southwest. Later, in 1875, he forged the New Goodnight Trail from Alamogordo Creek, New Mexico, to Granada, Colorado.

After failure in Colorado ranching, he relocated in the

Texas Panhandle in 1876, centering his activities at Palo Duro Canyon. The following year, in partnership with John G. Adair, the JA Ranch was formed. The million-acre spread was divided in 1887 on Adair's death, with Goodnight disposing of his share in 1890. As a stock-man, Goodnight made many notable contributions to the cattle industry, including better bred stock, and played a major role in bringing law and order to northern Texas. He died December 12, 1929, at his winter home in Tucson, Arizona. J. Evetts Haley, *Charles Goodnight, Cowman and Plainsman* (Boston, 1936), offers a solid biography.

JOHN GOODNOW (1858–1907), Indiana born, served in the Civil War with the 12th Indiana Volunteers, rising to the rank of lieutenant colonel. Subsequently he graduated from the University of Minnesota in 1879, making that state his home. Without prior diplomatic experience, he was appointed consul general in Shanghai in 1897, and successfully negotiated an important trade treaty with China in 1902. *Who Was Who in America*, I: 468.

WILLIS A. GORMAN, territorial governor of Minnesota, 1853–1857, began his military service in Minnesota as first sergeant, in 1846, as a Mexican War volunteer. Two days later, June 22, he was made a major. When he was mustered out in July 1848, he held the rank of colonel. With the Civil War, he was appointed colonel of the 1st Minnesota Infantry, April 29, 1861. In September he was appointed brigadier general in the volunteers. Mustered out in May 1864, he died May 21, 1876. *Army Register*, I: 466; Andrews, ed., *History of St. Paul*, pp. 24–29.

FREDERICK DENT GRANT, the son of the 16th President of the United States, Ulysses S. Grant, was born in St. Louis on May 30, 1850. Many of his early years were spent with his father in various military assignments, including the Civil War. In 1866 he was admitted to West Point, graduating in 1871. A variety of military appointments ensued, including escort duty, 1872–1873, for survey parties of the Texas Pacific Railroad across the Staked Plain and service with Custer during his 1874 Black Hills expedition. As his father's health began to fail, young Grant resigned his commission in 1881 to enter into business in New York and to assist his father with his memoirs. President Benjamin Harrison appointed him minister to Austria in 1888 and he continued in the post under President Grover Cleveland until 1893, when he returned to New York.

With the advent of the Spanish-American War, he was appointed brigadier general in the U.S. Volunteers, May 27, 1898. Duty in the Philippines found him first as commander of the 2nd brigade, 1st division, 8th Army Corps in April 1899. Subsequently, he was transferred to the 2nd brigade, 2nd division, in northern Luzon to protect and cover the flank and rear of General Arthur MacArthur's command. He remained in the islands until 1902 as commander of the 5th district in northern Luzon. On February 18, 1901, he received a regular commission in the U.S. Army. Returning to the states, he was posted to different commands. While commander of the Department of the East and Gulf, he died in New York City, April 12, 1912. *National Cyclopedia*, 15: 93–94.

JULIA GRANT was born in the White House, June 7, 1876. She married Prince Michael Cantacuzene, Count Speransky, at Newport, Rhode Island, on September 25, 1899. Her husband served as a major general on the staff of Grand Duke Nicholas in World War I. After the Bolshevik Revolution, Cantacuzene was manager of the extensive agricultural holdings of the Palmer Florida Corporation, headquartered at Saratoga. The couple had three children. Their marriage ended in divorce. *New*

York Times, March 26, 1955, p. 15, cls. 3–4; *National Cyclopedia*, D: 436.

FRANCIS V. GREENE, Class of 1870, West Point, was commissioned a 2nd lieutenant in the artillery, but transferred in 1872 to the engineers. When he resigned from service in 1886, he held the rank of captain. During the Spanish-American War he rose to rank of major general of volunteers. *Army Register*, I: 475.

JAMES A. GREGORY, Class of 1865, West Point, originally commissioned a 2nd lieutenant in the artillery, transferred in 1866 to the engineers and was promoted to 1st lieutenant. He made captain in 1874 and major in 1886. He died, July 31, 1897. *Army Register*, I: 477.

FRANCISCO GUILLEDO, who fought under the name Pancho Villa, had a short but successful career in both the flyweight and bantam divisions during the three years he boxed in America, 1922–1925. Nathaniel S. Fleischer, ed., *Nat Fleischer's All-Time Ring Record Book* (Norwalk, Conn., 1941), pp. 70–71.

IRVING HALE entered West Point as a cadet in 1880. Commissioned 2nd lieutenant in the engineers, June 15, 1884, he resigned from the service in 1890. With the advent of the war he was made colonel in the 1st Colorado Infantry, May 1, 1898; subsequently promoted to brigadier general, volunteers. He was honorably discharged with that rank in October 1899. *Army Register*, I: 467.

ABRAM A. HARBACK joined military service as a sergeant, 1st Iowa Infantry, on May 7, 1861. He was made a 2nd lieutenant in 1862, and gradually rose in rank: captain, 1867; major, 1894; lieutenant colonel, 1897. After the Spanish-American War he was promoted to brigadier general, in 1902, retiring on May 28 that same year. *Army Register*, I: 499.

FRANCIS BURTON HARRISON joined the New York volunteers, June 20, 1898, entering service with the rank of captain. He was discharged on January 31, 1899. *Army Register*, I: 505.

WILLIAM S. HART, famed actor and movie star, was born in Newburgh, New York, December 6, 1870, and grew up in the Midwest. His youth in South Dakota left an indelible influence on his subsequent life. He commenced acting on the New York stage at the age of nineteen and gradually established himself as a popular actor, becoming especially adept at portraying Westerners. Films beckoned in 1914 and he moved to Hollywood; many silent Western films marked Hart's motion picture career. He retired in 1925 and turned to writing. He spent his declining years on his Horseshoe Ranch near Newhall, California, where he died on June 23, 1947. *Webster's American Biographies*, p. 463.

GEORGE R. HARVEY, Alabama born, was educated at the University of Texas, Valparaiso University (Indiana), and the Kansas City Law School. He served for many years on the bench in the Philippines. Harvey arrived in San Francisco "on the last clipper plane to touch at Wake Island, before its capture by the Japanese early in the second World War." He died in Berkeley, California, April 9, 1952, at the age of eighty-four. His wife died in the preceding January. *New York Times*, April 10, 1952, p. 29, cl. 3.

HARRY HARVEY, born in New York City, June 4, 1873, received the Medal of Honor on July 19, 1901, for his meritorious conduct "in battle against the enemy at

Benictican, 16 February 1900." *Medal of Honor Recipients, 1863–1973* (Washington, D.C., 1974), p. 395.

JAMES JEROME HILL, Canadian by birth, was born near Rockwood, Ontario, September 16, 1838. As a youth he was forced to drop formal schooling and accidentally suffered the loss of sight in one eye. At fourteen he began clerking in a village store. In 1856 he went to Minnesota Territory, settling in fast-growing St. Paul. Starting out as a clerk with a steamboat company, ten years later he was a freight agent and general merchant. His steady rise to wealth mushroomed when he joined a syndicate which acquired the debt-plagued and construction-stalled St. Paul and Pacific Railroad Company in 1878–1879. Renamed the Great Northern in 1890, three years later the railroad was completed to Puget Sound, built without a single dollar or land grant from the federal government. Hill died in St. Paul, May 29, 1916. For an excellent account of his life, see Albro Martin, *Joseph J. Hill and the Opening of the Northwest* (New York, 1976).

HARRY HOUDINI. See Ehrich Weiss.

EMERSON HOUGH became a lawyer after graduating from the University of Iowa. But that vocation held little interest for him. Leaving his profession, he spent fifteen years wandering the West. From that experience he forged a new career as a writer, publishing his first book in 1895. All in all, he published twenty-five books, the most famous being *The Covered Wagon*. Born in Newton, Iowa, he died in Evanston, Illinois, April 30, 1923, at the age of sixty-six. *New York Times*, May 1, 1923, p. 21, cl. 3.

WALTER HOWE, a West Pointer, Class of 1867, held the rank of captain by 1891. He was appointed colonel in the 47th U.S. Volunteer Infantry, August 17, 1889, and ended his volunteer status with the rank of lieutenant colonel in 1902. *Army Register*, I: 548.

CHAUNCEY B. HUMPHREY, West Point graduate, was made a 2nd lieutenant in the 3rd U.S. Infantry, April 26, 1898. By March 2, 1899, he rose to 1st lieutenant. Transferred to the 17th U.S. Infantry, he was promoted to captain in February 1903. *Army Register*, I: 554.

LI HUNG-CHANG (1823–1901), most famous and powerful Chinese statesman of the late nineteenth century, was governor-general of Chihli Province (includes Peking) from 1870 to 1895. He toured the world, including the U.S., in 1896. For a short biography see Arthur W. Hummel, ed., *Eminent Chinese of the Ch'ing Period*, 2 vols. (Washington, D.C., 1940–1943), 1: 464–471.

HENRY CLAY IDE (1844–1921), born in Vermont, graduated from Dartmouth in 1866. A decade later he began his career of public service as state attorney, serving two years, followed in 1882 with election to the state senate. In 1891 he was appointed to the U.S. Commission to Samoa and served as Samoan chief justice, 1893–1897. He became a member of the Taft Commission in April 1900; secretary of finance and justice for the Philippines, September 1, 1901; vice governor, 1904–1905; acting governor, 1905; governor general, 1906. He entered business in New York City in 1907 and served as U.S. Minister to Spain, 1909–1913. *Who Was Who in America*, I: 616.

CHARLES ILFELD, born in Homburg vor der Hohe, Germany, April 19, 1847, immigrated to Taos, New Mexico, in the spring of 1865, following his older brother William. He worked for a time for A. Letcher. In May 1867 they formed a partnership and opened a store in Las Vegas. In September 1874 he bought out Letcher's interests and launched a notable mercantile career. He died in January 1929, leaving his heirs a chain of stores. William J. Parish, *The Charles Ilfeld Company* (Cambridge, Mass., 1961), details the success of this immigrant.

ALBERT KEEP, born in Homer, New York, April 30, 1826, became a director of the Chicago and Northwestern Railroad Company, in 1873, and also was elected president that same year. He served in that dual capacity until 1887 and then presided as chairman of the board, 1887–1901. He died in Chicago on May 13, 1907. *Who Was Who in America*, I: 659; *New York Times*, May 14, 1907, p. 11, cl. 6.

MYLES W. KEOGH, Irish by birth, entered the Civil War in 1862 by being appointed a captain of volunteers in Washington, D.C. By 1864 he was a major. At the end of the conflict, he joined the regular service as a 2nd lieutenant, 4th U.S. Cavalry, March 4, 1866, and was made a captain, 7th U.S. Cavalry, July 28, 1866. He received brevetted promotions three times for gallantry in the field during the Civil War. He was killed at the battle of the Little Bighorn in 1876. *Army Register*, I: 593.

FRANK B. KELLOGG (1856–1937) studied law in Rochester, Minnesota, and was admitted to the bar in 1877. He moved to St. Paul in October 1887, and developed an impressive legal reputation. Politics also commanded his attention. In 1916 he was elected to the U.S. Senate, but failed in a reelection bid. After a two-year stint as U.S. Ambassador to Great Britain, he served as secretary of state under President Coolidge, 1925–1929. After leaving office, he was awarded the Nobel Peace Prize in 1930 and served for five years as associate justice on the Permanent Court for International Justice. *Biographical Dictionary of the U.S. Congress*, p. 1150.

MIFFLIN KENEDY (1818–1895) and Richard King (1824–1885) were indeed "The Cattle Kings of Texas" by 1880. Their business association embraced a variety of other interests as well. Their ranching partnership existed only from 1860–1868: King had the land and cattle; Kenedy had money and cattle. The partnership made possible their rise to cattle kings. After the dissolution of the partnership each developed his own ranch. Mifflin Kenedy married Petra Vila de Vidal of Mier, Mexico, April 16, 1852. They had six children. Douglas, *Cattle Kings of Texas*, pp. 79–95; *Handbook of Texas*, I: 947.

JOSEPH J. KINYOUN (1860–1919) "laid the groundwork for the present program of medical and public health research carried on by the National Institutes of Health." Born in East Bend, North Carolina, he received his medical degree in 1882 from Bellevue Hospital Medical College of New York University. During his postgraduate training in Europe he was taught by Robert Koch, the great German bacteriologist. Returning to the United States, Kinyoun joined the Marine Hospital Service (now the Public Health Service) in 1886. He became the first Director of the Hygienic Laboratory and introduced bacteriology into the Marine Hospital Service. After leaving the service in 1903, he worked for a private research laboratory, became a professor of pathology and bacteriology at George Washington University Medical School, and ended his career as bacteriologist for the District of Columbia Health Department until his death. Ralph C. Williams, *The United States Public Health Service, 1798–1950* (Washington, D. C., 1950), pp. 249–250.

HARRY ALEXANDER LEONHAEUSER graduated from West Point in 1881. Commissioned 2nd lieutenant in the 25th Infantry, he rose slowly in rank. By 1889 he was 1st lieutenant; a decade later he was promoted to captain. With the war he was commissioned lieutenant colonel in the 15th Minnesota Volunteer Infantry, and shortly after promoted to colonel. He was mustered out of the volunteers in March 1899. *Army Register*, I: 629.

CHARLES F. LUMMIS was destined for a career as a newspaperman, author, editor, librarian, conservationist and preservationist. While on his famed walking trip from Cincinnati to Los Angeles, a distance of 3,507 miles covered in 143 days, he met Mariño Lebya in Golden, New Mexico, thirty-three miles northeast of Albuquerque, in the late fall of 1884. Lummis began his remarkable feat on September 11, 1884 and completed it on February 1, 1885. He vividly describes Lebya as a "known murderer," and records his gang's killing of an American doctor during his brief stay in Golden. Three years later, Lummis records Mariño's retribution. "A Mexican whom he had treated with great generosity, and upon whose friendship he relied, was bribed to kill him, or to assist a deputy sheriff in doing so. The precious couple met Mariño on the forest road a few miles from Golden, and the always alert outlaw challenged them. 'What? Don't you know me?' cried the false friend, riding up with a cordial smile and extending his hand. As Mariño grasped it, the traitor jerked him forward and the cowardly officer put a bullet through Mariño's brain from behind." *Tramping Across the Continent* (Reprint ed., Albuquerque, 1969), pp. 127–128.

Mariano Leiva (Leiba or Lebya) was serving seven years in the Leavenworth penitentiary; his sentence commenced in April 1882. It is clear that Lummis' Mariño Lebya is not Mariano Leiva, the culprit alluded to by Hoyt, even though Hoyt calls him Marino Lebya and compares his death to that of Jesse James, who was shot in the back by his friend Robert Ford, April 3, 1882. James was in his home in St. Joseph, Missouri, standing on a chair straightening a picture at the time. Settle, *Jesse James Was His Name*, p. 117.

ANTONIO LUNA Y NOVICIO was general of a division of the Army of the Philippine Republic and general-in-chief of military operations in the vicinity of Manila. Dean C. Worcester, *The Philippines Past and Present* (New York, 1930), p. 238n.

Aguinaldo subsequently had Luna eliminated because of his advocacy of conventional warfare against the U.S. forces instead of guerrilla tactics. Leon Wolff, *Little Brown Brother: How the United States Purchased and Pacified the Philippines at the Century's Turn* (New York, 1961), p. 209; *New York Times*, June 17, 1899, p. 7, cl. 1.

ARTHUR MacARTHUR, born in Springfield, Massachusetts, June 2, 1845, received his initial commission with the Civil War, 1st lieutenant adjutant, Wisconsin Infantry Volunteers, August 4, 1862. He ended the war with the rank of lieutenant and was brevetted twice for bravery in the field. Drawn to the soldier's life, he was appointed 1st lieutenant in the 17th U.S. Infantry, February 23, 1866. In 1890 he was awarded the Medal of Honor for his bravery at the battle of Missionary Ridge, November 25, 1863. On May 27, 1898, he was appointed brigadier general in the volunteers, and by August was a major general. He received like promotions in the regular army, January 2, 1900, and February 5, 1901. In various capacities, he saw extensive duty in the Philippines and served as military governor, May 5, 1900, to July 4, 1901. Thereafter he was posted to various stateside commands and was promoted to lieutenant general in 1906. Retiring two years later, he died in Milwaukee, September 5, 1912. *Who Was Who in America*, I: 759.

LUCIEN B. MAXWELL was born in Kaskaskia, Illinois,

September 14, 1818, son of an Irish-immigrant father and a French mother. The latter explains his given names, Lucien Bonaparte. His grandfather, Pierre Menard, was engaged in the fur trade; young Lucien followed suit. In the 1830s he began trading in the Southwest, using Taos as a base. A chance visit to St. Louis for trade goods, in 1842, resulted in Maxwell's employment as a hunter by John Charles Frémont, who was about to embark on his first expedition. He would serve again with Frémont's third expedition.

On June 3, 1844, he married María de la Luz Beaubien, daughter of a prominent Taso citizen and holder of a large Mexican grant of land. Eventually this would make Maxwell's name and fortune. By 1865, following the death of his father-in-law, Maxwell held 2,680 square miles of land (1,714,769.92 acres), making him the largest land owner in the United States. His vast holdings became known as the Maxwell Grant. He centered his ranching activities at Cimmaron, built a large house there, and lived in baronial style befitting a gentleman of his wealth and position.

Although he sold acreage from time to time, in 1870 he disposed of all his holdings, realizing a net profit of about $810,000. Investments in banking, mining and railroads failed to hold his interest. It was at this point in his life that he purchased from the U.S. government Fort Sumner and resumed ranching. He died there on July 25, 1875, a man of substantial wealth. He was survived by his widow, who died in 1900, and several of his children. Harvey L. Carter, "Lucien Maxwell," in Leroy R. Hafen, ed., *The Mountain Men and the Fur Trade of the Far West*, 10 vols. (Glendale, Calif., 1965–1972), VI: 299–306.

HENRY McCARTY, alias Billy Antrim, William Bonney, Billy the Kid, was probably born about 1859, the place in dispute. His mother was known as Catherine

McCarty during the time she resided in Indiana, Kansas, and Colorado before her marriage to William H. Antrim in Santa Fe, New Mexico, March 1, 1873. Her son acted as witness at the marriage ceremony and his name is recorded as Henry McCarty. It was by that name he was known when the family moved immediately after the wedding to Silver City. Later he took his stepfather's name and called himself Billy Antrim. He did not take up the name William Bonney (perhaps a family name) until he reached the Pecos Valley.

His mother died on September 16, 1874. Less than a year later he fled Silver City, having been jailed as a lesson by the sheriff for hiding a bundle of washing stolen from a Chinese laundry by an older man. Making his escape from jail, he headed west to Graham County, Arizona, in 1875. It was there he received his nickname Billy the Kid, or merely Kid.

Two years later, in August 1877, the Kid killed his first victim, Frank Cahill, an army blacksmith. He was jailed the following day when Cahill died. Making his escape, he fled to New Mexico and eventually made his way to the Pecos Valley, Lincoln County. Although he was a guest at John Chisum's South Spring River ranch, he was never an employee nor did he become a member of the Jesse Evans' gang. He found employment with John H. Tunstall.

His subsequent involvement in the Lincoln County War, which erupted with Tunstall's murder, and his career as a gunfighter and range thief has been carefully documented in Fulton's *The Lincoln County War*. Suffice it to note here that one of the components in that bloody and savage conflict was the killing of Sheriff William Brady and his deputy, George Hindman, April 1, 1878. Indicted for the crime, along with three others who were to become part of his gang, the Kid fled, leaving a trail of criminal activity wherever he went.

Hoyt recounts the events which led to his "arranged" arrest by Governor Lew Wallace, his jailing, and subsequent escape. More violence followed in his wake, as well as cattle stealing.

The Kid was captured with two gang members by a posse led by Pat Garrett on the morning of December 21, 1880, at Stinking Springs, three days after the same posse had ambushed the gang, killed Tom O'Folliard and almost caught Billy at Fort Sumner. On December 27, Garrett boarded the train at Las Vegas for Santa Fe with his prisoners, reaching the capital at 2:00 p.m. The Kid remained jailed in Santa Fe until March 28, 1881, when he was taken under a long-standing change of venue (two years) to Mesilla in Doña Ana County to stand trial.

On being convicted in territorial court of Brady's death, Judge Warren Bristol sentenced the Kid on April 13 to be hanged at Lincoln on May 13. Robert Olinger and Deputy Sheriff Dave Wood of Doña Ana County, with a posse of five men, escorted Bonney from Las Cruces to Lincoln, the journey lasting from April 16 to 20. The hapless condemned "was handcuffed and shackled and chained to the back seat of the ambulance" in which he was transported.

Six days after his return to Lincoln, the Kid killed his guards, Olinger and J. W. Bell, and made good an escape on April 28. Pat Garrett once again sought the fugitive, accompanied by two deputies. The Kid was finally located at Fort Sumner, staying with his friend Pete Maxwell. There, around midnight, July 13, 1881, Pat Garrett felled him with a single shot. He was buried the next day beside two of his gang, Charlie Bowdre and Tom O'Folliard, in the former military cemetery at Fort Sumner. Fulton, *The Lincoln County War*, pp. 68 *et seq.*

McCarty, *Maverick Town*, has a good chapter on "Billy the Kid," pp. 75–93. He incorporates much of Hoyt's details in his narrative.

CHARLES McCLURE, a graduate of West Point, Class of 1879, held the rank of captain by 1895. On April 17, 1899, he was appointed major in the volunteers and returned to regular rank as major in the infantry, March 1, 1901. *Army Register*, I: 657.

FRANK J. MEAD (not Meade) who was born in Greensburg, Indiana, in 1835, came to St. Paul in 1857. His career as a journalist included city editorship of the *Pioneer*, and as publisher of newspapers in Farmington and Shakopee, as well as in Nebraska and the Dakota Territory. His latter years were spent in Minneapolis, where he died on November 29, 1908. "Minnesota Biographies," p. 499.

PANTALEON MIERA was at one time a lieutenant in the infamous Sostenes Archeveque and Santos Benavides gangs in New Mexico and was a horse thief. He was captured in Bernalillo with a comrade in December 1880. Since the town apparently lacked a proper jail, the two prisoners were confined to the home of Constable Pedro Valdez. On the evening of December 29, the guards were overpowered and "the two thieves were lynched from a limb of a cottonwood which stood in the front yard." *The Daily New Mexican* (Santa Fe), December 30, 1880.

The clue to their capture rests in the tragic fate that befell Colonel Charles S. Potter, a member of the U.S. Geological Survey Corps. On October 14, 1880, leaving Tijeras en route to the New Placers, he vanished. His friends by the end of the year posted a $1,000 reward for his discovery if alive and $200 for the recovery of his body if dead.

It appears that Miera pawned Potter's gold watch and chain. When it was identified, Sheriff Perfecto Armijo of Bernalillo County proceeded to Bernalillo to investigate. The investigation cast suspicion on Escolastica Perea, who was arrested in Isleta. Brought to Albuquerque for questioning, he confessed to having been a witness to the crime.

Perea's story was that Potter, while on his way to the New Placers, met some men who advised him to take a short cut through Tijeras Canyon. Miguel Barrera served as his guide. In the meantime Mariano Leiva hastened to the home of "one California Joe, obtained arms, returned to the party, and shot Potter." After robbing him, the body was buried in the bed of a small stream about three miles from Tijeras. Barrera and California Joe were promptly arrested and taken to Albuquerque. On the night of January 31, 1881, a party of 200 men seized them and hung them from a beam in front of the jail. *Ibid.*, January 30, February 1, 2, 4, 1881. Miera, as already noted, suffered the same fate in Bernalillo a month earlier.

Leiva continued to elude capture until March. When taken, he denied being a party to Potter's murder. However, on August 18, 1881, he was tried for an earlier assault with a gun on Pat Garrett, which is described in Garrett's *The Authentic Life of Billy the Kid* (Norman, 1954), pp. 107–108. Convicted, Leiva was fined $80.00. Since the witnesses to Potter's murder were by this time dead, Leiva could not be brought to trial on that score, but did stand trial for stealing stock. Found guilty, he was sentenced to seven years. On April 5, 1882, he started for Leavenworth, Kansas to serve his time. *Las Vegas Daily Optic*, March 18, August 18, 19, 1881; April 6, 1882. Sheriff Armijo called Leiva "without doubt the worst villain within the bounds of the Territory." *Ibid.*, April 5, 1882.

JOSÉ ANTONIO MONTOYA, a resident of Bernalillo, is recorded in the 1870 U.S. Census as being fifty years of age. His household included his thirty-six year old wife, Lorenza, and three young sons, ranging in age from two to twelve. Personal wealth of $12,000 was reported.

WILLIAM C. MOORE became the second foreman in the employ of W. H. "Deacon" Bates and David T. Beals on the LX Ranch. Moore reputedly killed a brother-in-law in California. Fleeing to Cheyenne, Wyoming, he became manager of the Swan Cattle Company. Subsequently, he killed his Negro coachman and fled to the Panhandle "on a broken-down pony in 1877." He managed the LX until August 1, 1881, when he established a ranch of his own at Coldwater Springs in "No-Man's Land in the Panhandle of Oklahoma," stocked with company cattle he had stolen with the aid of two LX cowboys. He relocated soon after to the American Valley in western New Mexico. Charlie Siringo, while on assignment as a Pinkerton operative in Alaska in 1895, met Moore in Juneau, living under an assumed name. Siringo relates that while Moore was living in the American Valley in New Mexico, he killed two men. Outlawed with a price on his head, he fled. Margaret Sheers, "The LX Ranch in Texas," *Frontier Times,* 29 (February 1952), 130–131; Charles A. Siringo, *A Cowboy Detective. A True Story of Twenty-Two Years with a World-Famous Detective Agency* (Chicago, 1912), pp. 224–225.

MADAME MOUSTACHE'S real name was Eleanor Dumont. She came to Deadwood in July 1876.

PAGE BLACKWOOD OTERO, the eldest son of Miguel A. Otero and Mary Josephine Blackwood, was born in Washington, D.C., January 14, 1858. His younger brother, Miguel Antonio, served as New Mexico's territorial governor, 1897–1906. Page died in Los Angeles, California. Miguel A. Otero, *My Life on The Frontier, 1864–1882* (New York, 1935), p. 285.

HARRISON GRAY OTIS (1837–1917) volunteered for service during the Civil War, rising in rank from private

to captain. For bravery, he was brevetted major and lieutenant colonel. Leaving his home state, Ohio, he moved
west to southern California, first Santa Barbara, then Los
Angeles, and worked as a newspaper editor and owner.
He built his fame and reputation with the *Los Angeles
Times*, which he acquired full control of in 1886. Taking
leave of his paper, Otis was appointed brigadier general
in the California volunteers, May 27, 1898, and served
until July 2, 1899. He was brevetted major general of the
volunteers for his exemplary conduct at the battle of
Caloocan in the Philippines. *Dictionary of American Biography*, XIV: 100–101.

RANDALL PARISH, like Hough, went to the University
of Iowa. He, too, became a lawyer, beginning his practice
in Wichita, Kansas. In 1883 he went to Arizona and New
Mexico prospecting for gold. Subsequently, he became a
newspaper man working in Denver, Omaha, Sioux City
and Chicago. His first book, *My Lady of the North*, published in 1904, launched his career as a novelist. He died
in his native state, Illinois, at Peoria on August 9, 1923, at
age sixty-five. *New York Times*, August 10, 1923, p. 11, cl. 3.

ADELINA PATTI (1843–1919) was one of the great sing-
ers of her time. Born of Italian parents in Madrid, she was
trained in New York, where she debuted in 1859 to critical acclaim. After some years abroad, she returned to the
U.S. in 1881 and soon became extremely popular, commanding the highest fees. A coloratura soprano, her reputation as a singer is legendary. See Herman Klein, *The
Reign of Patti* (New York, 1920).

FRANCISCO PEREA (1830–1913) was born in Los Pa-
dillas, New Mexico. He received his higher education in
St. Louis and New York City. During the Civil War he
served as an officer with Union forces raised locally to

protect New Mexico. A Republican, he served one term as territorial deputy, 1863–1865. In 1881 he moved from Bernalillo County to Jemez Springs, Sandoval County. He spent the last years of his life as an Albuquerque resident. *Biographical Directory of U.S. Congress*, p. 1444.

JOSÉ LEANDRO PEREA, according to the U.S. Census for 1870 for the town of Bernalillo, New Mexico, was forty-seven years of age. He and his wife, Dolores, three years his junior, had eight children. His real estate holdings were appraised at $48,000 and his personal property at $360,000, making him one of the richest men in New Mexico at the time. His son Pedro later became a territorial representative in the U.S. Congress.

FREDERICK L. PERRY became a 2nd lieutenant in the Colorado 1st Infantry, May 1, 1898, and was promoted to 1st lieutenant on August 1, 1899. Discharged a month later, on May 8, 1901, he received a 2nd lieutenant's commission in the artillery corps. *Army Register*, I: 785.

ALLAN PINKERTON, native of Scotland, was born in a slum tenement in Glasgow, August 25, 1819. As a young Chartist activist, he fled to the New World with his newly wedded wife in 1842, settling at Dundee, Illinois. By happenstance, he earned a reputation as a citizen detective which won him appointment as deputy sheriff of Kane County, although he continued to maintain his cooperage business. An ardent abolitionist, he was deeply involved in underground railroad activities. Offered a deputyship in Cook County, the now committed lawman sold his business and moved to Chicago. In 1849 he was appointed the city's first detective. After a year he resigned and became a special agent for the U.S. Post Office, charged with cleaning up thievery in the Chicago postal system. Sometime later, the date is in doubt, he formed with a partner the North-Western Police Agency which became in time the famed Pinkerton National Detective Agency. Service in the Civil War only enhanced Pinkerton's reputation. In the postwar years his agency grew in size and prospered, especially from labor dispute cases. The pioneer detective died in Chicago on July 1, 1884. His sons, Robert and William, inherited the agency. James D. Horan, *The Pinkertons: The Detective Dynasty That Made History* (New York, 1957), 2 *et seq.*

JAMES E. PORTER, a native of Maine, entered West Point on September 1, 1864, and was commissioned a 2nd lieutenant in the 7th Cavalry, June 15, 1869. He became a 1st lieutenant in 1872. *Army Register,* I: 788.

LEBARON BRADFORD PRINCE (1840–1922), born in Flushing, New York, graduated from Columbia University in 1866. A lawyer by education, he entered New York City politics and served in the State Assembly, 1871–1875, and the Senate for one term, 1876–1877. In 1879 he was appointed chief justice for the New Mexico Territory, a post he held until 1882. He remained in his newly adopted home, becoming a staunch advocate of statehood. He capped his career as territorial governor, 1889–1893. *Dictionary of American Biography,* XV: 229–230.

RED CLOUD, a war leader and headman among the Oglala subtribe of the Teton Sioux, had been a major principal in the negotiations resulting in the Treaty of Fort Laramie, April 29, 1868, which created the Red Cloud Agency in northwestern Nebraska on the White River. From that date on he was a man of peace. He played an active part in the sale of the Black Hills to the U.S. in an agreement that was signed on August 15, 1876. He did not participate in the Sioux War of 1876–1877, remaining instead at the Nebraskan agency. Howard R. Lamar, ed.,

The Reader's Encyclopedia of the American West (New York, 1977), p. 1004.

ELIZABETH RINEHART was the daughter of the storekeeper Ira Rinehart whom Hoyt mentions.

ALBERT A. ROBINSON (1844–1918), Vermont born, graduated from the University of Michigan with a bachelor's degree in civil engineering and science in 1869 and immediately launched a lifelong career in railroading. From 1873–1890 he was chief engineer for the Santa Fe. From September 1880 to October 1881 he also served as division superintendent for the Santa Fe, Las Vegas to Santa Fe, Deming to El Paso. He rose to executive position of second vice president and general manager of the railroad, 1888–1893. On leaving that position, he became president of the Mexico Central Railroad Company. *National Cyclopedia*, 11: 203; *New York Times*, November 8, 1918, p. 15, cl. 3.

WILLIAM PENN ADAIR ROGERS, "Will" to his legion of admirers, was born and raised near Oologah, Oklahoma, when it was still the Indian Territory. As a working cowboy he made his theatrical debut as "The Cherokee Kid" in a wild west show in South Africa. When he returned to the United States, he became a vaudeville performer. By 1916 he was a star attraction in the Ziegfeld Follies. It was an easy step from the stage to motion pictures and radio. His southwestern drawl and wit made him a nationwide favorite entertainer. He also added to his following of admiring fans by his numerous writings and lecture tours. He died, age fifty, in an airplane crash near Point Barrow, Alaska, with his fellow Oklahoman, pilot Wiley Post, August 15, 1935, on a flight to the Orient. Donald Day, *Will Rogers* (New York, 1962), has authored a readable biography.

CASIMERO ROMERO (whose first name Hoyt incorrectly spells Casimiro), a sheepman and freighter, accompanied both by his family and that of Agapito Sandoval, moved into the Tascosa area in November 1876, from Mora County, New Mexico, where he had ranched for many years. Romero was "a cultured and wealthy Castilian," and took up land on the banks of the Canadian River "near a number of large springs." Later he resettled in Mora County, where he died in 1912 about age eighty. McCarty, *Maverick Town*, pp. 38–39; Roy Riddle, "Casimero Romero Reigned as a Benevolent Don in Brief Pastoral Era," *Amarillo News*, August 15, 1938.

EDGAR RUSSELL, an army career man, was commissioned a 2nd lieutenant upon his graduation from West Point in 1887. He was made captain in the volunteers as a signal officer and served from June 1898 to February 1901. On February 2, 1901, he was promoted to captain in the regular service. During World War I he was the chief signal officer for the American Expeditionary Forces and received the Distinguished Service Medal for his role in that awesome conflict. He steadily rose in rank, becoming a major general in 1922, the year he retired from service. He died in New York City, April 27, 1925. *Army Register*, I: 852; *New York Times*, April 28, 1925, p. 21, cl. 3.

JOHN A. SCHOFIELD, born in LaGrange, Missouri, graduated from Annapolis in 1898. Retiring with the rank of rear admiral in 1940, he died in Washington, D.C., March 19, 1949, at age seventy-three. *New York Times*, March 20, 1949, p. 77, cl. 1.

CORDENIO A. SEVERANCE (1862–1925), junior member of the firm of Davis, Kellogg and Severance, which was formed in 1887, after collegiate education in Northfield, Minnesota, read law with a distinguished Minnesota attorney and was admitted to the bar in 1883. In subsequent years the famed law firm went through a number of reorganizations, but Severance remained a senior partner until his retirement in 1917. The American Bar Association honored him with its presidency in 1921. He died in Pasadena, California, May 6, 1925. *National Cyclopedia*, 19: 143.

HORATIO SEYMOUR (1810–1886) was elected governor of New York in 1852 and 1862, serving one term each time. In the 1868 presidential election, running on the Democratic ticket, he lost to U. S. Grant by slightly more than 300,000 votes. *Webster's American Biographies*, pp. 937–938.

LIONEL A. SHELDON (1828–1917), though born in New York state, was raised and educated in Ohio. After attending Oberlin, he entered a New York state law school, graduating in 1853, followed shortly thereafter with admission to the bar and practice in Ohio. During the Civil War he served with distinction in the 42nd Ohio Infantry under Colonel James A. Garfield, and was brevetted brigadier general in the volunteers in 1865 for his meritorious service. Mustered out of service in December 1864, he settled in New Orleans and resumed his legal career. He served three terms in the House of Representatives, 1869–1875. In 1879 he returned to Ohio. His tenure as New Mexico's territorial governor spanned the years 1881–1885. Three years later he moved to Los Angeles, but in 1896 took up residence in Pasadena, California, where he died. *Biographical Directory of U.S. Congress*, p. 1590.

JOHN E. SHERMAN, JR., Ohio born, was the nephew of U.S. Senator John Sherman and General William T. Sherman. On May 24, 1886, he was appointed U.S. marshal for the New Mexico Territory. He took up his duties on July 20 and served until March 2, 1882, when he tendered his resignation. Keleher, *Violence in Lincoln County*, p. 185. Sherman's career as marshal is treated in Ball, *The United States Marshals of New Mexico and Arizona Territories*, pp. 79–106.

GEORGE F. SHIELS joined the California volunteers as a major surgeon, July 8, 1898, and served until discharged, June 10, 1900. For gallantry at Tuliahan River, March 25, 1899, he received the Medal of Honor. He earned his degree from the University of Edinburgh Faculty of Medicine in 1884, and became a Fellow of the Royal College of Surgeons, Edinburgh, in 1888, the same year he was licensed to practice in California. He joined the faculty of the University of California, Berkeley, in 1890, rising to professor of surgery. He accepted appointment to the New York Polyclinic Medical School and Hospital in 1904, and held a joint appointment at Fordham University School of Medicine in 1905. During World War I he again distinguished himself for bravery. He died in Palo Alto, California, age eighty, October 26, 1944. *Army Register*, I: 883; *Journal of the American Medical Association*, 124 (January 1, 1944), 53.

CHARLES A. SIRINGO was born in Matagorda County, Texas, February 7, 1855. He began working as a cowboy in 1871. As a cowboy, he helped establish the LX Ranch in the Panhandle. It was at this time that Hoyt met him. Siringo at the time was just a cowboy, not ranch foreman as Hoyt mistakenly recalls. When he was thirty, Siringo wrote his first book, *A Texas Cowboy, or, Fifteen Years on the Hurricane Deck of a Spanish Cow Pony* (Chicago, 1885), the first autobiography of a cowboy, hailed by Frank J. Dobie as "the most read non-fiction book on cowboy life." Later, Siringo was employed as a highly successful Pinkerton operative, from 1886 to 1907. Even after retirement to his ranch outside Santa Fe, he free-lanced as a detective. In December 1922 he sold out his New Mexico ranch. Suffering from a severe case of pleurisy, he moved to San Diego to live briefly. A few months later he moved to the Los Angeles area. For a time he resided in Long Beach, then moved to Hollywood, where he died on October 19, 1928. *Dictionary of American Biography*, XVII: 191–192; Siringo, *Riata and Spurs* (Boston, 1927), pp. 263–267.

JACOB HURD SMITH, born in Jackson, Iron Furnace, Ohio, in January 1840, enlisted at the outbreak of the Civil War and was commissioned a 1st lieutenant in the 2nd Kentucky Infantry Volunteers, June 5, 1861, rising in rank to captain by war's end. On March 7, 1867, he was commissioned captain in the 13th U.S. Infantry, the same day he was brevetted major for gallantry at the battle of Shiloh. By June 20, 1898, he was a lieutenant colonel in the 12th U.S. Infantry. On June 1, 1900, he was promoted to brigadier general in the volunteers, and made the same rank in the regular army the following year shortly before his retirement. He won the sobriquet "Hell Roaring Jake" during his Philippine service, which also brought him a court-martial. He died in San Diego, California, March 1, 1918. *Army Register*, I: 899; *Who Was Who in America*, I: 1144; *New York Times*, March 3, 1918, p. 23, cl. 1.

ROBERT A. SMITH was born in Boonville, Indiana, in 1827. After graduating in law from Indiana University in 1850, he moved to Minnesota in 1853, settling in St. Paul. He held a variety of offices—territorial librarian, 1853–1858; Ramsey County treasurer, 1856–1858; state representative, 1885; state senate, 1887–1889; mayor of St. Paul, 1888–1892, 1894–1896, 1904–1908; and postmaster, 1896–1900. "Minnesota Biographies," p. 719.

GEORGE M. STERNBERG (1852–1915), born in Oswego County, New York, took his medical degree at the College of Physicians and Surgeons (later a part of Columbia University) in 1860. On May 28, 1861, he was appointed assistant surgeon in the New York volunteers. At the end of the Civil War he remained in the army and had extensive duty in the American West.

In April 1879 he was detailed to the Havana Yellow Fever Commission, an assignment that established his reputation as an epidemiologist, although as early as 1875 he was publishing on the subject. Subsequently, he was a brilliant contributor to bacteriology and epidemiology, and an outstanding advocate of public health measures.

May 30, 1893, he was appointed surgeon general of the army with rank of brigadier general. In that capacity he established the Army Medical School, the nurse and dental corps, a tuberculosis hospital and many general hospitals during the Spanish-American War. He retired from service in 1902 and devoted his attention to social welfare activities in the nation's capital. *Dictionary of American Biography*, XVII: 590–592.

PUTNAM BRADLEE STRONG, appointed captain in the New York volunteers, May 17, 1898, was promoted to major in December. After his discharge, on February 2, 1901, he was appointed captain in the regular army's quartermaster corp, but resigned on July 15. *Army Register*, I: 932.

WILLIAM B. STRONG (1837–1914) was born in Vermont, but raised in Beloit, Wisconsin. After completing his public education, he entered the Chicago Business College, graduating in 1855. He commenced his railroad career as a station agent and telegraph operator. Strong worked for a succession of railroad companies prior to joining Santa Fe as general manager. He was promoted to vice president and, on July 12, 1881, elected president. He held that post until forced to resign in 1889. Retiring to Beloit, he subsequently moved to Los Angeles, where he died. L. L. Waters, *Steel Trails to Santa Fe* (Lawrence, Kan., 1958), p. 54n.

WILLIAM HOWARD TAFT, destined to become the 27th President of the U.S., served as the Philippines first civilian governor, 1901–1904, leaving that post to become secretary of war under Theodore Roosevelt, 1904–1908. He was Roosevelt's choice to succeed him, and Taft won over the Democrat's William Jennings Bryant in the 1908 election. *Encyclopedia of American History*, pp. 790–791.

BEN TURPIN, a New Orleanian by birth, was taken to New York City to live when he was seven. A natural comic, he started his career in burlesque. He became friends with Charlie Chaplin and made his first silent movie for him and Mack Sennett. He became a marvelous film comedian, his trademark being his crossed right eye, an accident of nature, not birth. He died July 1, 1940, at age seventy-one. *New York Times*, July 2, 1940, p. 21, cl. 5.

CHARLES H. UTTER received his sobriquet "Colorado Charley" in Deadwood by November 1876. Born near Niagara Falls in 1838, he grew up in Illinois. Venturing to the West, he became a widely known trapper; turned to mining and business during his many years in Colorado. He served as a guide, took up ranching, then moved into transportation by 1867. His friendship with Hickok dates from 1872, but as Utter's biographer affirms, there is no satisfactory proof that they were ever partners. The appearance of the word "Pard" on Colorado Charley's grave marker for Hickok "was simply standard designation of one good friend to another."

From Utter's biographer it would appear that he did not venture to New Mexico until the end of 1880, when he took up residence in Socorro, running a gaming table in the Monarch Saloon. When last heard of after his 1884 disappearance from New Mexico, he was living in Panama City. There his life's trail ends.

He may well have had Hickok's hat as Hoyt recalled, since it was Colorado Charley who had acquired the lot in Mount Moriah Cemetery and oversaw the reburial of Hickok in 1879. Agnes Wright Spring, *Colorado Charley, Wild Bill's Pard* (Boulder, Colo., 1968), provides full details.

LEWIS WALLACE (1827–1905) was a Hoosier by birth. During the Mexican War he served as a 2nd lieutenant with the 1st Indiana Infantry. In 1849 he was admitted to the bar, and in 1853 settled in Crawfordsville, which became his permanent home. He served in the state senate in 1856. During the Civil War he served with the 11th Indiana Regiment, first as colonel, and by 1862 as major general. President James A. Garfield appointed him governor of the Territory of New Mexico in 1878, a post he held until 1881. His statue represents Indiana in the U.S. Congress Hall of National Statuary. *Dictionary of American Biography*, XIX: 375–376.

ROBERT BRUCE WALLACE, a West Pointer, Class of 1890, was promoted to 1st lieutenant in 1897. On May 3, 1898, he was promoted to lieutenant colonel in the 1st Montana Infantry. Subsequently, July 5, 1899, he received the rank of colonel with the 37th U.S. Volunteer Infantry. Seriously wounded, as described by Hoyt at the battle of Caloocan, February 10, he finally died from his wounds on March 13, 1900. *Army Register*, I: 998.

THOMAS B. WEIR began his military career in the Civil

War as a 2nd lieutenant in the 3rd Michigan Cavalry in 1861, rising to the rank of lieutenant colonel by 1865. Mustered out of service, he was reappointed 1st lieutenant in the 7th U.S. Cavalry, July 28, 1866, and promoted to captain the following year. He died in service, December 9, 1876. *Army Register*, I: 1015.

EHRICH WEISS, born in Appleton, Wisconsin, 1874, destined to become famous as a superb escape artist and magician, adopted the name of Harry Houdini when he went on the American stage, a name derived from the French magician Houdin. His escape feats were extraordinary and were well publicized in the printed media. He died in Detroit, October 31, 1926, after surgery for a ruptured appendix, resulting in general peritonitis. *New York Times*, November 1, 1926, p. 1, cl. 2; p. 6, cls. 2–8; John B. Kennedy, "Houdini Made Himself the Master Magician," *Ibid.*, November 7, 1926, Pt. IX, p. 10, cls. 1–4.

LLOYD WHEATON began his military life as a sergeant in the 8th Illinois Infantry in 1861, but was a lieutenant colonel by November 1864. When the Civil War ended, he remained in service, being commissioned a captain in 1866. By 1895 he was a lieutenant colonel and by 1899 made colonel. He was appointed brigadier general in the volunteers, May 27, 1898, and major general, April 15, 1899. In the regular army he was made a brigadier general on February 2, 1901, a major general on March 30. He was decorated with the Medal of Honor, January 16, 1894, for his Civil War gallantry at Fort Blakely, Alabama, April 9, 1865. He retired from active duty July 15, 1902, and died in Chicago on September 18, 1918, age eighty. *Army Register*, I: 883; *New York Times*, September 19, 1918, p. 13, cl. 2.

CHARLES A. WILLARD, born in St. Johnsburg, Vermont, May 21, 1857, graduated from Dartmouth College in 1877 and took his law at Boston University, finishing in 1879. He practiced in Minneapolis and taught in the University of Minnesota's law department during the years 1887–1901. President McKinley appointed him justice of the supreme court in the Philippines in 1901. He resigned in 1904 and resumed his legal practice, until persuaded by President Theodore Roosevelt to return to the Philippine bench in 1904. In July 1909, he was appointed to the U.S. District Court in Minneapolis, which brought him back to the states. He died March 13, 1914, survived by his wife whom he had married in Manila in 1901. *New York Times*, March 15, 1914, p. 7, cl. 4.

RICHENS LACY WOOTTON (1816–1893) received the sobriquet "Uncle Dick" about 1858 when he visited Denver and was considered "a relic of a bygone age." Indeed, he had been in the Colorado area some twenty-two years. Long active as a fur trapper, he turned to a variety of other pursuits, notably freighting, with the decline of the fur trade. He eventually centered his activities in the area of the upper Arkansas River. In 1865, with legal authorization from the territorial legislatures of Colorado and New Mexico and in partnership with George C. McBride, he built a mile toll road over Raton Pass. It provided a comfortable income. The Atchison, Topeka and Santa Fe Railroad built over the pass in 1878 and compensated Wootton at the rate of $50 a month for putting him out of business. On his death, the company continued payment to his surviving wife. Harvey L. Carter, "Dick Wootton," in Hafen, ed., *Mountain Men*, III: 407–409.

WALTER WYMAN (1848–1911), a native of St. Louis, Missouri, received his medical degree from St. Louis Medical College in 1873. He entered the Marine Hospital Service in 1876 as an assistant surgeon and served in many of the service's hospitals until summoned to Washington, D.C., in December 1888, as chief of the quarantine division. June 1, 1891, he was appointed surgeon general and died in that post twenty years later. His contributions to public health were numerous and significant. Williams, *The United States Public Health Service, 1798–1950*, pp. 477–479.

RICHARD W. YOUNG graduated from West Point in 1882 and was a captain by 1885. He returned to serve as captain of Battery A, Utah Artillery, May 5, 1898, and was promoted to major in July. Discharged on June 28, 1899, he returned to civilian life. *Army Register*, I: 1067.

Place Notes

PLACE NOTES

BERNALILLO, seat of Sandoval County, lies seventeen miles north of Albuquerque. The name in translation means "little Bernal," and is probably derived from the Gonzales-Bernal family who lived in the district before 1680 and after 1693, following the reconquest of New Mexico in the wake of the Pope uprising. Use of "little" in the name perhaps applies to a Bernal who was short in stature or else junior to a senior Bernal. Another possibility has been suggested. The leading citizen of the area, Fernando de Chavez, and no friend of the Bernals, named his *hacienda* in memory of Fray Juan Bernal, who was martyred in the 1680 Indian uprising. T. M. Pierce, ed., *New Mexico Place Names* (Albuquerque, 1965), p 16.

BISMARCK was founded in 1872 by the Northern Pacific Railroad. The site on the Missouri River was first named Edwinton in honor of the chief engineer, Edwin F. Johnson. It was renamed in 1873 in the vain hope of attracting German capital to invest in the railroad. *Appleton's Guide to the United States and Canada. Illustrated* (New York, 1884), pp. 437-438.

THE CHUGWATER lies some fifty-three miles from Cheyenne. Dudley H. Snyder of Sabile Valley, in partnership with his brother, John W. Snyder, began importing herds of Texas cattle into Wyoming and disposing of them locally. The brothers were primarily responsible for establishing the cattle business in the area. J. H. Twiggs, *History of Cheyenne and Northern Wyoming . . .* (Omaha, 1876), pp. 53, 91.

COLUMBUS MEDICAL COLLEGE was organized in the summer of 1875 when the faculty at Starling Medical College split on the question of a professorial appointment. The new college was incorporated on January 17, 1876, and, indeed, its faculty roster included the most important doctors in Columbus, many with years of experience as medical college teachers. For the first seven years of its existence, Columbus Medical College was conducted in the Sessions Block on High Street and was affiliated with Hawkes Hospital of Mt. Carmel. Some 500 students were graduated from the college. In 1892 it merged with the Starling Medical College. By December 1912, Ohio Senate Bill 120 authorized the establishment of what is now the Ohio State University College of Medicine.

CROOKSTON, the seat of Polk County, was settled in 1872 and incorporated in 1879.

FORT BASCOM was established by Captain Peter W. L. Plympton, 7th U.S. Infantry on August 15, 1863. Acting on the orders of Brigadier General James H. Carleton, the commander of the New Mexico Department, he selected a site on the south bank of the Canadian River eight miles north of the present town of Tucumcari, forty-two miles east of the Texas-New Mexico state border. First named Camp Easton, after the department's quartermaster, it was changed in January 1864 to honor the memory of Captain George N. Bascom, 16th U.S. Infantry, who was killed at the battle of Valverde, February 21, 1862. In December 1870, it was abandoned; shortly after, the land was returned to the lessor. The name prevails today as Bascom. Robert W. Frazer, *Forts of the West* (Norman, Okla., 1965), p. 95.

FORT DOUGLAS was established on a bench just north of Red Butte Creek by order of Secretary of War Edwin

M. Stanton. It is situated east of Salt Lake City, which it overlooks. Colonel Patrick E. Connor, 3rd California Infantry, founded the post on October 26, 1862. Named Camp Douglas in honor of the famed Illinois U.S. Senator Stephen A. Douglas, it was designated a fort at the end of 1878. It is still in operation today. *Ibid.*, p. 166.

FORT ELLIOTT was originally known as "Cantonment North Fork of the Red River" when it was established February 3, 1875. But on June 5, a site near Mobeetie was chosen for relocation some twenty miles west of the Oklahoma border. It was north of and near the headwaters of Sweetwater Creek, a confluent of the Red River's North Fork. General William Tecumseh Sherman ordered its founding primarily to protect a route for Texas cattle to move to Kansas and to deter the re-entry of Indians into the Texas Panhandle. Major Henry C. Bankhead, 4th U.S. Cavalry, executed Sherman's order. After several changes, it was finally named on February 21, 1876, to honor the memory of Major Joel H. Elliott, 7th U.S. Cavalry, who died in action in late November 1868, in Indian Country, today Oklahoma. It was abandoned in October 1890. *Ibid.*, pp. 149–150.

FORT PEMBINA was established July 8, 1870 by Captain Loyd Wheaton, and was originally called Fort Thomas, for Major George H. Thomas, who died on March 28, 1870. It was designated Fort Pembina on September 6, 1870. Located a mile and a half south of the town, it was built on the left bank of the Red River of the North, just above the mouth of the Pembina River. Much of the post was destroyed by fire in 1895; it was abandoned and sold at public auction. *Ibid.*, pp. 112–113.

FORT SNELLING, prior to being named in 1825, a military post on the upper Mississippi River, was called by four different names and was relocated twice before a permanent site was chosen in 1820. The land was originally acquired from the Sioux by Zebulon M. Pike during his 1805–1806 expedition to determine the source of the Mississippi. Finally paid for in 1819, the first post was established on August 24, 1819. Construction on the permanent fort began September 10, 1820. The post and reservation were sold in 1857; the garrison was removed the following year. With the coming of the Civil War in 1861, the post was reoccupied and served as a training center. In the post-war years it continued to be maintained as a military facility and was not abandoned until 1946, when it was transferred to the Veterans Administration. Frazer, *Forts of the West,* pp. 67–68.

FORT SUMNER, situated on the east bank of the Pecos River, is the seat of De Baca County in eastern New Mexico. Its name was derived from the military fort established south of the present community in 1862. As part of the overall plans of Brigadier General James H. Carleton to contain the Navaho Indians, the fort's site was chosen by Captain Joseph Undegraff, 5th U.S. Infantry, and construction was executed by troops of the California Column, volunteers serving during the Civil War. In early 1864, Colonel Kit Carson, commanding the 1st New Mexico Infantry, dislodged the Navaho from Canyon de Chelley. By late 1864, three-fourths of the tribe, numbering 8,000, were resettled on the wastelands of the Bosque Redondo. Several hundred Mescalero Apaches were also confined there in 1863. But the project ended in utter failure. In 1868, the Navahos after four years of exile, a crushed people, were allowed to return to their homelands. The fort was abandoned and later sold at auction to Maxwell. *Ibid.,* p. 104; Robert M. Utley, *Frontiersmen in Blue: The United States Army and the Indian, 1848–1865* (New York, 1967), pp. 236–237, 242–247.

FORT UNION was established by Lieutenant Colonel Edwin Vose Sumner, 1st U.S. Dragoons, on July 26, 1851. The first post was built on a site some twenty-four miles northeast of Las Vegas on the west side of the valley of Wolf Creek, an affluent of the Mora River. In August 1861, Colonel Edward R. S. Canby, 19th U.S. Infantry, for security reasons, relocated the fort on the valley floor, a mile from the original site and east of Wolf Creek. Built of earthwork, it deteriorated rapidly, necessitating new construction. When completed, the fort served as the general supply depot for New Mexico. It was abandoned in early 1891. Today it is a national monument. Frazer, *Forts of the West*, pp. 105–106.

HOT SPRINGS is located seven miles northwest of Las Vegas. It is easily reached, since it is on US 65, one mile west of Montezuma. W. Scott Moore purchased the property from a man named McDonald, who received the original grant in 1840. Today the area is called Montezuma. Moore, a retired freight conductor with the Santa Fe Railroad, with his wife, Minnie, built "The Old Adobe House," which was the first hotel at what he hoped would become a fashionable spa. Stanley, *The Las Vegas Story*, pp. 292–293.

THE LIT RANCH was west and up the Canadian River from the LX Ranch where Hoyt was to work as a cowboy. It was carved out of the Panhandle by George W. Littlefield (1841–1920) in 1877. The ranch laid the basis for the owner's rise to wealth and position. He became an Austin banker and a philanthropist, benefitting the University of Texas. J. Evetts Haley, *George W. Littlefield, Texan* (Norman, Okla., 1963), offers a fine biography.

IRAPUATO, some 350 miles northwest of Mexico City, is located in Guanajuato in central Mexico. The city is on a small fertile plain in the mining region stretching between Celaya and León.

ROSWELL dates from 1869, when Van C. Smith and his partner, Aaron O. Wilburn, both from Omaha, Nebraska, founded a trading post at the confluence of the Rio Hondo and Pecos rivers. They constructed two adobe buildings which provided a general store, post office, and sleeping accommodations for overnight paying guests. When Smith filed the first land claim, March 4, 1871, he named the embryo town Roswell in honor of his father. In 1877, Captain Joseph C. Lea bought the entire town and kept it as a family possession for ten years. In February 1889, Roswell was made the seat of Chaves County. Pearce, ed., *New Mexico Place Names*, p. 138.

RUSH MEDICAL COLLEGE, chartered in 1837, did not actually open its doors until 1842. From 1898 to 1942 it was affiliated with the University of Chicago. In 1884 the Presbyterian Hospital was established as the major teaching hospital for the college, which subsequently was affiliated with the University of Illinois in 1971. Presbyterian Hospital merged in 1958 with St. Luke's (founded in 1864) and in 1969 the new hospital merged with Rush Medical College Corporation, forming the Rush-Presbyterian-St. Luke's Medical Center, and admitting its first students in September 1971. *1978–79 AAMC Directory of American Medical Education* (Washington, D.C., 1978), p. 78.

STAKED PLAIN is the southern portion of the Great Plains and spreads across most of the Texas Panhandle and New Mexico east of the Pecos River from the southeastern corner, north of Clovis. Josiah Gregg recorded, ". . . there is but one route upon which this plain can be safely traversed during the dry season; and even some of the watering-places on this are at intervals of fifty to eighty miles, and hard to find. Hence the Mexican traders and hunters, that they might not lose their way and perish from thirst, once staked out this route across the plain, it is said; whence it has received the name of *El Plano Estacado*, or the Staked Plain." *Commerce of the Prairies*, in Reuben G. Thwaites, ed., *Early Western Travels*, 32 vols. (Reprint ed.; New York, 1966), xx: 239–240.

TASCOSA, today a ghost town, is located in the extreme northwest portion of the Panhandle, south of the Canadian River, some thirty miles northwest of Amarillo. The name comes from Atascosa, which translates as gobby or quicksandy. It was the second village to be established in the Panhandle and was founded by three Mexican families. J. Evetts Haley, *The XIT Ranch of Texas and the Early Days of the Llano Estacado* (Chicago, 1929), pp. 35, 195–196.

Comment on
Jesse James and Billy the Kid

COMMENT ON
JESSE JAMES AND BILLY THE KID

Hoyt, in the original edition, pp. 111–112, inserted a lengthy footnote to his text to support his statement that he had personally met Jesse James in New Mexico. He states that James was there on an exploratory trip, which included a meeting with Billy the Kid in anticipation of a possible partnership. That lengthy note reads as follows.

In the summer of 1928, after I had written this account of my meeting with Jesse James and had told Mr. Harrison Leussler, the Western representative of Houghton Mifflin Company, of the incident, Mr. Leussler informed me that during an interview with the survivor of a well-known gang of outlaws, who now resides in Los Angeles, the one-time outlaw, now reformed, had stated that Jesse James was never in New Mexico and had never lost a part of any of his fingers. The inference was that either my story was a fake or I was mistaken in the identity of the man I met and described.

Although I never claim any great knowledge, I do claim that I intend to be very accurate about any statement I make. Taking into consideration all the circumstances of my meeting with Jesse James, I have always been entirely convinced that it was he without question. The man's statement disturbed me: it meant that if his assertions were true, mine must be wrong.

I left Mr. Leussler to keep an appointment with a friend in a near-by office building. There I had to wait a few minutes. Picking up a newspaper, I read of some action at law by Miss Jessie Estella James, granddaughter of the late Jesse James, represented by an attorney with offices in the building where I was sitting.

Making as nearly a bee-line to that office as possible, I introduced myself to the attorney, David H. Cannon, Esq. Mr. Cannon was good enough to give me a card of introduction to Miss James, who received me very graciously, but regretted that she could not give me the information I sought, inasmuch as her grandfather had been killed many years before her birth. When, however, she learned that I lived in Long Beach, she at once gave me a letter to her great uncle, John T. Samuels, half brother to her grandfather, Jesse James, who had resided in that city for some years.

I lost no time in calling on Mr. Samuels. I was cordially received and given all the information I wanted.

In reply to my questions, Mr. Samuels dictated and signed the following letter:

> 1421 East 10th Street
> Long Beach, Calif.
> August 10, 1928

To Dr. Henry F. Hoyt:

I am a half brother of the late Jesse James. He was not quite six feet tall, had blue-gray eyes, sandy hair, was square-shouldered and walked erect.

When about fifteen years old, he was with Quantrill. One day, while cleaning his cap-and-ball six-shooter, it went off accidentally, tearing off the end of the middle finger of his left hand at the first joint. Shaking his injured hand, he exclaimed 'Dingus' several times very emphatically, and his comrades at once nicknamed him 'Dingus,' a name that stuck to him the rest of his life. I never called him anything else.

I never heard him utter an oath in my life. When the war was over, he joined the Baptist Church at Kearney, Missouri, and was baptized there.

He had a habit of concealing the loss of the end of his finger and very few knew of it.

(Signed)

John T. Samuels

The letter which Hoyt reproduced, along with his own comments, is in the Houghton Mifflin Papers, Houghton Library, Harvard University.

The letter from John T. Samuels requires comment. According to William Settle, James did have a "tipless finger on his left hand." The biographer presents various explanations, including the one given here, and cites this in his note on the matter. *Jesse James Was His Name*, pp. 31, 206 *note* 9.

As to the nickname "Dingus," Settle writes: "He had used the word as an exclamation one time when part of his equipment pinched him painfully, and he was immediately dubbed with it." Settle dates this c.1865. *Ibid.*, p. 32.

In respect to tangible evidence bearing on James' presence in New Mexico the *Las Vegas Daily Optic*, December 8, 1879, printed this news item: "Jessie James was a guest at Las Vegas Hot Springs, July 26th to July 29th. Of course it was not generally known." Hoyt's account of meeting Jessie James includes an introduction by Billy the Kid. However, Miguel Antonio Otero, in his autobiography, published six years after Hoyt's had appeared, states that he met James at "The Old Adobe Hotel" at the Hot Springs, operated by a boyhood friend of the

James brothers, W. Scott Moore and his wife Minnie. Otero gives a very good description of James, noting he had blue eyes, and says he came directly from Kansas City to Las Vegas for the visit with his former Missouri boyhood friend. After the three-day visit, James returned to Kansas City. The purpose of the visit was to ascertain whether or not James might relocate in New Mexico, according to Otero. *My Life on the Frontier*, pp. 176–178.

Thus the evidence to support a visit of James to the Hot Springs rests on four months' delayed newspaper notice and two autobiographical accounts written in later life, published in 1929 and 1935 respectively. However, the two autobiographical accounts differ in one major respect: Hoyt includes Billy the Kid as an element in his version, while Otero does not. Hoyt also notes that James had the tip of a finger on his left hand missing and this defect is supported by James' half brother in a letter to Hoyt. Otero makes no mention of such a defect.

Since the *Las Vegas Daily Optic* provides the exact time of the reputed visit, the dates being cited by Otero (who no doubt obtained them from the newspaper), there is some evidence that would appear to impeach the story of the James visit to the Hot Springs.

At the 1882 inquest that was held in the wake of her husband's death, Zerelda Cole James, Jesse's widow, testified that they had married in Kearney,

Missouri, April 24, 1874, and had immediately gone
to Texas, centering their activities in the Galveston
area. After about five months, they returned to Kansas City and spent about a year there. Their next
place of residence was Nashville, Tennessee, where
their two children were born, In 1881 the Jameses
moved back to Kansas City for six months, and
from there to St. Joseph in November, where James
was fatally shot the following April 1882. Thus
their residence chronology appears to be: Texas,
May–September 1874; Kansas City, November
1874–November 1875; Nashville, November 1875–
May 1881; Kansas City, May 1881–November 1881;
St. Joseph, November 1881–April 1882. While residing in Nashville, James used the alias Thomas
Howard and that of J. T. Jackson on his return to
Kansas City. Settle, *Jesse James Was His Name*, pp.
117, 129.

If this meeting between James and Bonney took
place, it would have had to occur when James was
living in Nashville. The James' neighbors in Nashville later verified the fact that James was often gone
from the house three to four weeks, and sometimes
the wife and children too. So, there is an outside
possibility that James might have journeyed to New
Mexico and sought out Bonney. However, Settle,
James' biographer, although listing Hoyt's book in
his bibliography, nowhere gives credence to any
New Mexico trip or Bonney encounter.

Robert N. Mullin, who edited and saw through

publication the definitive study on the Lincoln County War authored by Maurice G. Fulton, when queried on the possibility of a Bonney-James meeting in Las Vegas, stated: "My notes indicate that when I was working with Fulton and researching for his book, he wrote me that after the close of the Dudley Court on July 5, 1879, Bonney hid out in the hills in DeBaca County, New Mexico, keeping out of the reach of Dolan's gunmen and other warriors of the Santa Fe Ring, until the latter part of August, when he barely eluded a detachment of the 9th Cavalry in Lincoln County and he was charged with keeping a gaming table in San Miguel County, but never apprehended. (The military were at the service of the Santa Fe Ring.) Fulton says, 'during the months of July, August and September, Bonney remained in hiding and never ventured from DeBaca County, except for an occasional night expedition to 'borrow' a few cattle.'" Mullin concluded: "I had so much confidence in Fulton's conclusions that I used the following wording in my *Chronology of the Lincoln County War*, without calling Henry Hoyt a liar: 'July 26–29 Bonney meets Jesse James near Las Vegas (according to legend).'" Personal letter, September 2, 1978.

The reader will have to judge for himself whether or not Jesse James did venture to New Mexico, met Billy the Kid, and was encountered by Dr. Hoyt.

Index

INDEX

List of The Lakeside Classics

The Lakeside Classics